Children in an Information Age

TOMORROW'S PROBLEMS TODAY

Other Titles of Interest

CHILVER & GOULD
Learning & Language in the Classroom

HUSEN & POSTLETHWAITE
The International Encyclopedia of Education

McGUIRE & PRIESTLEY
Life After School

PLOMP
Proceedings of the European Conference on Information Technology (EURIT 86)

SMITH
Computers & Education: CAL 83

ZETTERSTEN
New Technologies in Language Learning

A Related Journal

COMPUTERS & EDUCATION
An International Journal
D F Rogers & P R Smith

Computers have entered nearly every aspect and every level of education. In order to disseminate information on the wealth of experience being gained, *Computers & Education* sets as its goal the establishment of a forum for communication in the use of digital, analog and hybrid computers in all aspects of education. Although the principal educational applications of computers have been in higher education, there is a growing awareness of their role in secondary and indeed primary education, and papers which describe developments in these areas will be considered.

A prime requisite in developing any technology is the establishment of its supporting literature. For both scientific and nonscientific newcomers to digital, analog and hybrid computation, this publication serves as a reference standard against which goals can be set and the current state of the art assessed. The journal also features reviews of books and papers published elsewhere, meeting schedules and short courses being offered. Relevant papers are welcomed for editorial consideration.

Children in an Information Age

TOMORROW'S PROBLEMS TODAY

Selected Papers from the International Conference
Varna, Bulgaria, 6–9 May 1985

EDITORS

Academician Blagovest Sendov
and Dr Ivan Stanchev

PERGAMON PRESS
OXFORD · NEW YORK · TORONTO · SYDNEY · FRANKFURT

U.K.	Pergamon Press Ltd., Headington Hill Hall, Oxford OX3 0BW, England
U.S.A.	Pergamon Press Inc., Maxwell House, Fairview Park, Elmsford, New York 10523, U.S.A.
CANADA	Pergamon Press Canada Ltd., Suite 104, 150 Consumers Road, Willowdale, Ontario M2J 1P9, Canada
AUSTRALIA	Pergamon Press (Aust.) Pty. Ltd., P.O. Box 544, Potts Point, N.S.W. 2011, Australia
FEDERAL REPUBLIC OF GERMANY	Pergamon Press GmbH, Hammerweg 6, D-6242 Kronberg, Federal Republic of Germany
JAPAN	Pergamon Press Ltd., 8th Floor, Matsuoka Central Building, 1-7-1 Nishishinjuku, Shinjuku-ku, Tokyo 160, Japan
BRAZIL	Pergamon Editora Ltda., Rua Eça de Queiros, 346, CEP 04011, São Paulo, Brazil
PEOPLE'S REPUBLIC OF CHINA	Pergamon Press, Qianmen Hotel, Beijing, People's Republic of China

First edition 1986

Library of Congress Cataloging in Publication Data
Main entry under title:
Children in an information age.
Sponsored by the State Committee for Science and
Technical Progress of the People's Republic of Bulgaria,
... *et al.*
1. Computer-assisted instruction — Congresses.
2. Computers and children — Congresses.
I. Sendov, Blagovest. II. Stanchev, Ivan. III. Bulgaria.
Dŭrzhaven komitet za nauka i tekhnicheski progres.
LB1028.5.C514 1986 371.3'9445 85-28528

British Library Cataloguing in Publication Data
Children in an Information Age: Tomorrow's Problems
Today *(Conference: 1985: Varna)*
Children in an Information Age: Tomorrow's
Problems Today; selected papers from the international Conference;
Varna, Bulgaria, May 6–9 1985.
1. Education — Data processing
I. Title II. Sendov, Blagovest III. Stanchev, Ivan
370'.28'54 LB1028.43

ISBN 0-08-033890-9

Printed in Great Britain by A. Wheaton & Co. Ltd., Exeter

Foreword

Children in the Age of Information: Tomorrow's Problems Today was the theme of the International Conference held at the Druzhba Resort near the city of Varna, in the People's Republic of Bulgaria on May 6-9, 1985. The foremost objective of the Conference was to make possible an exchange of opinions and concrete results from research and applied work by scientists and specialists in the field of computer use in the instruction of children at school, in extracurricular activities and at home.

The International Program Committee made considerable efforts to invite to the Conference also scientists and specialists with reservations about the massive introduction of computers in education from the earliest years of instruction. The idea was in the course of discussion to make a still better and fuller elucidation of the numerous problems which the future development of informatics and computer technology raises as from now before teachers, psychologists, programmers and hardware designers, as well as before the strategists of educational policies.

Three hundred and fifty people took part in the work of the Conference: outstanding scientists and specialists from 40 countries and representatives of such international organizations as UNESCO, IIASA, WHO, IFIP and UNICEF. The large number of participants from East and West, from North and South contributed to establishing broad constructive contacts, to getting acquainted with the experience of countries already advanced in the field of computer-based instruction and to seeking new creative solutions for future work.

In accordance with the scientific programme, selected by the International Program Committee, 18 plenary sessions and invited papers, as well as over 100 scientific communications and specialized reports in the sections were delivered.

At an exhibition and various other scientific events arranged during the Conference, the participants were able to familiarize themselves with the equipment and programmes of different firms, research institutes and organizations active in the field of the computerization of education and to study Bulgaria's experience in organizing the school and extracurricular use of computers in the instruction of children.

The social programme gave the participants in the Conference a chance to enjoy the lovely Black Sea resorts around the city of Varna and to taste famous Bulgarian dishes, succulent fruit and vintage wines at cocktail parties and dinners.

The Conference was organized and held by the State Committee for Science and Technical Progress of the People's Republic of Bulgaria jointly with UNESCO, IIASA, the Lyudmila Zhivkova International Foundation and the World Health Organization.

This book the publication of which would have been unthinkable without the kind support of Pergamon Press and of Mr. Maxwell personally, contains the plenary and the invited reports as submitted by the authors for publication. The stream papers were published in two volumes totalling 800 pages by the Ministry of Education of the People's Republic of Bulgaria and placed at the disposal of the participants in the Conference at registration.

The book also includes the Message of Greetings by Mr. Todor Zhivkov, President of the State Council of the People's Republic of Bulgaria, to the participants in the Conference, and the recommendations unanimously adopted by those present to organize an International Programme and Centre on the Problems of Computerization in Education.

Lists of the members of the Honorary and the Program Committee, the reports of the four streams and the scheme of the scientific programme with the names of the speakers are appended as additional information for the benefit of those of the readers who were unable to attend the Conference.

In conclusion, the Editors should like to express their gratitude to the Lyudmila Zhivkova Foundation for the financial assistance granted and to Dr. Kiril Manov for his competent work to prepare this book for the press.

Sofia, July 1985

The Editors

CONTENTS

Address of Todor Zhivkov, State Council President of the P.R. of Bulgaria to Participants in the International Conference and Exhibition "Children in an Information Age: Tomorrow's Problems Today", 6–9 May 1985, Varna

Ladies and Gentlemen,

Comrades,

I am happy to welcome you all on behalf of the State Council of the PR of Bulgaria, the Bulgarian people and my own behalf and sincerely wish you success in your exceptionally interesting work.

It gives us joy that Bulgaria is host to such a prestigeous conference held during the current International Youth Year. It also makes us happy because this is one of the first conferences of its kind worldwide, attended by scientists from East and West and from the developing countries. We are happy to see amongst the renowned representatives of world science present here, our fellow countryman John Atanasoff - the inventor of the first computer in the world.

We also appreciate the fact that the conference and exhibition in Varna are jointly organized by UNESCO, WHO, the International Institute for Applied Systems Analysis and the "Lyudmila Zhivkova" International Foundation. The participation of such international organizations and institutes of high standing is in itself indicative of the significance of the problems you have undertaken to discuss.

In the course of several days, scientists from a number of countries will be discussing the application of computers in education, the raising and development of children. It seems to me the most important among these is the utilization of the opportunities computers offer us in developing the faculties of the young generation. What is to be done to facilitate children in unfolding the most natural and valuable of human qualities such as honesty, industriousness and respect for the labour of others through the mastery of new technologies. I trust that you, the experts in the field, share my deep conviction that we must encourage the education of children in the spirit of peace, understanding and friendship.

The People's Republic of Bulgaria engages actively in electronics and informatics undertakings within its abilities. We are implementing a national programme for education and training of young people to handle electronic calculators, and the mass introduction of the second, computer literacy. I hope the Bulgarian hosts and facilities in the conference have provided opportunities to acquaint you with everything socialist Bulgaria is doing in the sphere under discussion here. I am convinced that during discussions, more common ground will be broached, opportunities for future fruitful cooperation will be discovered.

I am pleased to once again convey my belief in the success of your conference and wish you all good health, energy and new creative achievements.

Inauguration Address of Academician Blagovest Sendov, Chairman of the International Programme Committee of the Conference

Comrade Yordanov,

Dear guests,

Colleagues,

As Chairman of the International Programme Committee and member of the Bureau of the "Lyudmila Zhivkova" International Foundation I am honoured to chair the opening session of the International Conference "Children in an Information Age: Tomorrow's Problems Today". As you already know this conference is organized by the State Committee for Science and Technical Progress of the People's Republic of Bulgaria, UNESCO, the International Institute for Applied Systems Analysis (IIASA), the "Lyudmila Zhivkova" International Foundation and the World Health Organization.

I would like to thank you all for the attention and interest shown.

I would like to convey a special word of thanks to our fellow countryman, Dr. John Vincent Atanasoff, the first man on the planet to come up with the idea of using electronics in the automated processing of information and the first to put it into practice almost half a century ago.

On behalf of the International Programme Committee I would like to thank all who submitted papers and accepted the invitation to take part in the proceedings of our conference and invest their prestige in making this conference one of the highlights in computer education worldwide.

With their scientific reports, participants will be able to share experience and views on various fields of computer application in education and extracurricular activities and will make a significant contribution.

The International Programme Committee had a difficult task to fulfil, within a short time, in drawing up the programme and evaluating the abstracts of reports. We hope this task has been successfully completed and the experience accumulated will be of service to us in the future.

I should have to avail myself of the opportunity to welcome you on behalf of the Bureau of the "Lyudmila Zhivkova" International Foundation and on behalf of its President Vladimir Zhivkov.

The co-sponsorship of the "Lyudmila Zhivkova" International Foundation in this event is not accidental. Moreover, this participation will lend a special meaning to our conference and hopes for future undertakings.

I would like to quote here part of the Constitutive Act of the Foundation stipulating its objectives:

1) To develop and popularize the highly noble ideas and undertakings of Lyudmila Zhivkova for the harmonious formation of children and youths, for the development of the creativity latent in man, for strengthening peace and understanding among peoples;

2) To encourage creative endeavour and to contribute to the dissemination of achievements in the sphere of culture, the arts, science and education.

I have quoted the abovementioned objectives to illustrate the proximity of Foundation purposes to the issues tackled by our conference. The harmonious and all-round development of the young generation, the promotion of child creativity, will be effected in a world saturated with computer technology. The most rational utilization of this technology for the achievement of that harmonious development is the major problem.

The "Lyudmila Zhivkova" International Foundation views its participation in holding this conference as the beginning of an eventual international programme with the participation of UNESCO, the International Institute for Applied Systems Analysis and other international organizations, on the problems of children in a computerized world. The viability and justification of such a programme will become evident in the results of our conference.

I would like to wish to all participants to gain more than they had initially expected from the conference. And to our foreign guests I would like to wish a pleasant stay in our hospitable country.

On the Start-up Course in Informatics and Computer Technology in the Curriculum for Soviet Schools

E. P. VELIKHOV
Vice-president, Academy of Sciences of the USSR, Moscow, USSR

I am very grateful I was given the opportunity to attend that Conference of great interest and importance to us.

I feel obliged to say, my intention is not to teach You, but rather to get myself informed, as I am not an expert in the field of educational informatics. As Academician Ershov could not attend this Conference, Academician Sendov suggested that I read the first Report.

In general this information treats the manner in which the Academy of Sciences of the USSR views the present Programme of the Soviet Union- "START-UP COURSE IN INFORMATICS AND COMPUTER TECHNOLOGY FOR SCHOOL CURRICULUM".

In January 1985, the Soviet Union adopted a Governmental Programme for Development of Informatics, Computer Techniques and Automation Means (concerning the near future as well as for the period till the end of this century). This Programme has the same status as the Energy Programme, or the Food Programme i.e. it is a basis for working out the five-year plans for the development of the national economy of the USSR. This Programme grounds itself on the fact that introduction of Data Processing Techniques is taking place and it will be continued at the same rate as well as the fact that it would influence all spheres of activities in the Soviet society.

Thus, that Programme, sets the training of young generation for life and work in the conditions of large-scale computerization of society, as one of the most important tasks.The Academy of Sciences of the USSR (within the frame of the Programme for development of the computer techniques) actively participates in the international cooperation in this field, and mainly in the cooperation of the Academies of Sciences of the socialist countries. Nowadays, a General Programme for electronization in the national economies of the socialist countries is being worked out. The Academies of Sciences of the socialist countries are actively working on the further development of computer techniques (this year a Joint Programme for Development of the Computer Techniques and Informatics of the young generations was worked out).

Meanwhile, we established an expedited cooperation in the field of computer techniques application in the educational process.

Our country has gained great and fruitful experience in using computer techniques in Higher-institute education, but application of computer techniques in schools raise many problems on principle.

The modern stage of computer techniques development is connected with its wide application in all spheres of social activities, and that sets the task of wide application of computers in school education, so that each member of our society is trained to use the computers.

The wide introduction of Computer Techniques in all spheres of human activities is determined by the appearance of microprocessors and the personal computers designed on their basis. These techniques really make possible that a new method to train the society for a new stage of the computer revolution is applied- a large-scale introduction of computer techniques in schools.

In 1985 the School Computerization Programme was discussed by the Polit-bureau of the Central Committee and a decision for a large-scale introduction of computers into school education was taken by the Central Committee of the Communist Party of the Soviet Union and the Council of Ministers of the USSR.

Nowadays, the Academy of Sciences of the USSR plays a very important role in this respect, as it is the one that has gained great experience in this field of activities and it disposes of the required staff. Thus it can render help to the Ministry of Education and the Academy of Pedagogical Sciences, to start the process of introducing computers in schools on a large-scale basis. I should mention, that during the last 8-10 years we gained great experience, based on the joint activity of few experimental schools and the Academic Institutes. One of the most complete experiments was performed in the Siberian Department at the Academy of Sciences of the USSR, headed by Academician Ershov. Now such experiments are being made in hundreds of schools jointly with various institutes, the Academy of Sciences of the USSR, higher-schools and institutes concerned with industrial activities.

The decisions, taken recently, are based on the experience gained as a result of that 8-year experimental period.

What idea do we have of the future and the final objective to introduce computers in schools ?

We think, that the main task is to train each child so that later on it could treat the computer as its permanent assistant in any kind of activities it would be involved. In this sense, the objective should not only set the task that students are to be taught of computers only as a tool, used in the education process, but it should be treated as a new, long-term stage in the educational program.

We consider that one of the main components in this sense is training of the student on the principle of unity in model building for the task to be solved, creation of algorithm for its solution and coding this algorithm for a computer. Thus, it is necessary not only to teach hardware and programming languages, but to teach techniques for the practical problem solving.

We think, that computers in school education would ultimately become the backbone of the whole curriculum. Thus three stages can be distinguished in this process.

FIRST STAGE- Comprehension stage, which begins at the age of 7 and lasts approximately to the age of 11. During this period the student for the first time gets acquainted with the new opportunities set before him by the friendly computers - conceiving them as a new assistant and a new friend in the educational process. Here, we think it is possible (on the grounds of the experience of the same New Sibirian Centre) to use a LOGO-type language (Ershov calls it ROBIK). At this stage about 2-3 hours weekly manipulation with the computer are required.

SECOND STAGE- It covers the age of 11-14, when the student starts getting acquainted with the more professional usage of the computer and more profoundly conceives the basis of the programming process, learning the aforementioned triad : problem model, problem solving algorithm and finally, program creation. So far, the student has been already trained to operate with the computer and the keyboard; the computer has already become its habitual tool. Thus, besides programming training (using more powerful languages) at this stage, it is possible to make a transition onto a wider scale of computer usage in teaching other school subjects - natural sciences and arts. Besides, students learn how how to use many application programmes, required for their future work (for example- usage of word-processing systems when writing compositions, electronic workbooks etc.).

At the end is the last stage (concerning the last two forms) - use of computers for Productive Toil. This training will be based on acquainting the students with application programme packages. This stage aims to give sufficient professional habits to use computers in typical practical situations.

In order to materialize that programme, it is necessary that in each school at least one class-room network (intended for 25-30 students, i.e. 12-15 PC) is established. We think it is reasonable that two students share one computer. To provide all schools with that techniques, we need more than 200 000 class-room networks and here we face a serious problem : the computer techniques is developed at a very fast rate, and it is desirable that our students have the opportunity of manipulating with the most up-to-date devices. Having in mind the scale of that task, one should rely neither on providing all the schools with class-room networks at once, nor on their simultaneous replacement with new computers. Thus, it is necessary to create many standards (of programming languages, hardware interfaces etc.) ensuring the possibility to achieve true portability of existing programs to new computers, and on the other side- the system for using computers in school should be open for novelties and should provide the student with an open environment through which he can find his own way in the school training process. This is our final objective.

Of course, we cannot immediately reach that objective. The first step, we are making now, is that by September 1st,1985 2,5 million students from the 9-th form will have been provided with a text-book (written under the edition of Academician Ershov) which sets the important task of creating a model of the surrounding environment, the algorithm for solving that objective task and finally, the manner of realizing that algorithm, by creating a programme suitable for that purpose, and give initial information about computer structure and programming languages. The introduction of informatics teaching in schools, since this year, is a very complex issue, as most of the students, cannot get an access to computers. Our task is that during the short period left, access of the students to computers (where that is possible) is provided from the beginning of the school year. This is the task in which the Academy of Sciences is actively participating.

Now, a textbook in Informatics for the 9-th form is under publication and next year a textbook for the 10-th form will be published.

Thus, we shall start introduction of computers in school education not downwards, but upwards, from the 9-th form onwards; then it will be propagated downwards and laterally. We think that at the beginning of that process, it will be helpful to use the method, already established in our country, the so called Centres of Education and Work. In Moscow there are more than 40 Centres for Education and Work, where students regularly go. In these Centres we shall provide classes which will ensure access of the students from the 9-th form,for two hours weekly. Depending on our technical opportunities we shall do our best to establish such Centres, where we have such personnel. This a completely real task, as we have to provide class-room networks for 40 Centres for Education and Work for the 40,000 9-th form students from Moscow. Similar work is being done in the capitals of the other Soviet Republics and in many other towns. The total number of such centres will depend on two issues: hardware availability and personnel.

The next step is using these Centres as ones for advanced learning and training centres for the future teachers. Further, we intend to gradually make a transition onto the establishment of class-room networks in special Centres, and that each school is provided with such a Centre. Then, when each student is given the opportunity of working in such class-room network, we shall reach the stage, mentioned at the beginning:when the student will be enabled to learn how to use computers not only for the purpose of computer training process, but for the training in other subjects- physics, chemistry, literature, history, writing of compositions, etc.

This is the task set before us now. This objective is of a large-scale, indeed. In a similar way, after the Socialist revolution, when we had to settle the problem with literacy in the Soviet Union (in which process the Academy of Sciences actively participated) now we have to solve the problem with computer literacy within a very short term.

The international collaboration is a very important issue in this objective. On the one side, an unified system, covering the educational process at all levels and giving equal opportunities to all students, is a very positive point, as we can direct great and centralized efforts, to create software suitable for that purpose. On the other side, each mistake will cost us much. Thus, we are interested in any kind of collaboration in the performance of the most large-scale experiment in this field.

It is well known, that most of the aforelisted situations have been disputable so far. The most important thing is the manner in which the computer should or could be used in the educational process and this requires a very profound check. The main check will start when use of computers on a large-scale commences, when the creative abilities of the students and pedagogists could be treated jointly with the opportunities the computer techniques give. In this sense we fully support the idea to create an International Centre (as it was suggested at the Conference) and the efforts made by UNESCO, the Institute of System Analysis, in order to establish international collaboration in this field. Here it is also very important to carry out a number of objective experiments, developing new ideas, concepts of the manner we would use computer in schools.

Usage of computers in school give new opportunities to children, provides them with a tool, helping them not only in the education process, but enabling them to get better acquainted with each other. The large-scale collaboration in this field is a noble and grand task, set before the scientists from all over the world.

The Academy of Sciences of the USSR pays great attention to the introduction of computers in school education. In 1983, a new Department was established at the Academy of Sciences - Department of Computer Techniques, Informatics and Automation. It joins the efforts of the scientists working at the Academy of Sciences and the ones working in Higher Institutes and industrial enterprises. Many institutes belonging to that Department carry out a large-scale work in the sphere of School Informatics : these activities are headed by Academician Ershov in Novosibirsk; in Moscow they are under the control of the Institute of Informatics, Problems, headed by Academician Naumov. The development of scientific grounds for teaching informatics and use of computers in school educational process is a very important component of the work carried out at the new Department of the Academy of Sciences.We shall be glad if an international collaboration on a large scale is achieved in this field.

Information Society and Education. Past Experiences and New Trends in Japan

SHOJI SHIBA
Faculty of SocioEngineering Group, Tsukuba University, 1-1-1 Ten Oh Dai, Sakura-Mura, Niihari-Gun, Ibaragi-Ken 305, Japan

1. CHANGES IN CHILD ENVIRONMENT

The socio-economic environment of modern children has changed dramatically in the past 30 years. The environment of a child in Japan 30 years ago was as shown in Fig.1-1. The father was the symbol of social authority for a child and teachers at school served as his or her main source of information. A child thus used to percieve the world through his father and teachers. Moreover, the existence of so-called "peer leaders" gave him or her experience of a simplified structure of adult society. In other words, such a system used to serve as a means of teaching the child about the structure of adult society through actual experience an a play situation. Furthermore, in the past, most children used to have younger brothers and sisters and in many homes a child was allowed to keep a dog or a cat as "followers".

There have been considerable changes in this environment since 1958 due to the introduction of television in the home. Fig.1-2 shows the proportion of households with black-and-white T.V. sets. By 1961, three years since the introduction of television in 1958, the percentage of households owning a T.V. had reached over 60%. Furthermore, in five years, the figure had exceeded 90%. Along with the 90% spread of black-and-white T.V. sets came the introduction of colour T.V. which began around 1966. By 1975, more than 90% of Japanese households owned a colour T.V.

The introduction of T.V. into the home on this scale had a great influence on children in Japan, different from that in other countries. Dr. Chie Nakane, a social anthropologist describes the difference in the structural lay-out of homes among

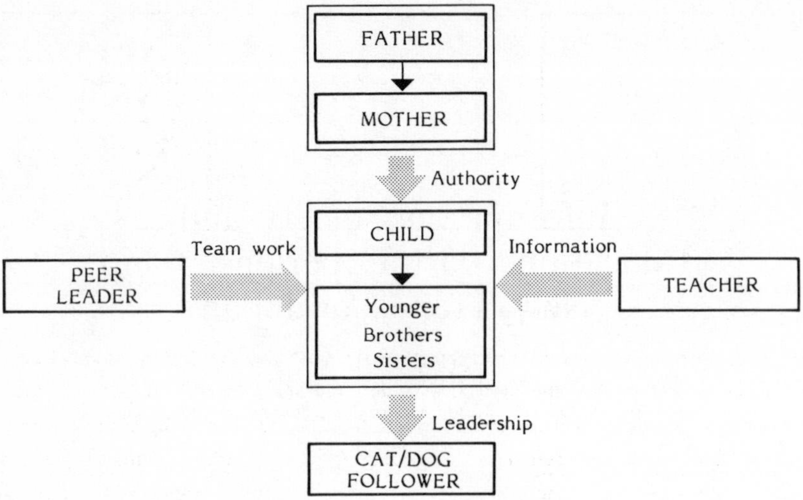

Fig.1-1. The environment of a child in Japan 30 years ago.

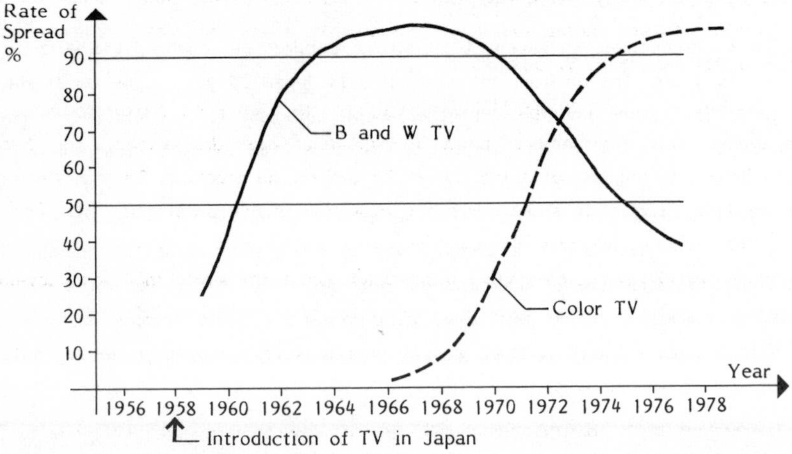

Fig.1-2. Spread of T.V. in Japan.

English, Italian and Japanese families as represented in Fig.1-3. In England, each member of a family has a private room and stays there most of the time. While there are common family spaces such as the living room and the dining room, the individual private rooms are the most important. On the other hand, in Southern European countries such as Italy, a common family room is more important than each private room. Members of the family spend most of their time during the day in this family room and the doors of their individual rooms are always left open,

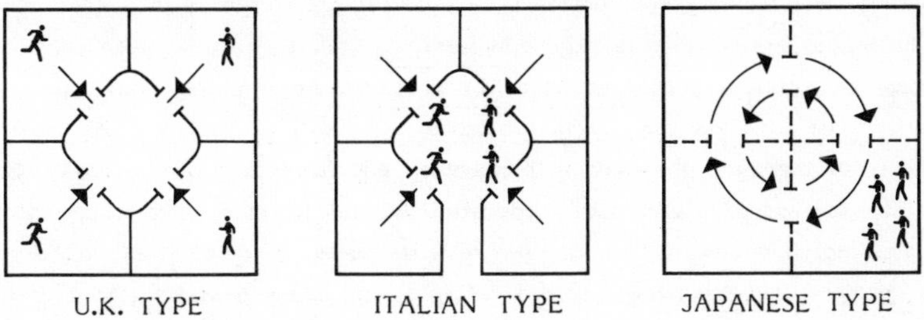

Fig. 1-3. Difference in structural lay-out of homes.

allowing others to enter without knocking. Furthermore, the family room is also open to other people beside the family. Japanese houses differ from both of these arrangements. In traditional Japanese houses, there is no such thing as a private room. Instead, the rooms are designated according to their function within the household, such as guest room, living room, kitchen, etc. Moreover, these rooms are not enclosed by walls but rather separated only by sliding doors which can be freely opened at any time. A family as a group lives together in a house. Usually a T.V. set is placed in the living room where all of the members of the family spend the largest amount of time during the day. Consequently, everybody sits in a happy family circle often with the T.V. turned on.

In this way, as T.V. gradually moved into the centre of Japanese family life, the earlier child environment shown in Fig.1-1 changed dramatically. The first of such changes is the loss of authority by the father and teachers. The newscasters on T.V. provide information about our social conditions much more articulately and skilfully than school teachers do. Furthermore, documentary programs about foreign countries provide much more vivid information about the world than some lessons at school.

In addition, fathers in T.V. dramas, which comprise 35% of all the available programs, are better looking and more pleasant than real fathers lazing at home. The drama fathers also appear to be more intellectual and sympathetic to children's requests.

It is therefore perhaps natural that with the introduction of T.V. into Japanese homes, fathers and teachers have lost their authority as head of the family and as a source of information. With such a shift in the power relationship, the order of authority for a child became T.V. - self - mother - father (teacher).

There has also been a change in the power relationship among children themselves. The significance of so-called "peer-leaders" in child society has been greatly enhanced. Previously, the structure of child society, centred on a "peer leader", used to serve as a stimulation of the general framework of society proper. However, today, children in Japan are exposed to acute academic competition from elementary school and even kindergarten onwards. In order to get a job with a good company, it is better to graduate from a good university. And, to enter a good university, it is better to enter a good high school, etc. Therefore, children must study extraordinarily hard to pass the special entrance examinations set by good upper level schools from the time they are in elementary and lower secondary schools, both of which are still part of compulsory education in Japan. Under such circumstances, a child does not have much time to play with its peers. It is said that, in Tokyo, 95% of six graders are attending "juku" or after school study sessions. There is just no longer a "peer leader" in today's children's world but instead a relationship based on the marks, which each child earns in a given school subject. Achievement in one subject is generally expressed in terms of standard deviation value. A child's social relationship with its peers is based exclusively on one narrow aspect of human ability called intellect represented by the oversimplified figures of "standard deviation". In other words, experience of mutual interaction among children as complete individuals is no longer possible in today's society. Instead, there is nothing but competition founded on intellectual ability.

Other changes in the child's social environment are found at levels below or subordinate to the child. As is shown in Fig.1-4, the number of persons per family (per household) in Japan has decreased from 4.97 persons in 1955 to 3.33 persons by 1980, a decrease of 1.64 persons in 25 years. In fact, nowadays families with many children are fairly uncommon and there are in fact quite a number of families with only one child.

Moreover, population concentration in urban areas has increased considerably over the past 25 years. In 1960, only 43.7% of the total population of Japan lived in the city. This grew to 48.1% in 1965 and to 53.5% in 1970; in 1975 the pique was 57.0% and in 1980 59.7% of the population lived in the city. In other words,

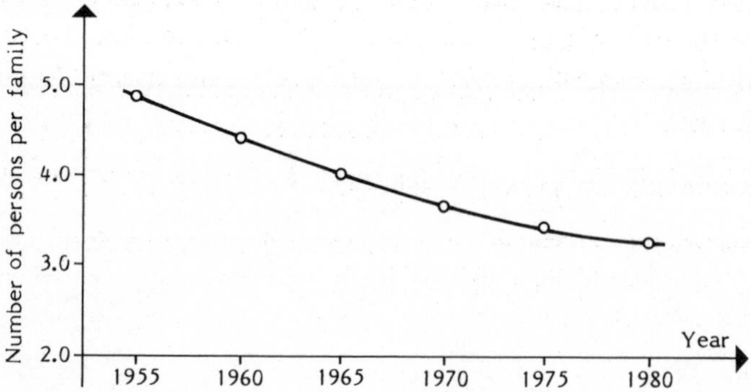

Fig.1-4. Decrease in number of persons per family.

60% of the total population was concentrated in the city resulting in a high population density in the city.

In such cities with a high population density, particularly in apartment buildings of various sorts, it is virtually impossible to keep pets such as dogs and cats. Consequently, many children do not have the opportunity to interact with a family pet which used to fufil the role of follower and friend for the children.

Figure 1-5 summarizes the socio-economic environment of today's children. T.V. is the most important factor both as a source of information and as a representative of social authority. The influence of father, mother and teachers at school has been largely suppressed, and comprehensive interaction with friends has disappeared; the friends of today's child are instead rivals in terms of simple scholastic achievement. On the other hand, with a decrease in number of siblings and pets at home, the child is being deprived to a large extent of environmental influences necessary for experiencing leadership and dependency as a micro social structure.

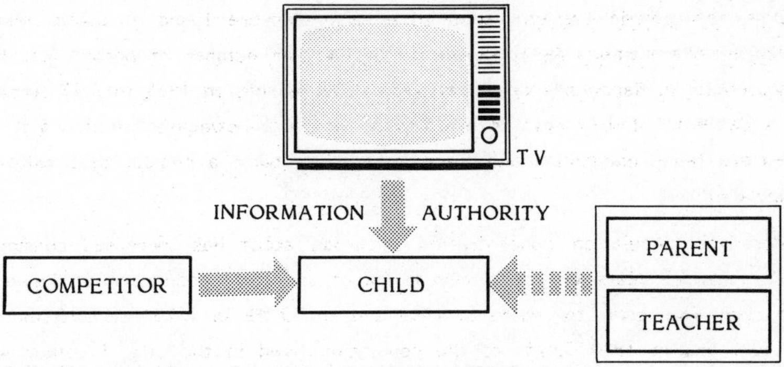

Fig.1-5. Socio-economic environment of today's children.

In other words, children in today's Japan are constantly exposed to information provided directly from a gigantic and more or less uniform source called the mass media, and are constantly subject to severe scholastic competition within their cohort group.

2. DETERIORATION OF JAPANESE SCHOOLS

Of course, such access to highly concentrated information from T.V. has many advanages for children. First of all, simultaneous broadcasting of the same information throughout Japan has served to equalize information availability for everyone. Regardless of family income or regional location, all Japanese children do have access to equal, high quality and the most up-to-date information. It is thus somewhat self-evident that such contact with high quality information should encourage children to acquire more sophisticated knowledge, beyond the framework of their daily lives.

Furthermore, the decrease in the number of children per family allows high parental investment in a child. Despite an increase in educational expenses, 94% of Japanese students advance to upper secondary school and 34% to university. One of the factors contributing to this positive phenomenon is the decrease in the number of children in each family as described in the previous section. In addition, the same factor also enables parents to invest in a child's extra-curricular interests and hobbies such as piano, swimming, and calligraphy. According to the statistics, at an elementary school in a suburb of Tokyo, 30% of the students are taking piano lessons and 24% calligraphy lessons.

The competition among peers of the same age group also provides an incentive for chidren to increase their intellectual skills. The results of studies conducted as part of an international comparison of children's mathematical ability have shown that Japanese children are ranked high both at elementary school and lower secondary school levels. While there are many factors contributing to such results, it can be safely said that academic stimulation through competition and review sessions at "juku" or after-school private classes has made a considerable contribution to improving the mathematical ability of Japanese children.

One of the visible signs of disturbance in the Japanese educational system is student violence both at school and at home. Fig.2-1 shows the results of nationwide studies conducted by the Ministry of Education in 1982. Violence of some kind occured in 13.5% of lower secondary schools and 10.5% of upper secondary school throughout Japan in 1982. Such cases of violence can be classified as those (1) directed towards teachers, (2) among students, (3) involving destruction of school property. At 775 schools, a total of 1,880 teachers experienced some violence by their students. Furthermore, a total of 3,042 cases of violence among students occured at 1,374 schools. The total cost of damage to school property amounted to 300,000 dollars. It is important to note that the number of such incidents of violence in schools has increased quite suddenly in recent years. During the compulsory elementary and lower secondary school period, students are not normally suspended from school nor required to study at home. However, such measures are taken in cases where a student is guilty of excessive violence and misconduct such as larceny, which may adversely affect the other students. The number of instances requiring these measures, which were traditionally considered exceptional, have increased dramatically between 1981 and 1982. During the same period the number of cases of "suspension" doubled and those of "home study" increased 4.8 times. While the number of cases of violence at school have fortunately proved to be decreasing over the past couple of years, this remains one of the major problems to be solved in the Japanese educational system.

	Number of Schools	Total Number of Schools	%
Lower Secondary Schools	1388	10252	13.5
Upper Secondary Schools	415	3954	10.5
Total	1803	14206	12.7

Violence directed Toward Teacher	775 Schools	1880 Teachers
Violence among Students	1374 Schools	3042 Cases 15517 Students
Destruction of School property	580 Schools	69140×10^3 Yen $= 300 \times 10^3$ doll.

Fig.2-1. Student violence.

Along with violence at school is the increase in so-called "bullying" among students which has become commonplace at schools in recent years. According to a study conducted among 2,299 lower secondary school students, 82.4% had "either seen or heard about 'bullying' at their schools". The most common types of "bullying" include "persistent teasing about negative traits and weak points", forced isolation, and "destruction and hiding of personal belongings".

Furthermore, the number of drop outs from school is increasing, according to an investigation undertaken by the Ministry of Education.

3. RANKING BY STANDARD DEVIATION AND EDUCATIONAL STANDARDIZATION

These various types of disturbance at school cannot be explained as having one or two simple causes. However, the phenomena are not completely unrelated to the change in child environment over the last 25 years, as illustrated in Fig.1-1 and Fig.1-5. The decline of the father's authority following the introduction of T.V. at home, the decrease in or lack of interaction among siblings as a result of the reduction in family size and the consequent weakening of the educational effect of the home, are some of the causes of the current disturbances witnessed at school. Other possible causes may include loss of actual social experience among children in a neighbourhood, and excessive emphasis on academic competition. This competition, which is based on nothing more than the evaluation of intellectual ability, is believed to have tremendous adverse effects on today's children. Some even say that there is a monstrous creature called "standard deviation" living in all Japanese homes and schools.

In Japan there are several organizations which set large-scale standardized tests for college entrance on a nationwide basis throughout the year. Between 250 and 300 thousand students, for instance, are said to take each of the tests set by a certain organization.

Upper secondary school students wishing to go to college take these standardized tests for college entrance almost on a monthly basis, often taking several set by different organizations. These tests are quickly corrected and summarized by the testing organizations. The results, standard deviation and entrance possibility for universities proposed are all sent to the students by post. This may perhaps appear not too different from the Educational Data Processing systems available in many other countries. In Japan, however, such standardized tests and standard deviation values are more than just criteria for checking one's aptitude and deciding the future direction of one's studies. For Japanese students, unlike students in other countries, they are the essential "tools" for uniform education and selection by competition. There are almost 400 colleges and universities in Japan. Each of them is supposed to be founded on the basis of its own original educational philosophy. Nevertheless, the universities are ranked and classified solely according to the numerical value of standard deviation of entrance possibility. For the upper secondary students then, what counts is not so much the features of a particular university but its value in terms of standard deviation. They are forced to compete for their entrance to higher ranked, i.e. "good", universities.

Furthermore, upper secondary school teachers give academic guidance to their students by comparing the standard devation value of each university as provided by the testing organizations and the standard deviation of the results of tests taken by a particular student. Schools, students, parents and even the universities themselves are being controlled by this monster "standard deviation".

Such a "belief" in standard deviation is not limited to college entrance. It also affects all those involved when a student enters an upper secondary school from a lower secondary school which is still a part of compulsory education in Japan. At present, 94.3% of students attend upper secondary school. When the lower secondary school teachers give academic guidance to their students, they likewise rely for their major sources of information on the ranking of upper secondary schools according to standard deviation information, provided by the testing organizations and on the average standard deviation of the student's standardized test results.

In other words, the teachers strongly recommend an upper secondary school appropriate to the standard deviation value of a particular student. Here again, the students are being ranked for their future upper secondary school according to a single scale called "standard deviation". This phenomenon is not limited to particular regions but is in evidence throughout the whole of Japan.

The ranking system based on standard deviation has greatly distorted the original purpose of education. Perhaps the greatest distortion lies in restricting the basis for student evaluation to mere academic ability instead of introducing more varied and comprehensive criteria. Furthermore, such ability is determined solely by the standard deviation value of the results of a set of written tests. This basis prevails throughout the whole of Japanese education, from elementary school, lower and upper secondary schools and university.

The situation described above is a result of technical developments in computer-aided educational data processing, and of the expansion of the new educational information industry, which provides data on entrance possibilities. These are some of the side-effects of an educational system of the modern developments in information technology.

4. MOVES TOWARDS EDUCATIONAL REFORM

I have so far discussed the disturbances at school and the evaluation of students by the limited criterion of standard deviation. These problems in the present Japanese education system are serious, and there is general agreement throughout Japan on the need for some educational reform. In other words, the educational system established after World War II is no longer capable of accommodating the changes in our society such as rapid industrialization and the development of a so-called "information society". Therefore, in September, 1984, a "Committee of the Ad Hoc Council on Education" was set up by the government to meet the requirements of the new era, the modern information society. Since its establishment, a number of positive arguments have been put forward for educational reform in Japan. This Ad Hoc Committee was established under the direct supervision of the Prime Minister. Its purpose is to draft a plan for educational reform in order to accomodate various social changes resulting from recent economic developments and advances in science and technology. Such changes include reorganization of industrial and employment structures, greater access to information, urbanization, an increasingly aging society, and internationalization. Extensive discussions are at present being held on the subject and on April 24, 1985 the committee published its Interim Report.

5. INTRODUCING COMPUTERS IN EDUCATION

In the previous sections, I have outlined the changes in child environment and the state of the educational reform plan in modern Japanese society, which is currently undergoing transition to an information society. It must be borne in mind that a particular type of development in information technology may have a quite different impact when applied to education, depending on the cultural and socio-economic conditions of different countries. A success in one country cannot be directly transferred to another country without modification. The impact can differ considerably according to the current educational needs as well as the social and organizational conditions for accepting information technology in a given country.

This section is devoted to a discussion of the current situation regarding the educational use of computers, and its relationship with social and institutional factors in Japan.

So far, the Ministry of Education has been responsible for promoting the use of computers in the Japanese education system. Its efforts have taken two major directions. The first is to provide basic instruction in information processing technology for commercial and technical courses in upper secondary schools. This was started in 1970 to provide for industrial or vocational education to meet the requirements of modern technological advance.

There are, in all, 46 prefectural governments in Japan. The aim was to establish an Information Processing Education Center in each of those prefectures, where commercial and technical upper secondary school students can learn about computers. In the past 15 years, 37 prefectures have managed to establish such a Center. The Information processing Education Center in the Gifu prefecture is a good example. This Center, established in 1973, is currently run by 12 employees. The computer at the Center is FACOM M-150-F (4MB). All upper secondary school students following commercial and technical courses in the Gifu prefecture receive practical training in computer skills at this Center. The content of the training includes, as shown in Fig.5-1, an initial Introduction to Computers, Data Processing, Programming and further courses in Management Science, Systems Analysis and Gaming. The major part of the instruction is centred on programming, using languages such as BASIC, FORTRAN and COBOL. The courses on Management Science and Systems Analysis have thus been developed to train the students beyond mere education in computer languages. The courses in data processing are divided into those for accounting systems, Banking systems, etc., and to stimulate busines developments. 6,331 people visit this Center each year and a total of 105,046 man-days of practical training being given.

In addition, this Center trains high school teachers in the use of computers. There is a Teacher Training Program at the Center shown in Fig.5-2. Teachers without any previous knowledge of computers start their training course with an Introduction to Computers (1 day) and proceed to the BASIC (2 days) and then

SUBJECT MATTER	
1. Introduction to computers	
2. Data processing	
3. Programming	BASIC FORTRAN COBOL
4. Introduction to statistics	
5. Linear Programmin	
6. Systems Analysis	
7. Gaming (marketing)	
8. Drawing by Computer	

Fig.5-1. Subject matter at the Gifu Center for students (on commercial and technical courses in upper secondary school).

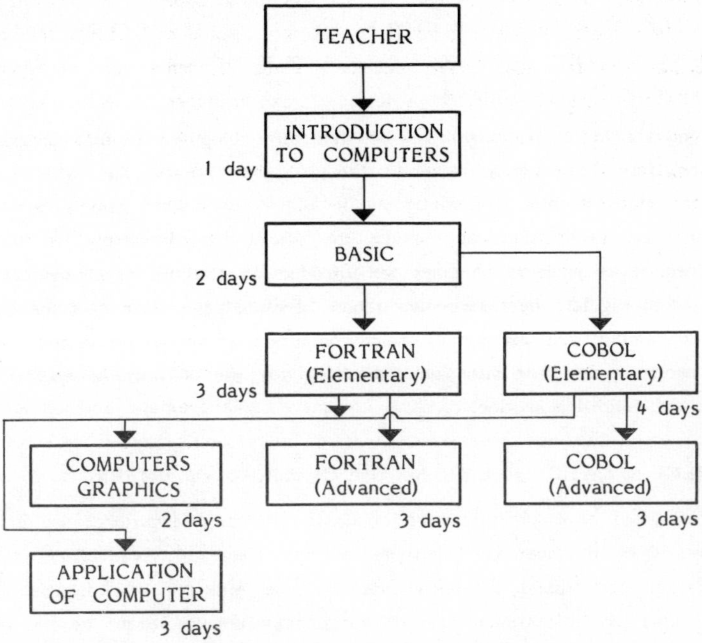

Fig.5-2. Teacher training program.

to the COBOL or FORTRAN courses (3 or 4 days). Besides these courses, there is also a three-month course for specialists in information processing at school. Except for this longer course, all the courses are offered during the summer vacation, between July and August. In 1984, new courses on processing methods for class scheduling and grading and on PASCAL were also established and a total of 257 teachers have received training at the Center.

As mentioned, there is a Center of this kind in most of the prefectures in Japan, contributing to the improvement of computer literacy at high school level. Furthermore, in recent years, an increasing number of high schools have been linked up to the Center by an online system, thus following similar training at each individual school. Some Centers have also expanded their roles beyond mere computer language training and are supplying CAI information as well as storing various educational data for public use. The establishment of such Centers represents the major and the most effective means so far employed to introduce computers systematically into Japanese schools. While such efforts deserve high commendation they are still not nearly sufficient for the wider purpose of improving computer literacy among upper secondary school students in general. One of the major drawbacks lies in the fact that attendance at these Centers is not open to all high school students but is restricted to those following commercial and technical courses. This is perhaps inevitable given that the Centers' original purpose was the modernization of vocational training. However, the total number of commercial and technical high school students in Japan is only compared to those in regular courses. Computer training at these centers is virtually closed to the students in regular upper secondary schools.

Given this fact, one might ask whether any computer training programs are currently offered at regular schools through other means, and what computer education conditions are like, not only in upper secondary schools but also at elementary and lower secondary levels: the answer, unfortunately, is that there are no large-scale projects on computer introduction directed at elementary, lower secondary and regular upper secondary school levels. If this is in fact the case, the only other possibility is the use of micro-computers which have developed considerably in recent years. The situation concerning the use of micro-computers is discussed in the following section.

6. CURRENT SITUATION REGARDING USE OF MICROCOMPUTERS

Two studies have recently been conducted on the educational use of microcomputers. One of them is "Attitudes on the Use and Availability of Microcomputers in Educational Establishments" by the Ministry of Education (MESC) and the other is "Educational Use of Microcomputers in Japan" by the National Institute for Educational Research (NIER). The results of these studies should indicate the current situation regarding the use of microcomputers in Japanese schools. (See "Audio Visual Education in Japan", No.23)

As is evident from the information given above, microcomputers are not being introduced in most Japanese elementary and lower secondary schools. On the other hand, although the 56.38% rate of introduction at upper secondary school level appeares impressive, in reality, only 2% of schools have more than 20 microcomputers and most have less than 3. Therefore, the Japanese educational system is far from actually using computers in class. In other words, the introduction of microcomputers in Japanese schools is still at a very early stage.

A similar situation has also been indicated in the results of research conducted by NIER.

While the introduction rate of microcomputers may at present be low, many teachers are endeavouring to study the possibilities of introducing microcomputers into schools.

Although few in number, some schools are actually introducing CAI and CMI into their classes. MESC of Japan set up a Special Research Fund for CAI research more than ten years ago and has continuously supported its development. It is with this constant support from MESC that research in CAI and CMI has been conducted in Japan as indicated previously. I have also described the vigorous efforts of MESC to establish Educational Centers for computer training in each prefecture in Japan. Through its support for CAI/CMI research and its efforts to establish the Educational Centers, MESC is without doubt making a major contribution to a wider introduction of computers into Japanese schools in the future.

7. NEW MOVES TO INTRODUCE MICROCOMPUTERS INTO SCHOOLS

From the beginning of the 1980s, microcomputers have become very popular throughout Japanese society, even with children. Fig.7-1 shows the results of a study of experience with the use of microcomputers among 6th, 8th, and 11th graders. Approximately 20% of the students have some kind of contact with microcomputers. Since microcomputers are unavailable at most of the schools, these figures indicate that quite a number of computers are already available in private homes. Such contact with microcomputers is mostly through playing games with programs already on the market, with only 3 - 4% of the students writing programs themselves. Nevertheless, the results of this study reveal an important aspect of the use of microcomputers in Japan - computers are being made available to students not through school but through individual homes.

A new movement has emerged in the educational world as a result of the popularity of microcomputers throughout society.

Grades	Computer used		Computer not used
	create programs	only use ready made programs	
6 th.	3.9%	14.5	81.7
8 th.	4.6	15.1	80.4
11 th.	3.7	10.0	86.3
Total	4.1	13.4	86.2

Fig.7-1. Experience in the use of microcomputers among students.

In fact, the results of the study on "Attitudes towards the Educational Use of Microcomputers" conducted by MESC show that 60 to 70% of teachers are positive about introducing microcomputers into schools.

This general climate of acceptance of microcomputers throughout society is further enhanced by the mass media, T.V. in particular, both among adults as well as children. As already mentioned in Section 1, T.V. is a very powerful means of communication in Japan. "Knowledge about microcomputer will be as indispensable in the near future as a driving licence is today! " -- this is becoming the almost anonimous opinion of Japanese society.

News items concerning the introduction of microcomputers into schools abroad accelerate increasing acceptance of this view. "U.S.S.R. Planning to Introduce 1.2 Million Computers for School Education by the Year 1990", "France Establishes a Plan for 1 Million Computers in Schools", and "Computer Education Revolution in U.S." -- such headlines not only make people conscious of the low rate of computer introduction into Japanese schools, but also further stimulate public demand for increased educational use of computers. Against this background, on 12 March, 1985 the Subcommittee on Educational Broadcasting, the Council on Social Education, and the Ministry of Education, Science and Culture published the final report on the "Educational Use of the Microcomputer". In it there is a statement saying that "computer education is a prerequisite for the harmonious co-existence of humans and technology in an information society, for us humans to mantain our human dignity without becoming slaves to computers." To achieve such a goal, the report states that the following conditions should be met:

1. Distribution of information, including actual examples, of computer use in schools.

2. Promotion of research into various ways of using computers and methods for evaluating the advantages and disadvantages of these.

3. Promotion of training in the use of microcomputers.

4. Development of software.

5. Preparation of various data bases so that they can be retrieved by any school.

6. Development of hardware.

7. Cooperation by related organizations.

Furthermore, the report emphasizes the great importance of training those involved in education in the use of microcomputers in order to determine appropriate educational applications for schools, and lays down standards for training in the Educational Use of Microcomputers.

8. WHO IS TO BE IN CHARGE OF INTRODUCING MICROCOMPUTERS IN EDUCATION?

As described in the previous sections, Japanese society is now starting to introduce microcomputers for educational purposes. Is school the only vehicle for this? The answer is No. While we must continue to put our efforts into promoting wider use of computers in schools, it is difficult to imagine rapid progress in schools in the immediate future in the effective use of computers for educational purposes.

One of the reasons for such a pessimistic view of the Japanese situation stems from the general lack of vitality in the present educational system, which is caused by the attitude of many of the teachers. While there are teachers who are seriously committed to the task of educating their students, their number is gradually decreasing. In contrast, there is an increasing number of teachers who regard the work simply as a means of earning money in exchange for a given number of hours' work.

The second reason for the lack of vitality in education is insufficient motivation or incentive on the part of the schools themselves. In Japan, most of the elementary, lower and upper secondary schools are state schools. Teacher status is guaranteed and students must enter their assigned schools. In other words, students do not have the freedom to choosing their own school and teacher and there is thus no competition among teachers or schools. In these circumstances, the lack of vitality in the educational system as a whole is perhaps a natural consequence.

The third reason is the limited freedom of each teacher to change the content of what is taught. This is not because of strict regulations imposed by the Ministry of Education. The reason for this inflexibility is in fact the influence of the "monster" or the excessive emphasis on standard deviation values. Since both schools and students are evaluated by means of standard deviation, educational activities tend to focus solely on improving this rating. The general content of the school curriculum does not therefore allow teachers any opportunity to practise free or creative education.

Coupled with the lack of vitality in the schools is the lack of adaptability to new technology among the teachers. In addition, there is a tendency for teachers to resist any new changes. Another problem is financial -- whether a large investment in state education is possible given the current deficit in the national budget.

Bearing these factors in mind, it is doubtful whether schools and teachers are at present competent enough to take charge of promoting the use of a new type of information technology, namely microcomputers, for educational purposes. Although quite a number of individual teachers are in fact eager to implement the introduction of computers into schools, it will take several years to change the whole, nationwide school system. The problem does not lie in the hardware or software of computers but rather in what is called the "human ware" and "heart ware", the nature of humans themselves. While software or hardware problems can be technically resolved in a fairly short period, the human element requires a long period of time to accept any recognizable changes. In retrospect, our consideration of the educational use of microcomputers has laid too much emphasis on the existing school system. There is a saying in Japanese, translated roughly as "new wine comes only in a new bottle", meaning roughly, in English, "You can't teach an old dog new tricks." In order to develop the use of new information technology it is necessary to establish a new system appropriate for this purpose.

I believe that one should look for this new system not to the state, but to the private sector which is constantly revitalised by free competition. Successful management of such a system in the future information society depends on the following conditions, summarized in the following 5 key phrases:

1. Small-scale, franchised system

   Education for children is more effective in small classes. However, small classes lack the ability to develop hardware and software for educational purposes. This problem can be resolved by means of the franchise system. It is the only management system which combines the advantages of both individualization and standartization at the same time.

2. Using the energy and abilities of women

   The life of Japanese women has changed considerably in the past 35 years. As is shown in Fig.8-1, a woman's life forty years ago was devoted to her husband and children. However, the Japanese woman of today has almost 30 years of "freedom" during her life after her children have grown up. The employment of such women, wishing to work for self-fulfilment in the later years of their lives, is beneficial both to the women themselves and to their newly-independent children.

3. Direct and immediate feedback

Direct and immediate feedback must be available in both directions. In other words, while it is obvious that the instructors must provide direct feedback

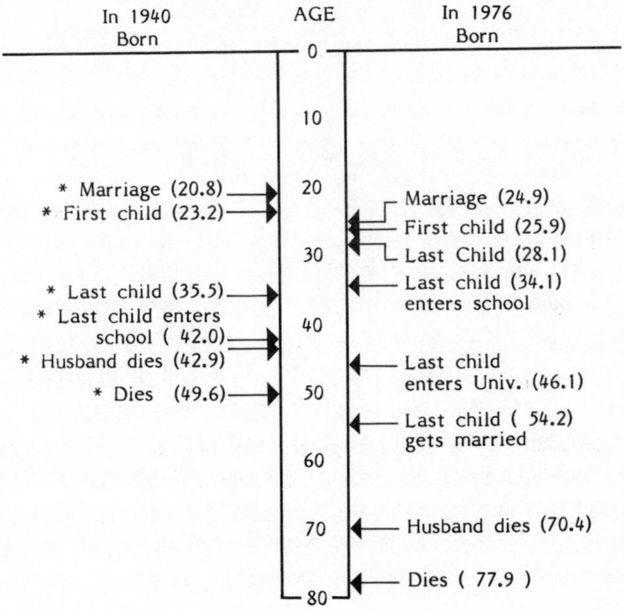

Fig.8-1. Life of women in 1940 and 1976.

on the children's performance, it is equally important that the children or their parents provide immediate and direct feedback to the instructors about their methods of education. The present education system in Japan lacks this latter feedback loop to the teachers. Students cannot quickly or easily change schools although they may be dissatisfied with the teaching methods. This is one of the reasons for the decline in the current educational system and it discourages self-improvement on the part of teachers.

4. Strong corporate culture

A powerful educational philosophy is necessary to bring together all the individual classes under a franchise system. In particular, it is important for each of the separate classes to have complete faith in the social meaning of providing education in new information technology. A clear corporal identity and continuous intensive training for all the instructors are probably essential requirements for extending the corporate culture to all of the franchised classes. It is this strong faith in computer instruction which promotes the spread of new education and develops the abilities of children in society.

5. Reasonable profit

Obviously, some kind of reasonable profit is necessary to continue successful management. However, excessive profit results in harmful side effects. The people who work within the system must be those who find the experience of teaching children rewarding not only in financial terms but also in personal terms through watching and participating in the development of children.

Is there any Japanese company which meets the five requirements above?

The answer is Yes. There are in fact several such companies in the service industries, most of which have proved to be surprisingly successful. One of these is the Kumon Institute of Education Co., Ltd. The Duskin Co., Ltd. is also an example of this kind of management system. All of these have successfully grown up over the past 22 to 25 years. Kumon has promoted its teach-yourself system in arithmetic and mathematics through a franchise system and Duskin established a company which rents dust control goods through distribution and collection by visiting individual households. Both of these companies are characterised by their emphasis on individual classes or stores run mainly by female managers which are horizontally linked under the same corporate culture and by the practical franchise system. The management system of Kumon which is also an education industry provieds a good example for our present purpose (an Outline of Kumon is presented in Appendix IV).

Arguments for introducing computers for educational purposes often tend to centre on the discussion about hardware and software. Furthermore, they tend to assume that introduction to computers will be achieved through schools. However, for the use of computers in education to be truly effective it is necessary to (1) create a new type of educational institution outside the scope of traditional schools; and (2) employ a new management system which will enliven this new type of institution and promote the educational reforms necessary for the coming society. In Japan, at least, widespread introduction of computers for educational purposes would be possible only with such a management system. I believe that this new management system, provided it fulfils the five key requirements outlined above, could quickly and positively effect the improvements needed in the Japanese system of education.

Children and Computers. Myths and Limits

J. HEBENSTREIT
Computer Science Department, Ecole Superieure d'électricité, Plateau du Moulon, F-91 91D90 Gif sur Yvette, France

The very first computers were designed exclusively for high speed calculations as is shown by the title of the book by Professor Brillouin published in 1948 when he returned to Paris from the USA: Les calculatrices géantes américaines (The American giant calculators).

The opinion current at that time was that these machines, because of their price and difficulty of use, had no commercial future and would be used only by a few large military or industrial laboratories for their specific needs in high speed calculations.

A number of technological and technical innovations in the late forties and early fifties produced a dramatic change in the way computers were used.

The invention of the ferrite core which enabled bulky electronic tubes to be replaced by tiny passive elements, and the advent of magnetic recording on tapes, drums and disks which enabled huge quantities of information to be stored, led to the development of smaller and cheaper machines.

Finally, the advent of the transistor in the early fifties resulted in an impressive reduction in volume and price and an enormous increase in the reliability of the computer.

All these factors combined to produce a rapid increase in the number of computers installed; but contrary to all predictions, while this increase proceeded rather slowly in the area of scientific calculations, its growth between 1960 and 1970 in the area of data-processing in large companies, was explosive.

It should be mentioned at this point, mainly for the benefit of the younger generation, that the automation of data processing is not as recent as some people believe and did not begin with the advent of the computer. In fact the invention of the punched card by Hollerith at the end of the nineteenth century to accelerate the census of the US population resulted in the birth of a strong industry for world-wide production and sale of complex electromechanical devices for high speed manipulation (i.e. merging, storing, etc.) of standard punched cards where information was coded and stored in the form of holes.

Two big international companies with sales in the million dollars or million francs range dominated the market until 1940. One was IBM, founded in 1921, and the other was the Compagnie des Machines Bull founded in France in the early thirties, based on the patents of the Norwegian engineer Frederik Bull.

Both companies rapidly realized that the speed of data processing could be increased considerably by replacing the electromechanical machines which manipulated the cards (i.e. physical objects) where the information was coded by computers with a system where that same information was coded in the form of electrical signals. In fact, the installation of computers as data processing systems was very easy because most large companies and organizations were using large quantities of punched-card equipment as a management tool well before 1940.

For these companies and organizations, the change to computers was in general no more than a replacement of the earlier electromechanical equipment by faster and more modern machines and was not considered as a radical innovation (it should be noted that at that time computer manufacturers developed the necessary application software themselves and gave it away to their customers, which simplifies the problem of computer installation considerably).

Teaching computer science (1960-1975)

The increasing use of computers in data processing and scientific calculation was reflected in the manufacturers' catalogues which offered two lines of products, one for data processing and one for scientific calculations; neither of these two lines were found in education.

Since the first computers were used for scientific calculations, the computers bought by universities were installed quite logically in the mathematics departments.

Towards the end of the fifties, the computer science curriculum consisted of 30% FORTRAN, 50% numerical analysis and 20% mixture of ferrite cores, Boolean algebra, automata theory, computer structure, etc.

Data processing was largely neglected in universities despite the fact that 90% of the computers installed were used for data-processing. The alleged reason was that data-processing applications were trivial (file storing and merging, accounting, etc.) and did not give rise to any interesting problems.

Interestingly enough however, these very "trivial" problems led an increasing number of scientists to switch from scientific calculations towards subjects which are today considered as the very core of computer science (optimal processing of increasing volumes of data, optimization of computer use through multiprogramming and time sharing, real-time systems, sharing of large files, etc.).

However by the late seventies the distinction between data-processing and scientific calculations had vanished and the core of knowledge had been built which included the fundamentals of both applications as shown by the striking resemblance of almost all curricula in computer science all over the world.

Informatics in the eighties

The history of technology shows that the form and initial use of a new product is strongly conditioned by the past (the first cars looked like horse-drawn carriages and the electrical engine first designed to replace steam engines had to wait 50 years before finding its place in vacuum cleaners, washing machines, type-writers and electric shavers).

This general statement is of course true for computers. Since the beginning and even up to a few years ago, a company could not afford to buy a computer because of its price unless the machine was to replace a large quantity of manpower; consequently, the main use of computers was in the replacement of people for large-scale manual operations in big companies (printing payrolls, management of orders and invoices, etc.) exactly along the lines of the first industrial revolution.

To speak of children and computers at that time would have been pure nonsense.

However, during the last 10 years or so, because of the tremendous fall in the price of computers due to the advent of the microprocessor, the whole philosophy of the use of computers has changed dramatically.

In big companies, analysts are today studying the content of the job of each person from the shopfloor to the chairman of the board to find out which part or parts of each job can be automated; and each person is given a micro-computer or a terminal to assist him in automating one or other part of his job, either to save time or to enable him to improve the quality or quantity of his work.

We are entering the era of computer assisted activities (Computer Aided Design, Computer Aided Manufacturing, Computer Aided Drafting, Computer Aided Management, Computer Aided Medical Diagnosis, Computer Aided Office, etc.) which is also called CAX, where X stands for any activity.

Ten years ago computers were used to replace people on the lines of taylorism where hundreds of people prepared punch cards to feed the machine. Today we are entering a period where computers are becoming personal tools sitting on the desk of each professional and allowing him not only to save time by asking the computer to take over all the tedious parts of his jobs but also to do much more and attack more difficult and more complex problems than was possible before.

The rapid increase in the number of computers used in all professions and at all levels of activity (the production of microcomputers for 1984 is around 4 million and is going to increase sharply this year) has already had a number of consequences.

The first of these is the shortage of informatics professionals, that is those who design and manufacture the hardware and the software which computer users will buy and use.

The second consequence is, at least in developed countries, a kind of growing awareness among the general public of the key-role of informatics in the society of tomorrow which has been inspired and encouraged both by the mass-media and in official speeches.

This in turn had led governments in almost all developed countries to make proposals or decisions to introduce computers throughout the whole educational system from kindergarten to university.

Moreover, because of the falling price of computers and the way manufacturers and retailers advertise their products, a growing number of parents are feeling increasingly guilty if they do not buy a computer for their children.

Despite some dissimilarities in scope and methods, all proposals or projects to introduce computers in education fall into one or other three "scenarios".

First scenario : computer awareness/computer literacy

In the first scenario, children are to be taught about computers, how they work, how they are used, they social impact, and the way they change jobs; last but not least they are also to be taught programming (the British Micro-electronics in Education Project even includes micro-electronics) and all this before the age of 12 or 15.

This scenario looks like some emergency decision to confront the massive onslaught of microcomputers. It is over-simplified because there is not much sense in teaching the state of the art of informatics to children who will be adults in 10 years from now, given that no-one is able to predict what informatics will look like in 10 years from now (Who was able 10 years ago to predict 500 $ computers, computer networks, integrated service networks, electronic mail, extensive data-banks, etc.

In my opinion this scenario is not only useless, but is harmful because the time spent on these topics could be better used to teach much more fundamental subjects like mathematics, sciences or oral and written expression which are more than ever necessary to turn out the highly adaptable people needed by our and fast-changing society.

In some places, it is suggested that one should go even further and teach programming and/or algorithms.

The teaching of programming

Some people argue that it is necessary to be able to program a computer for two reasons:

(a) If you do not know a programming language you will be like an invalid in a computerized society,

(b) If you do know a programming language you will be able to find a well paid job.

These two arguments were valid years ago but do not apply any more:

(a) Citizens of the computerized society will not write programs, but will use computers in the CAX mode with pre-written cheap software which will be sold by the hundred thousand copies (remember that VISICALC software has sold over 400,000 copies).

(b) If companies can afford to by microcomputers they cannot afford to have their employees writing programs instead of getting on with their work. Moreover, those people who will be hired to write programs will need to be specialists in programming which has little to do with the simple knowledge of a programming language.

Other specialists argue that programming has intellectual merit and compare it to Mathematics or even Latin. Training in programming would teach children:

(a) To "think logically" (whatever this means),

(b) To formulate solutions in a clear, exhaustive and unambiguous way,

(c) To be careful and pay attention to detail,

(d) etc.

From an objective standpoint, these people are indulging in wishful thinking.

The truth is that we would like future programmers to have the abovementioned qualities but experience has shown that training in programming, however intensive, has not succeeded in developing these qualities in people who did not have them beforehand.

The incredibly large number of reports on the poor working methods and the low productivity of professional programmers are proof of this, as are the harsh aphorisms well known in professional circles.

I shall quote only two of these:

"If we could manage to allow programmers to write their software in a natural language, we should see that the majority of them cannot write";

"In software, the first 90% of a job takes 90% of the time; the last 10% also takes 90% of the time".

Some people argue that this has been true up to now because we have not been able to teach "good" programming but that the "new" programming methods or this or that new "miracle-language" or "miracle-system" is going to change the situation.

This may well be possible but remains to be proved.

Moreover, which language should be taught?

the respectable one (FORTRAN),

the easy one (BASIC),

the educational one (PASCAL),

the useful one (COBOL),

the modern ones (LISP, PROLOG, SMALLTALK, ...),

and which will be the standard one in ten years from now?

Will it be a natural language and in this case will it be Japanese?

Some specialists agree with the argument that a programming language is not really important but insist on teaching algorithms.

The teaching of algorithms

The teaching of algorithms is intended to teach children:

° to formulate a problem correctly,

° to analyse the problem and break it down into relevant sub-problems,

° to solve the problem by writing the correct algorithms,

all this is also sometimes called "problem solving".

Now problem solving is an interesting concept. It was formalized in the 17th century by René Descartes who suggested breaking a problem down into sufficiently small subproblems which could be solved at a glance, and the only thing we have done since then is to add new keywords like "step-wise refinement" or "divide to conquer" which is just a form of paraphrase and do not add anything new.

This is not surprising since the general concept of problem solving is so general that it has almost no semantic content.

Apart from academic problems, and even in this case, the solution of any problem depends heavily on the particular discipline in which the problem is formulated and is close in form and content to the handful of paradigms characteristic of that discipline.

There is very little in common between solving a problem in astronomy and solving a problem in biology except that is each case there is a "problem-solving" problem. At that level of generality we may take the view that the concept of problem-solving has no semantic content, unless it is applied to a given discipline, in which case problem solving is a bag of tricks and not a method.

In fact, what is common to the proposals for teaching programming and teaching problem-solving is the idea that there are "informatics methods" for solving problems and that the ultimate in problem solving is to write a computer program that solves the problem.

This is a completely abnormal view of problem solving in general and represents nothing more than an attempt to produce theory from what has been the practice of analysts and programmers for the last 20 years or so. The classic problem solved by analysts and programmers was to automate a procedure or a set of procedures carried out by hand (like establishing payrolls or sorting files, etc.) by means of a computer program. It is not surprising that these people have tried to produce a theory from their daily activities.

Unfortunately the general act of problem-solving cannot be reduced to the specific task of automating procedures and the teaching of programming and/or algorithms is thus of no use except to specialists in informatics.

The real challenge facing us is totally different. In our fast-changing society new problems are arising all the time, and our role should be to prepare children to solve problems which we do not even know today, firstly, by developing insight, intuition and imagination based on a solid understanding of the basic paradigms of science and secondly by helping them to identify which part of a problem requires their own intellectual effort and which part can be assigned to the computer as an assistant. As Terry Winograd said "Computers should not be regarded as a mathematical abstraction but as systems with which people interact".

It is my opinion that computers can be used in education for that purpose and I shal return to this subject later.

Second scenario: the computer as an intelligence amplifier

Despite my opposition to the teaching of programming to children, not so much because it is harmful (as some people think) but mainly because it is a waste of time, I still believe that some aspects of programming can be useful in the education of children, provided more research is done on various aspects which I am about to comment on.

With computers, children can carry out certain experiments which would otherwise be completely impossible:

(a) children can make drawings on a screen with a light-pen; if the computer draws a straight line through any two successive positions of the light-pen, are the drawings different from what children draw with a pencil on a sheet of paper? If there are differences, are these significant?

(b) if having drawn any closed line, the computer is able to fill in the closed surface with any colour, does this change the way children draw?

(c) if different basic drawings are available through a menu of icons (houses, trees, flowers, ships, windmills, boys, girls, animals, etc.) do the drawings which the child produces by assembling the various elements have any psychological significance?

(d) what is the impact of a text-processing package on the speed of learning to write and speak? What is kept and what is lost when children switch to hand-writing? Is there an interconnection between the two activities?

(e) does the possibility of typing a description of something to be done (a few instructions) and to have it done later on request change the concept of the passage of time (past, present, future). How does this compare with the "programming" of a toy like "Big track"? Is there a difference from the child's point of view?

(f) producing a drawing on a screen, storing it in memory and calling it up again later is one level of abstraction above producing a drawing on a piece of paper and storing it in a physical location where it can be found again. How does this change the way a child conceives the concept of storing for later access? What distinction does he make between storing in a computer and storing in a physical location? How does he understand the need to name an object before storing it in memory?

(g) Piaget has emphasized the importance of the fact that the child becomes progressively conscious that he is a performer compared to outside objects. A computer with a program can become a performer while still being an object. Does this change the way a child understands the outside world and his relationship to that world? If it does, what does it change?

There are more questions along these lines but they are all open questions and very little research has been done up to now. We hear some wonderful stories to the effect that "Children love computers" and "They cannot stop typing on the keyboard", including the story about that slightly dyslexic little girl who refused to write because she did not like her handwriting and who suddenly started writing novels when she got a text processor (her parents would have been better advised to take her to a doctor to cure her instead of letting her dyslexia increase!).

All this is true, but they are special cases not the general rule; there are moreover other special cases where children are very reluctant to use computers. In general, children do not love or hate computers; when they can access one, they play a while with it and then change to other games.

Some experts hold the view that if you give a child a computer and a programming language (preferably a "miracle-language") he will become creative and explore and find out lots of things by himself, rather than use software packages which are accused of "programming the child".

This is an over-optimistic view of mankind in general and of children in particular, reminiscent of Jean Jacques Rousseau's "gentle savage" corrupted by civilization.

What happens statistically is that children play with computers as long as they can achieve sophisticated and/or surprising results with a minimum of effort (think of video-games) and that they stop playing as soon as they have to put in much effort to insufficiently rewarding results. It is therefore useless to believe that children will spend a long time on computers if their only aid is a programming language.

Third scenario: Computer assisted activities

In this scenario the role of the computer is that of an assistant to be used as a set of resources and services. In other words, the future user of a computer will be no more concerned with computers per se than the citizen of our "electronic" society is concerned with electronics.

What he will be interested in is the quality and variety of services available at his terminal which will be an outlet for a complex network system of communication, information and processing. The use of such a terminal will be socially accepted if and only if its use is sufficiently simple, which means compatible with the usual behaviour of people in our society.

The history of informatics of the last twenty years illustrates the considerable efforts made by professionals to simplify the use of computers in order to put the machine at the service of man instead of obliging people to learn a complex set of details, relating to the machine, which was in fact putting man at the service of the machine. We still have further to go in that direction to realize the statement of Arno Penzias (Nobel Prize in 1978) "We must teach computers to understand people".

The computer as a source of services and resources is going to play a major role in education and there are now in many countries various projects in progress to use computers for educational purposes.

In the early sixties the main role of computers in education was to replace teachers. The so-called tutorial mode simulated as accurately as possible the role of the teacher in the classroom giving lectures, asking questions, correcting answers and so on. Evidence of this trend is seen in the numerous publications of that time which tried to show that computer-based education was cheaper than institutional education.

The reason for the popularity of the tutorial mode was the high price of computers which made their use economically feasible in education only if they were able to replace teachers.

The tutorial mode is not bad in itself. It may be very useful in a number of circumstances (children who have to stay away from school for a given period, repetition for the less gifted, learning check-list types of activities like maintenance, control, etc.); but it is by no means the solution because it is quite ridiculous to try to reduce all educational processes in all their complexity to that kind of rudimentary mechanism, which is much more likely than anything else to develop conditioned reflexes in children. The fact that it has been implemented by means of advanced technology and with reference to Socrates does not change the situation.

Education is, on the contrary, a complex process where the aim of teaching is to help each child to acquire knowledge, not for the purpose of memorizing it and being able to answer questions, but for the purpose of helping each child to build for himself a coherent mental views of the world around him so that he can act on this very world with increasing chances of success; in this situation, there is a wide variety of possible uses for computers at each stage in the educational process, not only for the child but also for the teacher.

We have already mentioned the growing tendency to use computers in the CAX mode. If we apply this to education then we have two performers: the teacher and the child and each of them can be assisted by the computer in their tasks.

Computer Aided Teaching

Very little has been done in this direction up to now and therefore very few software packages (which I shall call "teachware") are available to help teachers to improve their teaching in the classroom.

One interesting application is the "electronic blackboard" where the teacher uses the keyboard to show texts and pictures. Many different uses are possible:

- increasing the number of examples,
- simulation of experiments,
- presentation of cases where an unknown rule is applied and asking the class to find the rules, etc.

Some experimental teachware has been developed in France and has produced extremely interesting results.

In one of these experiments (age 13-15) the teacher shows a triangle where two points are fixed and one of the points can be moved via the the keyboard. He asks how this last point should be moved to produce a triangle with the same area as the original one.

After discussion between the pupils a move is proposed.

If the area of the new triangle is equal to the original one, the proposed point appears green and the computer gives a "beep"; if it is not the case the new point appears red and nothing happens. New discussion, new point, etc., until a line of green points, parallel to the fixed side, appears on the screen; this, with proper commentary by the teacher, allow him to introduce the formula of the area of the triangle, which at the same time justifies and explains what is shown on the screen.

What this factual description is unable to describe is the excitement in the classroom, the vividness of the discussions between pupils before making a decision and the pleasure of those who guess that all the points lie on a straight line. What is important here is the emergence of a new type of teaching where the computer plays an active role in the hands of the teacher. What is also important is the change introduced in the relationship between the teacher and the pupils, where the teacher is not the one who teaches the truth and gives poor marks for a wrong answer. On the contrary he is encouraging the intuition, the imagination and the creative thinking of the pupils and leaving the computer to show whether a pupil's proposal is right or wrong, with the subsequent demonstration which helps to explain why some ideas were right and others not. This example provides only a slight insight into the wide range of possible uses of the computer by the teacher and much more research is necessary in this direction.

Another possible use of the computer to assist the teacher in the classroom is "guided discovery" which is the teacher's version of a game called "Microworld". For this purpose the teacher uses a software package simulating an experimental phenomenon (physics, chemistry, biology, demography, geography, etc.). Pupils work in groups on a terminal where they can change the parameters of the phenomenon while the teacher goes from one group to another.

This has many different objectives:

- to put children in a research situation i.e. to construct an explanatory model of what has been observed. This is a real genuinely inductive way of reasoning and requires creative thinking at a fairly high level of abstraction (children are working on the symbolic representation of a real event),
- to verify that children apply the experimental method correctly: experiment, hypothesis, verification of the hypothesis, verification of the hypothesis through experimentation, new hypothesis, etc. with examples and counter examples,
- to verify that children apply a strategy to make their experiments converge on a conclusion and are not playing by trial and error,
- to help children to become independent in a situation which requires constructive thinking in the search for a solution.

Another interesting possibility for the teacher is the use of small data-banks; these can be used in many disciplines, the main purpose being to show that there are methods for asking the right questions and for refining these progressively and that there are also methods for distinguishing between relevant and non-relevant facts in the answers given by the computer.

Computer Aided Learning

Here we are interested in the assistance which a computer can give to the pupil.

I shall only mention video-games or the so-called educational games, because apart from what I have said previously about the psychological impact of the specific properties of the computer, they have on the whole little educational value.

Besides these, the tutorial mode or the drill and practice mode can help the less gifted children at home to improve their performance provided its use is supervised by the parents: I know few children who will volunteer to work outside lesson-time, even on a computer when it becomes daily practice.

A more interesting possibility is a text processing system with a reference dictionary which can be used to improve spelling or can encourage children to write, either because it comes out neatly printed or can be sent directly through electronic mail.

Dictionaries or encyclopedias on computer, including video-disks, are much more likely to be used by children because they no longer need heavy books accessed by alphabetical order but can obtain immediate answers to any question with moving pictures on the screen.

Finally the most interesting is probably still to come as shown by a recent experiment in France. The example I shall describe is in elementary chemistry but it can be used in any discipline. The software is an expert-system in chemistry but it is not used to answer questions. Instead of asking a question, the user submits a chemistry problem to the computer and asks the computer to explain step by step how it solves the problem. This is the first example I know on computer of learning how to solve a problem by watching a computer solving the problem and setting out in sequence the rules which are followed to find the solution. This new direction seems very promising at least for simple problems and should be further investigated.

Long term implications

The using of computers through the various techniques described is aimed at improving present education by giving children more independence, increased powers of critical thought and more scope for creativity.

Moreover, if children are encouraged to work with computers, they will become familiar with their future environment in tomorrow's society and with the variety of tools which they will have at their disposal.

This computerized society is no figment of science fiction; it is already a reality in an increasing number of industries in the form of CAX tools.

These tools give their users increasing power over their environment by allowing them to solve problems which they would have been unable to solve, and by allowing them to master more and more complex problems; it is thus essential to familiarize children with these tools, not by giving them lectures on computers or programming but by giving them the opportunity to use these tools in the widest possible variety of situations.

Knowledge about computers and programming is generally useless as a means of achieving because writing a program of 50 to 100 instructions does not enable the user understand anything about a data-bank, how to access it and how to use it; just as knowing how to pilot a plane is totally irrelevant to what one needs to know to fly from Paris to Varna on a commercial airplane.

In the first case, it is necessary how to control a plane with its problems of mechanics and aerodynamics, with its take-off and landing procedures, etc. In the second case since there are specialists to pilot the plane, the passenger is not concerned with these problems; what the passenger has to know is how to read a flight schedule, how to plan flight connections, how to make a seat reservation, the address of the air terminal, the duration of the ride to the airport, the maximum weight of his luggage, etc.

The image of the user in front of his computer with a programming language as his only resource is a thing of the past. More and more computers are integrated into complex systems of information, communication and processing, ranging from the local working station, with dozens of sophisticated software packages where instructions are sent by the hundred thousand, to local, regional and international networks. Each user will therefore be linked to thousands of other computers with access to information and software packages available all over the world which he will be able to down-load in his own station for further use. This multiplication of increasingly sohpisticated software tools which will be accessible from any professional or private terminal is the major characteristic of the computerized society - the society our children will live in and for which we have to prepare them.

The invention of printing has allowed the knowledge accumulated by past generations to be put at the disposal of everybody in book form and has therefore contributed to the general progress of knowledge.

The advent of information, communication and processing systems represents a radical change because these not only allow faster and easier access to that accumulated knowledge but also enable methods and techniques to be put into operation through the use of software packages written by others, which is a completely new concept.

Up to now we have had to memorize the description of methods and techniques from books and try to apply these methods to each problem encountered.

By adding information, communication and processing systems to printing we are, without always realizing it, allowing the era of discursive information (the description of what we have to do to solve a problem) to enter the era of operational information (how to chose the software package which when implemented by a computer will provide the solution to the problem).

If we analyse the implications of this radical change three point emerge:

(a) it is absurd to believe that there will one day be software packages to solve all the problems or answer all the questions which men will ask,

(b) the numerous software packages being developed today are packages which will assist men in the solution of problems by providing a tool for automatic processing of certain parts of his problem,

(c) the use of these software packages is not an easy way out. One must first of all learn how to use them and in addition have sufficient mastery of the subject matter concerned to be able to make a critical appraisal of the results produced by the computer (no software will ever allow a TV-repair man to design VLSI circuits).

The contents, techniques and methods of all present-day educational systems from elementary school to university are based implicitly on the hypothesis that, for solving the problems which are given or will be given to the student, the student will have at his disposal his brain, a sheet of paper, a pencil and possibly some books. This very hypothesis is never explicitly stated but forms the very basis of all educational systems.

If, as I believe, in the very near future any pupil or student will have permanent access to systems of information, communication and processing where thousands of software packages will be available to help him to solve his problems, then it is clear that the preceding hypothesis is no longer valid.

In other words, more general access to systems of information, communication and processing will progressively challenge the methods, techniques and content of all systems of education from elementary schools to university because each access itself brings into question all knowledge and skills as we define them today.

Learn to think differently

One often hears these days that our problem is to integrate informatics into all disciplines but it should be evident at this stage that those who attempt to achieve this objective by teaching programming or algorithms are addressing the wrong problem.

If informatics is not the science of computers, it is not the technique of programming either. The computer is a machine and programming is a technique. Both together are tools for the processing of information which is the major subject of informatics.

When I speak of integrating informatics into all disciplines I am not concerned with computers or programming but with information processing in the broadest sense and what it can bring to the user.

The major trend in informatics in recent years is the rapid emergence of computer-aided techniques (what I have called CAX) which are, strictly speaking, processing systems of an increasing degree of sophistication in a constantly expanding number of areas (electronics, avionics, medicine, biology, mechanics, architecture, office work, etc.).

Some experts belittle this phenomenon by calling it "press-button informatics" but I believe that it is the most important development since the invention of the computer.

It is important for two reasons. First of all it is going to give us more and more powerful tools which will inevitably challenge all existing knowledge and skills and secondly it will affect everyone in their professional and private lives.

It is obvious that these tools, because they relieve the user of lengthy and detailed routine work, also require him to be more imaginative, more intuitive, and more creative so as to invent alternative solutions to be tested on the computer; they also require him to have the capacity to judge critically any result produced by the computer which in turn involves a different and deeper type of knowledge. However even a superficial analysis of the content of education shows that a large part of education is devoted to the teaching of analytical methods which result in the breaking down of a problem in successive steps to the level where each sub-problem can be solved by hand.

This is not only normal, it is essential in a situation where there are no resources other than paper and pencil.

Given the fact that the vast majority of analytical methods are algorithms, however, it is clear that sooner or later we shall have software packages to implement these methods automatically and everybody will be able to use them including schools.

Since it is highly probable that, in the not too distant future every school child will have a computer in his pocket just like he has a pocket-calculator today (the very first first pocket calculator was put on the market only 13 years ago at a price of 700 $ US) with a wide variety of powerful software packages, it is clear that our present system of education will at all levels become increasingly inappropriate. It is not too early therefore to begin to think about the sort of modifications which should be introduced in the content as well in the method of education (as is already the case in certain states of the US).

It has often been said that informatics would effect profound changes in our intellectual habits as a result of its intrinsic logic and that to accelerate these changes it was important to teach the techniques of informatics to everybody, particularly children. The implicit assumption was that we could prepare our society for the unavoidable changes by teaching algorithms to everyone through top-down analysis, data-structures, rigorous logical thinking, iteration loops, recursion and proofs of programs.

The difficulty here is that this very proposal is nothing more than an attempt to rise to a respectable level of culture and to convey to the whole of society what has in fact been the essence of professional programming activities over the last 10 or 20 years. An even greater difficulty is that this type of proposal is exactly the type of conditioning by the past which has coloured the invention of every new tool, as I suggested at the beginning of my talk.

But the greatest difficulty of all is that this type of proposal is contrary to the most recent trends in the evolution of computers towards widespread CAX activity. The more general use of computers <u>is</u> going to change our mental habits but not because of the above mentioned reasons.

What is going to happen is that as a result of economic competition or because of the simple need of industrialized countries to survive, more and more sophisticated informatics tools will be introduced.

What is going to happen is that everyone will have to use, professionally, at first and later in his private life tools so powerful that they would have been unthinkable 10 or 20 years ago.

This will inevitably lead to changes in the formulation of problems because they will be solved through the use of much more powerful tools, and this will lead people quite naturally to think differently (long distance travel problems are considered differently today from what they were before the invention of the rail road, the car or the airplane and this has profoundly changed the way we look at the world in general).

The advent of CAX tools and their more general use in the next ten years is going to challenge all our skills, and the teaching of computers and programming is by no means the answer to that question. The question does in fact go much deeper, namely how are we going to change our whole system of education to take into account the existence of these powerful tools and how are we going to integrate these in a new set of coherent curricula at all levels so as to educate everyone from elementary school through to university to make the most efficient use of these tools.

Terry Winograd has said that "There is one thing which computers cannot do and which people do quite naturally: "think" but it has also been said that the way we think is to a considerable extent conditioned by the nature of the tools we use".

The advent of CAX tools is opening up a whole new era where men will be relieved from a considerable amount of routine intellectual activity and mechanical thinking; this gives us for the first time in history a unique opportunity to use education to develop insight, imagination and creativity which are more than ever necessary to make the best use of these tools.

Dr. Hamming has said that "The purpose of computing is insight and not numbers". I would like to paraphrase his statement by saying that the ultimate purpose of computing should not be to turn people into servants of the computer but to develop in people those qualities which are unique in men: in other words, the ultimate purpose of computing should be to help people to become more human.

The Future of Electronic Learning for Children

MARY ALICE WHITE
Electronic Learning Laboratory, Box 426, Salisbury, CT 06068, USA

I will try to give you a summary of what I see as a development in technology for children in the United States as I see them. When I use the term "electronic learning", I mean learning delivered by any electronic system but predominantly at the moment that is computers, although I think it will change fairly quickly to computers and videodiscs. I am familiar with what is happening in many public school systems in the United States as I spend a fair amount of time talking with public school officials and state education agencies but I would not try to represent myself as an expert on all the school systems. What I tel you is what I think is happening as seen by other experts besides myself.

If I were to summarize what is happening in the United States' public school systems in terms of delivering education through electronic technology to children, I would say that I see three different levels of involvement. Let me describe them to you briefly. I am talking now about the use of computers as a form of teaching and learning to children in our public schools in the United States. Level One , I would characterize as based on the concept of the computer as peripheral to education. The schools' systems that belong to this level see the computer as something that is not directly involved in education and very possibly have been pressured into becoming involved through parent organization which are very active.

From an organizational point of view, Level One requires the least amount of change from the school organization and the least amount of investment of money, the least change to its power structure and it certainly is the least politically dangerous, at least over the short term. The political problems that are faced by school systems at Level One is that the parents shall become uneasy about the lack of involvement and will demand more. Educationally, it represents the least use of the computers for education and it could meant that teachers and pupils will be left behind other school systems that are moving much more rapidly. I think it should be said that many school systems fall into this Level One, not out of choice but because of lack of money. But I am trying to define here those systems that do have a choice, but who conceptually can only see the computer as peripheral to education. They represent, in my view, a total lack of understanding of technology's power to educate. It means that their pupils are probably getting less than thirty minutes per week per pupil on any kind of computer and what they are getting is fairly superficial in terms of a little bit of computer literacy.

In the United States the term "computer literacy" can mean almost anything from letting children begin to learn how to use a keyboard, to a short lecture on the history of computers, to an introductin into a programming language such as Basic. It is a hodge-podge and represents, in my view, very little serious educational effort.

Level Two, as I see it, is based on the concept that the computer is an adjunct to education, not peripheral but an adjunct. Organizationally this does not interfere with the schedule or the staff assignments. it requires a little more money than Level One but not a whole lot. It requires some teacher training. It can be dropped or expanded in response to pressures so that if parents groups want more, then the school system can increase the role of computer as an adjunct. It might be compared to trying to put the computer and all technology into little boxes that don't interefere with the current work of the school. It means that if you need to, you can add more boxes, or if you need to, you can take away some of the boxes. It's an add-on or a cut-back type of response.

Educationally, it means more access to computers than Level One, but in my view, little involvement in serious educational content. Conceptualy, I think it shows still no understanding of technology's power to educate. In Level Two schools you will see LOGO used as anything from a serious attempt to introduce some logical thinking to LOGO used as "busy" work in the back of the room. You will see some more computer literacy. You will see some drill and practice software used probably for children who are a little bit behind in their work. There will be some content course software,but the assortment of software, again seen as an adjunct to education, is not going to have instructional impact. The instructional time per week per pupil probably is in the range of a half hour to an hour per week.

Level Three represents those schools who have the concept of the computer as a subject for study much as any other course in the curriculum is a subject for study. Organizationally this level does require adjustment in the schedule because a course has to be scheduled. It requires additional teacher training. It requires the addition of new courses in the curriculum that deal with the computer and it probably means hiring a computer technician in a central laboratory or resource room where many of the computers are kept.

Educationally, Level Three at least gets the computer into the curriculum. It exposes students to advance programming languages in high school such as Pascal and Forth. It means a competent computer teacher must be hired or trained. Usually there is a curriculum coordinator who is given repsonsibility for coordinating the computer into the curriculum. Conceptually, Level Three sees the computer as another subject in the curriculum which means that it is accepting the computer in terms of being a traditional course and therefore, it is fitted into the traditional structure of the school.

It has the advantage of at least getting the computer into the school as a respectable subject to be studied. If you walk into such schools, you see Basic being taught in the elementary school, and Pascal and Forth at the high school level. You will see some simulations being used in science and in history. You will see a range of computer courses being offered for advanced students at the high school level. The instructional time that will be given will depend very much on whether a student is interested in pursuing computer science as a course content. But the level per pupil throughout the system is probably well over an hour per week and maybe as much as three to four hours per week.

Level Four may appear in the same school system as Level Three. I don't wish to imply that these are separate paths necessarily. Level Four has a different concept than anything in Levels One, Two and Three. Level Four sees the computer as a learning tool, not as a subject for study, not as an adjunct and not as a peripheral to education. Here we are getting much closer to the idea that technology is conceptually central to the role of education.

Organizationally, Level Four which sees the computer as a learning tool requires much more change from the school organization. It requires the adaptation of software and utilities into appropriate parts of each subject area, by which I mean English, math, science and social studies. It means absorbing the computer into the early grades usually as a word processing tool. It may require more time from the existing courses in the curriculum and it may require more hardware and it certainly will require more software, and most of all, it requires more teachers throughout the school system to be computer competent. If one assumes that the computer is a learning tool, then it changes immediately the responsibility of the teacher to use it as a learning tool in whatever subject he or she is teaching. This means a very fundamental change in teaching skills and in the use of the computer within each of the subject areas.

Educationally it means that the computer is being used as a word processing tool for crunching numbers. You will see word processing software in such schools. You will see spreadsheets, you will see data bases, you will see simulations, you will see computers used as a tool for scientific study and used, for example, for sensors in experiments. You will see it used as a statistical tool. In my experience, you are more likely to see this at the higher levels and the university level than you are at the kindergarten through twelfth grade public school level. Conceptually this is more imaginative, as far as it goes, in saying that the computer is a learning tool whose uses are still, in my mind, at the primitive stage. As far as time is concerned, I would think that children involved at a Level Four would be getting at least two hours per week use out of the computer as a learning tool.

Level Five has a different concept than any of the previous four. It sees the computer as an educational delivery system. In fact, it sees it as the new educational delivery system. This is a fundamental change in concept and is radical in the sense that it goes to the root of the concept.

Organizationally it means a fundamental change in the structure of the school organization, in the schedule, in use of space, in the scope and sequence of the curriculum, in staffing, in costs and in financing. It means a change in the entire school organization which can be expected to resist such change.

Educationally, if you walked into such a school, you would see that the computer would be delivering a large part of the curriculum, varying from thirty minutes per day per pupil to up to three hours per day per pupil. It leaves the teacher free to concentrate on higher order skills and on instruction beyond basic skills. It is intended to expand the productivity of the learner and to individualize learning. There are few such schools in my country. I have seen only one but it is a very different and a very exciting kind of school Conceptually, it seems to me, it is the challenge that is before us.

In my view, these technologies, by which I mean not just the computer but the computer plus video disc, plus videotape, plus fiber optic communications systems, represents a fundamental change in learning and teaching and therefore, a fundamental change in how education will be delivered. In my view, it is a waste of time to think of these technologies as peripheral to education or as an adjunct to education and not even as a subject for study. I think the future will demonstrate the technologies to be used (1) as a learning tool and (2) as an educational delivery system.

Let me comment first on what I see as the future of the technologies and then secondly, the future of the U.S. public school system in terms of electronic learning for children. The future of the technologies, it seems to me, tells us that the computer has pretty much crested as far as its invasion of the home market and possibly the public school market in its present form as a microcomputer. I expect to see the development of much larger computer systems to deliver large curricula as a delivery system. The laser disc, I think, is definitely on its way in some form, probably within three years according to the people I talk to. We will see 500 megabyte compact discs available, which means enormous capacity to store print, pictures- both still and moving, graphics and sound, which brings into question the future of databanks via electronic networking. It seems to me that if students can have this enormous data base available to them at their elbow, that networking and telecommunications will not be so prominent.

I do see, however, the development of fiber optic transmission systems which are moving ahead in several parts of the country, and I am told that they are economicaly viable now so that in five years we can expect to see them moving at least into the corporate offices. Engineers with whom I talk tell me that we will be having before ten years or so, a unit that will sit on our desk at home which will combine what used to be a telephone with what is now a computer,a monitor and a laser disc, so that delivered into our homes and our offices will be an instrument to bring us text, voice, graphics, imagery, sound,still and moving pictures and with the capacity to communicate back and forth to her people through this system being called ISDN- which I think is a terrible name for it- The Integrated Systems Digitalized Network.

Another technology that we see coming is the use of interfaces like the Macintosh on most of the computers because moving an icon around with a mouse is a whole lot easier way to deal with a computer than having to participate in a series of textual commands. Only engineers like textual commands. A human being prefers an easier way of doing it and the computers need to become much more human.

I see a movement at the university level in particular to develop learning tools from these technologies, both computer and video disc. As many leading universities in the United States are getting wired, such as Brown University, Carnegie Melon,Drexel, University of Michigan, we are seeing the optimum ratio come into existence of one computer per student and one computer per faculty member. Under these conditions, I think we are seeing now and will see increasingly, many different uses of the computer as a learning tool- not just in the sciences, not just in mathematics, but in history, in the arts, it must, in fact in every part of the curriculum as faculty and students learn to explore it as a learning tool. I hear now of the development of hypertext which means that we can see a piece of text on the screen and decide that we wish to have more information about a particular piece of it and can bring then in depth by branching much more information on a particular subject, and so to speak, follow our nose down through the text so that the text that is delivered can be as much in-depth as the reader wishes or in some reform. I see the development of expert systems which will allow us to trace the process of judgement made by experts in arriving at a decision and leads to the possibility that we can train other people to do the same and thus become experts.

Finally, I see a future technology that will be cóncerned with building a curriculum using both computer and video disc. It is going to be expensive. It already is. A current estimate at WICAT (in Orem, Utak,USA),to build one course is $ 1 million. I don't think that is going to change substantially. But I believe this will happen because we will find out fairly soon that microcomputers are like mosquitos stinging at the curriculum and just don't deliver enough breadth and depth to make a difference.

Let me turn now to describe what I think may be going to happen in the public schools in the United States, and I speak here essentially of the public schools and kindergarten through twelfth grade when children are five years of age to about eighteen or nineteen years of age.

I see several things happening which, in my opinion, are going to change fundamentally and drastically our public school system. I must say that I have many concerns about these changes. I have to report to you that I think they are likely to happen.

1. I see deregulation coming for public schools. Up to now it has been very difficult for a pupil to move from one public school system to another simply because he wished to do so. Most public school systems are designed for students coming from one particular geographical area which has been used to help to disaggregate our schools. But I think the mood in the country is such that just as we have deregulated the airlines and deregulated the television networks and are moving toward the delivery of private hospital care as opposed to public, I think we are going to see a move to deregulate the schools. An example of this is that recently in the legislature of Minnesota, a plan was introduced to allow students in the eleventh and twelfth grade of high school to select to go to another high school the last two years and to take with them the state monies and the local monies that were assigned per capita to that pupil. It is hard for me to stress sufficiently how different an approach this is in the United States public school system. When this was introduced last fall, I am told that nobody thought this piece of legislation would have a prayer of getting through but I am told that it was voted in the Minnesota Senate recently and lost by only one vote and has yet to come before their house. Similar legislation , I am told, has been introduced in Colorado and in Tennessee, so I think we will see a move

to permit pupils to flow back and forth among the public schools at their own choice, carrying with them state and local monies so that public schools will begin to be in competition with each other for the first time. Hopefully this would mean that public schools would attempt to compete with each other in the quality of the education that they deliver and that this would have a beneficial effect on not only quality but on cost. I think the move is primarily one to improve quality and not cost.

2. Productivity in education is going to be, I think, an overwhelming issue. It comes from several sources. One source is a feeling in the United States that our work force is not doing terribly well in terms of competing with other work forces around the world. We see our economy losing shares of its markets overseas. We see workers who don't have the requisite skills needed for new production techniques. There is a feeling that our industry is slipping behind and is stuck in an old mold. This in turn causes the schools to be criticized on the grounds that they are not delivering workers with the right kinds of skills and ability to make decisions.

There is another move that says we have thrown billions of dollars at the schools since the 1960's and it hasn't made a bit of difference except that some of the scores on the S.A.T. have gone down. The S.A.T. is an exam taken pretty much throughout the country for admission to college and is considered a mark of how well students are prepared. These scores have gone down since the 1960's slightly and are now coming back up a bit. But the critics of the schools argue, with some justice, that all this money hasn't made a bit of difference as far as improving the amount of education or the quality of education in our public schools.

The critics of our public school system point out that the brighter women have left the schools because they now have opportunities to go into law, medicine and business. They also point out that we have a generation of women teachers now in their upper 50's who are about to retire who will no longer be in the schools, and yet those coming into the schools to make a career of teaching are showing S.A.T. scores in the high 300's which is a very low score indeed. It is a grave concern that the ability of the people coming into the teaching profession is so low. One answer, of course, is that there are much better alternatives for young people than a career in teaching. Those who argue for increased productivity. at least hose who I think make some sense, will agree that it is unlikely that we can increase teacher productivity. That is my view, that teacher productivity is about at its limit. Having been a teacher a good part of my life, there are just so many minutes in the day that you can spend on so many people in face-to-face talking of any kind. And unless we can invest new hours, I don't see that we are going to get much more productivity out of teachers. But I do agree with those who feel that the real breakthrough is going to come with learner productivity.

I think that learners can move much more quickly on an individualized basis than they are now doing and that is one of the great hopes of these technologies.

A third issue is the equity issue in which I think every responsible person worries about those who cannot afford the technologies and those schools that cannot afford to buy computers, or video discs, or anything else. it is a great concern that many of our children who live in poor school districts in large cities, many of whom are children from minority backgrounds, are going to be left way behind in the acquisition of the skills of technology but more importantly, be left behind as far as the delivery of education through the technologies. It is quite possible, I believe, that those who urge the need for productivity in the schools are also going to be joined by those who are going to argue for equity and that the combination of the productivity issue and the equity issue isn't going to make a ground-swell or public opinion that move the schools into competition with other forms of delivery.

Fourth, I see a move toward the development of private schools run for profit by corporations in the private sector. I think there are a number of reasons that this will happen. I have just said that I think that the productivity issue and the equity issue will be two of the driving forces. Schools run for profit can probably deliver education at a current cost of about $ 3,000 per year per pupil. This compares to the average in New York State, for example, which is a state that spends a lot of money on its pupils of $ 4,700 per year per pupil. The argument can be made that using the technologies as a delivery system for education that private schools can be set up and run at lower costs than public schools can be set up and run at lower costs than public schools and can deliver a superior quality education, which is to say that they will be more productive. There are a number of corporations that I know are considering this because they see it as an opportunity to make money and as an opportunity to use technologies, sometimes their own, in the service of education. I believe that we will see national chains of private -for-profit schools within five to ten years in the United States and that they will be in a position to compete with the public schools. There are those who feel that one reason the public schools have not been more productive is that they don't have any competition in effect. Something like 85% of our children attend public schools and only 15% attend independent schools or religious schools. The lack of competition means that there are no other standards by which to compare educational effectiveness and these private for profit schools would purport to offer such a comparison.

Fifth, I think as we move toward a more critical attitude toward the public schools and more demand for proof of effectiveness that we will move away from credentialing teachers and move into much more competency based licensing. In our country we tend to give a teacher a credential when she has completed a certain course of study coming into teaching but I think that will change and instead we will require that teachers demonstrate certain competencies instead.

Sixth, I see the rise of museums and libraries as alternative sources for technology in learning. Museums and libraries are much more flexible as organizations than are our public schools, usually because they are much smaller units, often run locally, and they can adapt quickly to changes- much more so than the public schools. At the present time, we have libraries that are renting out video tape cassettes, for example, to the users of the library, and we have museums that are using all of the technologies to deliver exhibits. Some of the most exciting things that are going on, I believe, will be found in our libraries and our museums in terms of moving into technology.

Seventh, I see the rise of centers for educating pre-school children. We have a number of such centers now but they are a mixture of day care centers that simply take care of children while their parents are at work, to nursery schools that intend to give various kinds of pre-school instruction. There is a sense in the country that education before kindergarten or first grade is well worth the long term effects based on some studies that have been done recently about the effects of headstart. Perhaps the more driving force is the fact that so many of the women are now working. Somewhere between 50 and 60% of all mothers of children under six are now at work and this percentage is increasing, so there is a great need for places where children can be not just kept but hopefully taken care of an educated. There is also the beginning of a population boom that we will be a 14% increase in the elementary population which will help to drive this. At the moment, there are something like 1,000 Kindercare Day Care Centers and another chain called La Petite in mostly the west and midwest of our country. About a third of the pre-school centers are welfare, that is they are paid by public funds and two-thirds are paid for by private means. One of the reasons that I believe you are going to see an entry on a national scale of pre-school centers is again the opportunity some private corporations see for using technology to educate young children and also to make a profit.

Eighth. As we move from the older industries into the new ones, as we move what we call the "smoke stack industries,. the rusting factories one sees around Cleaveland and Detroit, and into the more technological industries and service industries, there seems to be a gread need to retrain workers from one kind of occupation to another. I believe we will see that the rise of life-long learning is a serious sense in which one will get retrained for one, two or even three careers during a lifetime. This suggests the rise of certain forms of adult education, again using technology to help deliver those skills and knowledge.

Ninth. Finally what I think we see coming is the end of an era in which the publich school has been seen as the major educational system. It is my view that we have had another one for a long time, called television which reaches something like 2½ billion people in 162 countries. I think that is the tip of the iceberg. I believe we will see very imaginative ways of developing an educational delivery system based on all the technologies: computer, video disc, whatever is invented, and that these will absolutely change the nature of what we call the public schools. I think this will happen becayse of two things, 1) the technologies are now here, although we haven't learned to use them very well in my opining; and 2) a growing public dissatisfaction with the current public school system which costs more and more and more, and which in the view of the public, isn't doing that much better a job and certainly is failing to attract bright young people into that field. Given that and given the concern that exists about the American economy's inability to compete as it once did, I think you will see great forces at work to open up the public school system to deregulation, to competition, to private enterprise , and to the uses of technology.

I view all this with a great mixture of feelings. On the other hand, I am excited about the technologies as I do think that they can deliver a type of instruction that we have never seen. I have heard about individualized instruction all my life and it was only recently that I actually saw it when I saw thirty children in a computer room and each child was absolutely on a different part of the curriculum and I might say enjoying it and learning. WHen you realize the children get 1/360 of their school time in terms of individual instruction, which is to say, they get ½ day per year of individual instruction which amount to one week in their total educational career from kindergarten to twelfth grade, then perhaps you could share with me my concern that individualized instruction is one of the great areas where we can improve and I think with the use of technologies. It is the learner's productivity, I believe, that will go up. All that is very exciting.

What disturbs me, of course, is the moving away from a public school system that has been responsive to the public, that has been locally controlled to a large extent, that has been part of the citizen's power to direct. If it moves into the private sector, I worry about some of the values that may become part of the curriculum. I worry about what will be left out. I worry about who is going to be able to afford such schools. I worry about the type of citizenship training that will come out of such schools. I worry about their responsiveness to the consumer.

So it is with mixed feelings that I see these things coming but I have to say to you, I think they are coming. They represent, in my mind, the fundamental change that the technologies offer, combined with a period when there is national dissatisfaction with the public schools. I think the two mean inevitable fundamental change.

Some Education Policy Responses

TIBOR VASKO
International Institute for Applied Systems Analysis (IIASA), A-2361 Laxenburg, Austria

INTRODUCTION

The process of education is as old as the human race. All through human history this process has become increasingly formalized and socialized (one milestone being, for example, the introduction of compulsory education). These steps made the responsibility of education for the future of the whole society (a Nation) more explicit. In spite of the fact that this responsibility has not been questioned for centuries, there are many recent documents monitoring the disqueting state of the educational process which may not fulfill this responsibility. These signals are coming even from countries which devote considerable resources to education. Some countries following this pattern of management of socio-economic issues are contemplating national programs to enhance the efficiency of the educational process.

Because of its importance, education is an inherent part of development strategies in most countries, industrially developed or developing. Appropriate institutions (ministries) are designing policies aiming to influence in the desired direction the behaviour of individual actors in education processes. The efficiency of individual measures taken in achieving the selected objectives is difficult to predict because the educational process at large is a complex social phenomenon. To study it in order to acquire better understanding and to use this knowledge for designing more efficient measures to manage it is not an easy task because several disciplines are involved. The resulting semantic and methodological differences make it sometimes difficult to achieve a fruitful communication through interdisciplinary barriers. Because cultural and comparative studies might bring a specific insight into the process. This by no means proves that one could easily transfer experience from one country to another.

SOURCES OF INCREASED INTEREST IN EDUCATION

Many sources seem to have a common denominator - economy. One long-term source of growing interest in modern education is created by even faster scientific and technological development. With an increased amount of information circulating in the national economy and in modern products, as proponents of "information society" point out , the knowledge to handle information by computers is considered particularly important.

More generally speaking, the importance of an educated labour force has been known for centuries, but more exact explorations made by Dennison (1962),using methods which became known as " growth accounting",concluded for the USA,that :

> Increased education is not only one of the largest sources of past and prospective economic growth. It also is among the elements most subject to conscious social decision.

Five years later the study was repeated for Europe and reached a similar conclusion (Dennison 1967):

> The increase in education has been a principal source of growth in the United States and it is important to know that European countries have not been achieving more rapid growth by raising the education of the labour force more rapidly.

More recently Drs. Millendorfer and Hussain (1985) tried to correlate the labour force qualification by means of neoclassical production function and, as they claim (see Figure 1) found a reasonable correlation between economic growth (in GDP / capita) and qualification of the labour index (including developing countries).
Recent economic decline has only increased this challenge. I am inclined to call these "pull" factors.

These are even more valid for modern technologies. After serious studies Soete and Freeman (1984) expressed the important view that education and training in a high technology environment are sometimes a more important ("intangible") investment than the physical capital investment and should not be considered as consumption or current cost.

Out of curiosity I cannot avoid a quote from the early work of K.Marx made around 1857 when he wrote referring to the increase in the free time of society: "The savings in work-time are equal to the increase in free-time, i.e. time for the full development of an individual, who acts back on the productivity of labour as the greatest productive force. He can be considered from the point of view of immediate production process as the production of capital fixe, this capital is the man himself." (Translation and italics are mine).

"Push" factors include implications of the fact that resources devoted to education are large and in some national institutions the management of funds predominates. Higher expenses are recorded for vocational training than for general education. Authorities responsible for education strive to decrease the use of those resources and yet to meet increasing requirements. This is another factor pushing innovation into the education process.

Educational policies have to deal with intricate economic, political, managerial and technical problems where the introduction of computers is only one issue among many others. To illustrate it I would like to mention a most recent interesting study of educational policies of seven countries (Hough,J.R.,1984) where no one explicitly mentions the introduction of computers.

SOME POLICY RESPONSES

Education is always responsible for the capability of the future society and is therefore, part of overall policy supporting economic and social development. The application of computers is again embedded into national educational policy. A fragmented overview of some policy responses of different countries is outlined in the following paragraphs.

UNITED STATES OF AMERICA

In the USA pioneering efforts in computer applications have been developed and a clear vision of applying computers to education has been pursued . Numerous studies supported by the government (US Office of Education, National Science Foundation) and several foundations (Exxon, Sloan) have tried to make this vision a reality.

At the same time opposing views were voiced arguing that computers are expensive gadgets which do not increase the quality of education.What is more, rigidly programmed machines may lead to idiosyncracies and cause teachers to select only those problems which can be comfortably taught by computers.

A more recent message from the US President's Commission on Excellence in Education is contained in the title of its report "A Nation at Risk." It cites the ideas of an analyst (Paul Copperman) that :

> Each generation of Americans has outstripped its parents in education, in literacy, and in economic attainment. For the first time in the history of our country, the educational skills of one generation will not surpass, will not equal, will not even approach, those of their parents.

They recommended many measures (divided into five groups) to reattain the supposedly lost excellence in education.

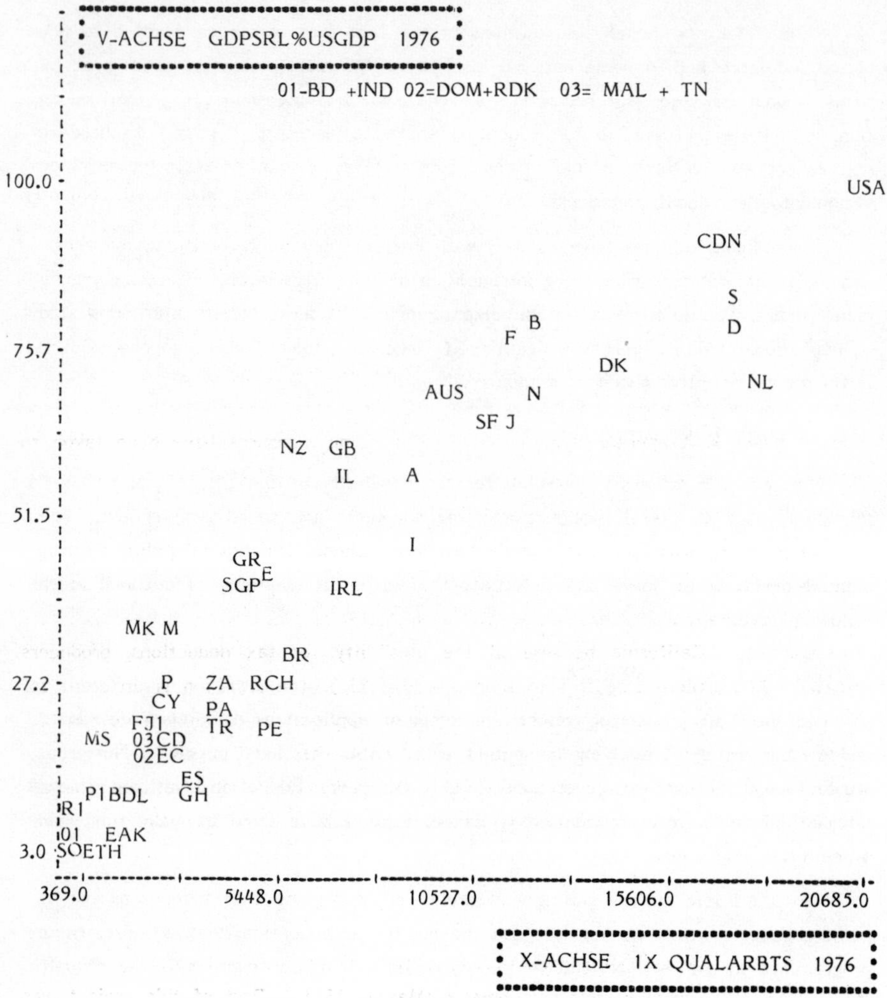
V-ACHSE GDPSRL%USGDP 1976
01-BD +IND 02=DOM+RDK 03= MAL + TN
100.0
75.7
51.5
27.2
3.0
USA
CDN
S
D
B
F
DK
NL
AUS
N
SF J
NZ GB
IL
A
I
GR
SGP E
IRL
MK M
BR
P ZA RCH
CY
PA
FJ1
TR
PE
MS
03CD
02EC
ES
P1BDL
GH
R1
01 EAK
SOETH
369.0
5448.0
10527.0
15606.0
20685.0
X-ACHSE 1X QUALARBTS 1976

Fig.1.

On the other hand, the volatile and fast-changing situation only extends the spectrum of differing views on the same problem. A recent US National Science Foundation Study "educating America for the 21st Century" puts education among the national goals and adds that "Almost any statement made today will, therefore, be obsolete in a few years, if not months."

There are excellent analytical studies depicting the real impact of computer based education at college level in the USA (Kulik, Kulik, Cohen,1980).

In 1983 it was estimated that the number of microcomputers in American schools was over 100.000 which could be taken as an indication that virtually every school in the USA had a microcomputer (in the USA there are 83,334 public and 21.749 private schools, and 3.453 colleges). However, the distribution of computers is not uniform allover the country. In spite of this number of computers there is no overall policy on computer applications, though some measures have been taken to promote the computerization of schools (for example, a 25% tax write-off is available for equipment supplied to colleges).

The distribution of computers depends on individual states as the state is responsible for education. For example, in Minnesota there was one computer for every 50 children. There are states where only 50% of the schools have computers. For example,in California because of the possibility for tax deductions, producers donated 13.000 microcomputers to schools (in 1983). The situation is different for university education, where some universities already require a student to own a microcomputer and others are to follow soon. Some of these universities expect to interconnect microcomputers into networks (Bereiter 1983). However, in general, affluent children in the USA find more home support for microcomputers than in many other countries.

JAPAN

Applying computers to education is a part of the national strategy in Japan denoted by the term "Information Society" (Masuda 1971). Part of this project was a Computer - Oriented Education in an Experimental School District (cost $ 266 million). This plan conceived of an experimental school district conducting computer-oriented education in pre-school,kindergarten,primary school, junior and senior high schools, university playing a central role. The plan includes rationalization of school office work, an individual education guidance system, computer-oriented education, and an educational science research center. The project planned to help solve problems concerning future computer-oriented education, measuring the educational effect of the intelligence network, planning a standard education system, and developing a new individual educational system. It was conceived as an educational sys-experiment, permitting objective scientific data collection and analysis of differences between the computer-oriented,private instruction,problem -solving type of educational system and the contemporary uniform group education system.

In the early stages, a computer-aided instruction (CAI) system model classroom has been tested in primary schools under the direction of Tsukuba University; training programs in computer operation and programmming were begun in state commercial high schools. But Japanese children are already in contact with computers when they attend kindergarten, which they attend until they reach the age of five (in Japan there are 14,893 kindergartens). From five until 12 years of age they attend elementary schools of which there are 24,945).They are followed by lower secondary schools (10,780) and then by upper secondary schools. Ninety percent of the population continue their education until the age of 18. State education in Japan follows a national curriculum and private schools provide education for 7 percent of the population.

It is claimed that no other nation's children devote so much time to computers as Japanese schildren. However, some critics have pointed out that education in Japan has been too application oriented, not fostering creative, logical and philosophical thinking. To remedy this is one of the tasks of the new, almost legendary, fifth generation computer project in Japan.

FRANCE

The French national Experiment in Educational Computing started in October 1970 but initially focussed on secondary education. France is also following a national curriculum, which has the advantage of a coordinated approach with related teacher education. One of the recent schemes assumes 10,000 computers in Lycees. The standard of the future is eight computers and a printer in each classroom.

FEDERAL REPUBLIC OF GERMANY (Gorny 1983)

As education is not a federal issue its policy is handled by individual states, which allows for regional differences. It is reported that Bavaria has gone furthest toward computer literacy and compulsory informatics at the lower Secondary level. All gymnasiums specializing in mathematics are offering 28 hours of informatics in the 10th class within mathematics lessons. Special teacher training programs have been initiated for elementary schools (Grund and Hauptschulen), gymnasiums (5-13-th school year) and vocational schools. There are (in Bavaria, for example) 3-4 microcomputers in each classroom.

Computerization is finding a foothold relatively slowly in educational policy for several reasons- one reason is that the complicated procedures, generated by the complicated structure, take their time to filter through the necessary stages (teacher training, curriculum development, etc.)

UNITED KINGDOM

The National Development Programme in Computer-Assisted Learning began a sustained effort in 1973 in the United Kingdom, with a modest budget of 2 million pounds sterling. In 1982 a new scheme (3 million pounds sterling) was started to persuade every secondary school to buy a microcomputer. This scheme seems to have been a success: in the first year 80 percent of state-run secondary schools bought a microcomputer (with a 50 percent subsidy from the government). In 1982 a similar scheme (estimated to cost 9 million pounds sterling) was focused on 27,000 primary schools.

SWITZERLAND

In this conferederation decisions on education lie in the hands of 26 sovereign states. A coherent policy was introduced in 1975 when the Training Center for Swiss Teachers in secondary education set up an informatics coordination group (Morel 1980).

- to begin the introduction of informatics into secondary schools;
- the computer as a tool for different subjects in secondary schools;
- what hardware and software should be used.

AUSTRIA

Computers in Austria are used predominately in post-compulsory education. At this stage there are three main types of schools which give access to university, and also post-compulsory vocational schools which do not give access to university. The curriculum, which is drawn up by the Ministry of Education and Arts, states that "the aim of the subject is to promote knowledge and the ability to solve different problems with the aid of computers. "Computer education for teachers was also introduced. There are also projects, (computer camps) organized by a professional society (The Austrian Computer Society) which aim to teach more creative use of the computer, beyond numerics, during vacation periods. In the past year much has been done, for example, microcomputers have been given to gymnasiums (3-8 according to size).

SOVIET UNION AND SOCIALIST COUNTRIES

Computers were introduced into schools very early on, starting at university level in the early 1950s (first generation computers). Later secondary schools were also given computers, generally a microcomputer. At the same time the curriculum was changed, to accomodate several courses on programming and computer science at different levels. New specializations have also been introduced.

In the mid-1970s more elaborate schemes were worked out. To illustrate the point , we can describe the scheme approved by the USSR Ministry of Higher Education dated January 12,1978 - the so-called " Automated Teaching Systems". The scheme is based on two stages. The first (up to 1982) aims:

. to develop computer systems custom-made for schools;

to initiate research and development into the psychological and educational issues raised by the application of such systems;

. to work out a methodology for developing algorithmic and semantic structures of teaching courses and appropriate monitoring systems. Among the first are some aspects of physics, chemistry, mathematics, and programming languages;

. to develop languages for teaching, user control languages, and interactive (dialog) programming languages.

The second stage relies on interconnecting the individual functional systems into an integrated network.

Last Year (Pravda, january,1984) a major policy paper was presented in the USSR on "Basic reform directions of general and vocational schools" initiated by the Central Committee of the Communist Party of the Soviet Union (CPSU). The paper states that the great problems at the end of this century and the beginning of the next will be solved by those who are sitting behind school desks today. Among the many recommendations intended to improve the efficiency of education is the need to:

> ... equip the students with the knowledge and skill to use modern computer technology, to secure wide applications of computers in the educational process and, to build for this purpose special school and interschool cabinets.

On March 28 ,1985, the Politbureau of the CPSU and the government approved a decree which proposes to introduce, into all secondary schools, a new subject "Basis of informatics and computer technology" and also to use computers extensively for teaching other subjects, and to start courses for training teachers.

Computers should also be used in out-of school environments, in technical creative activity, youth clubs, centers of culture, etc. It was stressed that the inten sive mastering of computers by the younger generation would be an important factor in speeding up scientific and technical progress.

To help to implement this program , the results from many projects which are now underway in the whole Soviet Union will be used.

Similar programs are being introduced in the other socialist countries.

BULGARIA

Concentrated efforts are now underway to apply computers to education. It is being coordinated by government bodies like the State Committee for Science and Technology, the Academy of Sciences, the Ministry of Education, and also Youth Organizations. This conference is one product of this acitivity. It will be reported in detail. I refer to Vasko (1985).

OTHER SOCIALIST COUNTRIES

In the other socialist countries the introduction of computers started in the earlyearly 1950s at university leve. Later, secondary schools were equipped with microcomputers. Now with the wide availability of the 8-bit micro-processor, microcomputers are being widely applied to secondary schools. A strong interest is also devoted to vocational training which is being coordinated with secondary school education. The activities of professional organizations are also important : one,for example, in Czechoslovakia, created 39 regional centers to disseminate knowledge on the use of computers to the widest audience. Similar activities are being performed in Hungary by the Neumann Janos Society.

SOME THOUGHTS ON THE SITUATION IN DEVELOPING COUNTRIES

I must start with the usual disclaimer- that developing countries represent a very heterogeneous society. Therefore, only a few generally valid claims can be made. Obviously, much research remains to be done. On the other hand, there are many who are sceptical regarding the use of computers in educational issues in developing countries since, even in developed countries the situation does not seem to have been mastered. On the other hand, there are those who see a potential for developing countries (Aiken, Oualid 1983).

Microcomputers were labelled as solutions looking for problems. Could some solutions be accomodated by the problems of developing countries? Potential problems singled out are:

- increased access to education, both inside and outside urban centers, thus helping to increase the potential of the educational system;
- helping to fight iliteracy;

There is increased hope that the falling prices of computers may lead to their easier acquisition by developing countries. Developing countries should get all the help possible, but their own role cannot be replaced in an activity as culturally dependent, bound as education. The message of technology transfer from developing countries to developing countries , even if small, supports this view.

TENTATIVE PRELIMINARY CONCLUSIONS

In my paper I have tried to present an exhaustive report on the state of the introduction of computers into education in individual countries. I have presented instead part of the situation. Nevertheless, some preliminary conclusions can be attempted and I am sure that with the information gained from this conference one can try to suggest some general, and hopefully relevant conclusions.

1) As with the general application of computers to the other softer areas, for example, management, we could detect several stages of computer-usage (Nolan 1973; Nolan 1975).

Stage I	initiation	(acquisition)
Stage II	contagion	(intensive system development)
Stage III	control	(proliferation of control measures)
Stage IV	integration	(user/service orientation)

Different countries can be in different situations, but even within a country institutions might be at different stages. For example, in several countries computerization at university level is at higher stage than that at the secondary or elementary level. Yet it is important to analyse and identify the present situation system-wise before making any policies for the future. So much for the dynamics of the process.

2) One can detect several directions as far as approaches are concerned.Perhaps the most distinct ones are:

- . the computer as a tool or aid;
- . informatics as a scientific branch, and the computer as one means of implementation.

There are also, of course, mixed strategies.

3) At the organizational level, strategies for computerization are dependent on the structure of the national educational system and its management. However, the causal relations seem to be unclear. They run from fragmented policies (Netherlands, Rushby 1981), to more coherent ones (FRG, UK), to centralized ones (France, USSR).

4) Components of the policy are among others:

- Overall educational policy strategy, centrally defined. (Japan,France,USSR, etc.):
  - . including- standardized hardware, software ,courseware;
  - . teacher education;
  - . curriculum;
  - . guidelines;

- Financial support :
  - . special funds, grants,etc. (UK,France,USSR,etc.);
  - . tax allowances (USA);
  - . subsidies (UK);
- Organizational response:
  - . the creation of specialized institutions;
  - . funding of R&D in existing organizations;
- Societal measures :
  - . involvement of parents (Austria, Bulgaria)
  - . use of leisure-time activity;

All of these measures have the ability to guide and enhance the known positive aspects of the use of computers in education. Education systems seem to be particularly resilient to innovations. Although the computer is very specific, its impact, in spite of wide studies, is not well known. It has recently been pointed out that the impact of television is only now becoming apparent after 30 year use. I would subscribe to the claim of the Armenian Socialist Republic's Minister of Education who said :

> Miracles are not taking place. Especially in education. It takes hard work to teach pupils useful knowledge, but it is clear that the computer can help.

(Achumyan 1984).

REFERENCES

Achumyan,S.T. (1984) Introduction to: Application of Microcalculator in Elementary School. Erevan, Luyc Publishing House (in Russian).

Aiken,R.M. and A.Dualid (1983) Microcomputers as Educational Tools. In Information Processing 83 edited by R.E.A. Masen. Elsener Science Publishers, B.V. North-Holland, IFIP.

Bergel,H.(1984) Tax Incentives for Computer Donars is a Bad Idea. Communication of ACM, 27 (3) : 188-192.

Denison,E.F. (1967) Why Growth Rates Differ. Washington, DC: Brookings Institute.

Gorny,P. (1983) The New Information Technologies and Education.Implication for Teacher Education.Country Report 2.Federal Republic of Germany,Association for Teacher Education in Europe, January, Brussels.

Hough,J.R. (1984) (Ed.) Educational Policy. An International Survey.London and Sydney; St. Martin's Press, New York.

Millendorfer,J. and M.Hussain (1985) Structural Changes in World Economy: Regional Issues and Consequences. In Restructuring Interdependent Economies edited by T.Vasko. CP-85-22. Laxenburg, Austria: International Institute for Applied Systems Analysis.

Nolan, R.L. (1973) Managing the Computer Resource: A Stage Hypothesis. Communication of the ACM, 16(7) :339-405.

Nolan,R.L. (1975) Thoughts About the Fifth Stage. Databse 7(2):4-23.

Rushby,N. (1981) Microcomputers in the Classroom in Continental Europe. Pages 5-13 in Microcomputers in Secondary Education : Issues and Techniques edited by J.A.M. Howe and P.M. Ross. London: Kogan page and New York: Nichols Publishing Co.

Vasko,T. (1985) (Ed.) Children and Computers. Selected Papers from the Meeting on Children and Computers,2-3 May, 1984, Albena,Bulgaria. CP-85-8.Laxenburg, Austria: International Institute for Applied System Analysis.

The Content and Place of New Information Technologies in School Education

M. M. EDMUNDSON
Education Consultant, 31 Marshall's Drive, Saint Albans, Hertfordshire AL1 4RB, UK

1. A point which has to be kept in mind when considering the use of new information technologies (NITs) in education, is the variety of national education systems which exist throughout the world. Each country will of necessity relate the problems of the NITs in education and their solution to the system with which they are most concerned. Many of the issues for education brought about by the rapid growth of new technologies are common to all countries but the response and the solutions to the problems are "system dependent".Nevertheless, experience gained in one country can be helpful to another even though the latter will in the end, have to approach the problems in a different way. In this exchange of ideas and experience, UNESCO has a significant role to play. What has to be accepted is that education systems themselves will have to make some changes if they are to meet the challenge of the NITs. This calls for a degree of flexibility both in government policy and in the professional attitudes and response of teachers. This calls for a degree of flexibility both in government policy and in the professional attitudes and response of teachers. This paper refers to experience in the UK and "education" means the years of compulsory primary and secondary education plus those additional years of secondary education which extend up to, but do not include, further and higher education. i.e. the age range 5-18.

2. The new information technologies have grown out of the rapid developments over the past two decades in the science of microelectronics and its applications in many technological fields. Of these, the development of the microcomputer is so far-reaching, that (in education at least) it transcends most if not all other electronic applications and has to be given special consideration. Indeed, many people may believe that in education, the reference to "NIT" is synonymous with "microcomputer". This is understandable but in my view wrong, because there are

many facets of the microelectronic revolution besides the microcomputer which must filter into appropriate areas of the school curriculum.

3. Children readily adapt to the use of new technologies in education. Often they adapt more readily than do the teachers. Children quickly reveal remarkably mature skills in handling and programming the microcomputer if allowed to do so freely. These skills are usually most prominently displayed by pupils in the upper half of the ability range but there is not necessarily a close correlation between pupils who are normally classified as academically the brightest and those who reveal the greatest affinity and the greatest skill with the micro. Some research in this field would be valuable.

4. In the UK many aspects of the education service are decentralised and permit a good deal of autonomy at regional and local levels. Central government has no absolute authority over the curriculum. Many decisions about curriculum are left to the headteacher and staff, with the approval of the school governors. England and Wales are divided into approximately 100 Local Education Authorities (LEAs) which are responsible for the education service in each county or region. (Scotland has a separate education system with its own ministerial officials.) In simple terms, the education service in the UK may be described as a triple partnership between central government,local education authorities and professional teachers.

5. Interest in computing goes back to 1970 when a few enthusiastic teachers (mainly maths. teachers) began to design and introduce courses for their pupils which dealt with the principles and applications of computers. They were usually called "computer studies" courses but they were non-vocational in character. Pupils who took these courses could take a public examination (as with all their other subjects) and the total number of entrants at all levels rose from about 7000 in the early 70s to over 100,000 in the summer of 1984. By 1980 these courses had led to the appointment in many secondary schools of a "head of computer studies". The NIT programme has highlighted the need for every school to have a "computer specialist" teacher on the staff- a point discussed later in this report. In most secondary schools this specialist is also the Head of Computing/Computer Studies; in others, and in the primary schools, it is usually an enthusiastic teacher who has agreed to take over these specialised new duties.

6. The media, especially the newspapers and television, have helped to create a climate of interest in homes throughout the country which has also benefitted the schools. In the last two years the personal microcomputer has become a tool or a toy in a large number of homes. The news-stands display dozens of different magazines devoted to microcomputers and/or electronics and a moments observation shows that these are purchased by customers of all ages.

7. It can be argued therefore, that the climate in the UK was a particularly favourable one by 1980 and an important factor contributing to the relatively rapid developments that have taken place in schools and in teacher training in the past three years. The process may be called "raising the level of public consciousness" about new technologies and is a point for any country to bear in mind when preparing the way for educational innovation in this field. However, the most important element in the whole process has been government support and the allocation of money over and above the normal education budget.In 1980 a national project was started which became known as the Microelectronics Education Programme (MEP). (The Scottish Microeletronics Development Programme in Scotland.) A director and his support staff were appointed and the director published a strategy document in April 1981. The main effort of the MEP was directed in 3 ways:

a) An extended programme of in-service teacher training plus appropriate modification to initial training courses.

b) A mechanism and structure for writing and publishing software which taps the best professional ideas.

c) A country-wide information network which keeps all parts of the education service in touch with developments.

d) Provision of hardware (through the Dept. of Industry)

8. The MEP strategy encouraged interest in, and advised on, work in 4 domains,briefly described as :

a) The computer as an aid throughout the curriculum. Computer based learning

b) The computer as a tool; its applications and uses in society, industry and commerce. Computer studies.

c) Computer aided information systems - databases, information ,storage and retrieval, electronic office.

d) Electronics and control technology. Robotics.

14 regional centres were established,distributed geographically as evenly as possible. Each centre has become the focus for advice and information for a group of local education authorities. The centres fulfil many roles; for example, they assist with in-service training courses for teachers; they publish a newsletter for all the schools in their area; they help with software production; they are equipped with a library and a variety of computers which teachers can use; there is a range of peripheral devices for teachers to test and try out for themselves, such as printers, robots, and so forth. In the past 3 years many local education authorities have established their own well equipped centres for their teachers and almost all LEAs now have an adviser for computing in schools.

9. In-service teacher training has proceeded vigorously. About 120,000 teachers have now been on courses ranging from 1 day to 1 week, covering many aspects of microelectronics and microcomputers in education and this programme of training continues. Introducing NITs into schools throws an enormous burden on teacher training programmes. In general, training must proceed at a number of levels. The following are illustrative; some topics may be covered at levels other than those suggested or in more than one level.

a) Awareness training - introducing the naive teacher to the new technology with examples of its potential in the classroom.

b) Second level training concentrating on particular applications of the micro in school. For example, its use in the science laboratory, or in the workshop or in the teaching of history or geography and so forth.

c) Third level training: understanding and using software tools, databases, communication systems etc. Relating the use of new technology to the psychology of child development and learning. Integrating the micro into the school environment. The user interface.

d) Courses for teachers of computer studies which will include things like computer architecture, programming languages, computer applications, social implications etc.

e) Training in microelectronics and in the application of the micro in industry and commerce. E.g. Computer control of machinery, robotics, wordprocessing and other techniques of the electronic office.

f) Training the trainers- courses for LEA advisers enthusiastic teachers and similar staff to enable them to run other courses for less experienced teachers The cascade effect increases the total number of courses available nationally.

g) Courses to meet particular educational needs: the use of micros in primary education; their use for remedial teaching and with the mentally and physically handicapped.

h) Courses to train technicians to provide first-line maintenance of micros and other equipment associated with the NITs. In the UK some of these are provided by the computer manufacturers at moderate cost.

10. The MEP and the SMDP have been responsible for ensuring that the full range of courses as set out in the previous paragraph have been (and continue to be) provided. Some are organised by their regional and national co-ordinators, others are the responsibility of the local education authorities helped by MEP and SMDP funding. The courses are best organised regionally and locally so that teachers have the minimum of travel and inconvenience when attending. Sometimes the course is held in normal working hours with the teachers released from classroom duties for this purpose. Frequently the time a teacher spends on a course is partly in "working" time and partly in "own" time. The two national projects have

also produced self-instructional packs so that teachers can help themselves by studying these materials most of which are supported with readers, case-studies, tutor-books on how to use the microcomputer, a sample range of courseware,slides and video-tapes. The Open University has also produced a modular distant-study course dealing with the use of the micro in the classroom and with micro-electronics and the principle of the mircroprocessor. The latter includes a circuit board for experimenting with the processor, including its application in computers and control.

11. The MEP third field of activity is that of production of software (some-times called courseware) i.e. applications programs of all kinds which will assist teachers in many parts of the curriculum - maths,science, language,geography, economics and so on. In the UK a number of educational software centres receive financial aid from the MEP and they are producing some very good software. All of them are linked with publishers who have the facilities to produce and market the materials efficiently. The average program costs about £10. There are of course other producers of software, many of whom were or still are, teachers who are taking advantage of the demand. For some teachers the NITs have provided a new outlet for their talents.

12. In addition to support from the Department of Education & Science, education has received government support through the Department of Trade and Industry. The DTI has provided money to equip schools with hardware. First they offered every secondary school a micro at half price. This was later supplemented with other peripherals including a printer, software, a robot vehicle and other devices. Primary schools are able to buy a micro at half price and included is a self-instructional pack for teachers and a range of software (about 40 programs) to get them started. The DTI has also provided all the teacher training institu-tions with money for hardware and software so that young students in initial training can be introduced to the new information technologies as preparation for their future work.

13. Schools also have other funds with which they can purchase micros if they wish. Most have done so and a recent survey shows that the typical secondary schools now has 9 or 10 computers; some schools have as many as 15-20 often placed together in a "computer room" and interlinked by what is called a "network". By 1986 it is estimated that the DES will have spent £21 million on the microelectronics programme and the DTI a further £21 million on hardware and software. The BBC micro is proving to be by far the most popular choice of the teachers and about 85% of all primary schools have selected this model.

14. The introduction of NITs into school requires a teacher to make considerable modifications to his teaching style and to the way his time and energy

are allocated to various duties. The use of software in the teaching process requires suitable advance preparation and follow-up: Are the educational aims of the program in line with the teacher's objectives for that lesson? Are materials available (books, apparatus, opportunity for research, access to a data base etc.) which will enable the pupil to gain the maximum benefit from using the program and to follow it with other appropriate activities? Does the software blend into the curriculum smoothly from the learners point of view or is it crudely "added-on" with little obvious relevance. A common mistake is to allow the pupil to feel the use of the micro is a form of "reward" rather than a fundamental experience. Does the teacher have the skills of communication for discussion and debate which a particular program calls into play if it is to be effective with the learning group? Although the load on the teacher may be increased in some ways, e.g. in the advance preparation needed for a lesson using the micro, in other ways for example during the actual lesson itself the teacher may have more time to devote to individual pupils.

15. Introducing microcomputers into the classroom also makes special demands on the teacher's professional skills and on his/her organisational abilities. This is true whether a single micro is brought into the classroom or whether a computer room fitted with many micros is available for class use. The teacher's diagnostic and observational skills are particularly important. Properly used, computer based learning can provide a diagnostic analysis of a pupil's performance which gives the teacher an insight into the child's strength and weaknesses on which further work can be planned. There is general agreement that the NITs frequently demand the following new skills of the teaching staff. Some of these merely require the application of existing skills to the new context of information technology. Some may be of special importance to the "computer specialist" but in varying degrees, most of them are the concern of all teachers :

The ability to operate NIT equipment including the development of keyboard skills.

The ability to write software.

The ability to identify and correct simple faults in both hardware and software.

The ability to teach about the NITs.

The ability to instruct others in the use of the technology.

The ability to give advice to others about purchasing,care and use of NIT equipment.

The flexibility to adapt to the new possibilities afforded by NITs.

The development of new applications of NITs.

The ability to use NITs effectively in the management of learning, assessment and school administration.

16. The use of micros in a school inevitably requires one member of the staff to be designated "computer specialist". This is the person to whom other teachers turn for help and advice and who assists with the in-school education/training of their colleagues. Few teachers at present possess the educational and technical knowledge which ideally, the post calls for. This is why more often than not, it is the enthusiast who takes over this role and learns many of the required skills as he(or she) goes along. The computer specialist keeps in touch with developments outside the school and with the local education authority adviser. He keeps abreast of software development and is able to advise colleagues on suitable programs to meet their needs. It is a wise precaution to have a second teacher sharing these specialist duties so that in the event of illness of resignation of the senior specialist, most of the services can continue to be provided for the rest of the staff. All teachers, not only computer specialists, have to learn to make educational judgements about software. One teacher trainer reports: "Once teachers have some familiarity with the technology and are investigating the use of computer based learning (CBL) with their classes, almost inevitably they express disappointment at the small range and uneven quality of many of the published materials. Much published courseware, including some intended for "awareness training" is educationally thin and can cause teachers in the formative stages of CBL to be sceptical, even dismissive of the technique. A necessary part of this formative training is to point out and discuss good and bad features of program designs. Does the program have significant educational aims, or merely serve as a minor aid and leave the conventional practices of teaching and learning undisturbed ? What are the guarantees that the programs will develop learning, or could the instruction of design, perhaps evolving from Educational or Instructional Psychology, should underpin the development of the various types of program? A good deal of courseware currently available cannot withstand such scrutiny; it seems limited and appears to have evolved in idiosyncratic ways. Software is the key component of computer based learning, for it is the medium through which the educational experience of the teacher is released into the classroom, and the tool by which he/she can develop the educational potential of the computer. Without software which engages th educational mind of the teacher and enlarges his/her repertoire, training of new skills is superfluous.

17. There are other ways in which the new technologies are being introduced into school curricula. Some schools have experimented with "awareness courses" in the 12-14 year age range. They are a valid curricular response to the changes in the world around us : robots in engineering, computers in graphic design, micro-

processors in the supermarket, programmable devices of all kinds from washing machines to video recorders, teletext systems for communication and so forth. There is no fixed patterns for these courses. Some teachers use the micro to illustrate its versatility, so that pupils learn without going into great technical detail, how to interface the micro with other technology to control it, or to measure data and display it graphically. The pupils experiment with the microprocessor to operate model traffic lights or control a model train. Other courses concentrate more on gates; they design their own circuits, etch the copper laminate and make a simple printed circuit board which when fitted with the chips and other components, makes a burglar alarm, or a sensor for switching on the house lights when it goes dark. The staff who teach these courses usually have a technical or scientific background; above all they have an enthusiasm for the NITs which they can pass on to their pupils. I have no qualms about young children learning to program the computer; it is now a fundamental skill if the pupil is to master the computer and use it as a tool on which to sharpen and develop his/her own intellect. Children who will live well into the 21st. century must develop the power to use the computer, in the sense of bidding it to do one's will.

18. The educational reponse to the NITs may be summarised briefly as follows:

1. School cirricula may now include new topics such as microelectronics, computer studies, information systems etc.

2. Established curricular subjects such as mathematics, science, humanities, etc. can use the microcomputer to assist learning and conceptual understanding and as a diagnostic tool to help the teacher plan the best course for a particular pupil.

3. Although not mentioned earlier, the micro can be used in the general organisation of the school- record keeping, printing class lists, time-tabling and so on.

Some countries may wish to give higher priority to using the micro in the teaching of basic skills - numeracy and literacy. Software appropriate for these objectives would be required and in many cases the micro could help the teacher to distribute the work-load more effectively. New software packages are becoming available which will help teachers to prepare computer based learning materials without requiring them to have any knowledge of computer programming.

19. If lessons are to be learned from the use of other educational technologies in the past, we have to be aware of both the pedagogical issues in today's curricula as well as the organisational and methodological constraints for both teachers and pupils, and apply our knowledge to the use of the new information technologies in the classrrom. Based on my own experience I single out the following as important for consideration in the microcomputer age:

1. Teacher-teacher and especially teacher-pupil relationships.
2. Software issues.
3. Organisational matters in the school and classroom.

A very large slice of the vocation of teaching is concerned with personal relationships- with colleagues, with pupils, with parents and so on. Every reasonable teacher has experienced that immensely rewarding feeling of satisfaction and achievement resulting from a superb interactive lesson with a class of children. If only there were more lessons like that; thanks goodness there are some . I see these relationships as essential in the year 2000 as they are today and therefore I see the importance of the micro in schools mainly in that context- how they can improve interactions and relationships. Microcomputers are valuable tools; they will not replace teachers in the forseeable future. We strive to make programs more user-friendly, by which is implied more human. But a machine is a machine; a computer is pre-ordained by its program however sophisticated it may be. In the right context, one raised eyebrow has still more thought provoking power than a screenful of computerised questions.

20. Teachers usually agree that their main job is to prepare pupils for life, not just for examinations; to train them how to learn is as important an objective as learning the details of a relatively narrow syllabus. Social pressures work the other way; examinations are important and priorities become reversed, however well intentioned the teacher may be. Long term aims are frequently sacrificed for short term goals. Memorising the algorithm (in whatever context or subject) which will improve the chances of examination success is often 'safer' than slogging away for the conceptual understanding which would last a lifetime. I believe that I have glimpsed within the microcomputer a tool which will narrow the gap between these conflicting pressures on teacher and pupil. It is for these reasons that I support most strongly those programs which assist with conceptual understanding. Programs would vary from a few lines (or even none at all) to the more conventional sophisticated package.

21. Predicting the future is risky; much of what happens with the development of new technologies in schools will depend on the level of investment afforded. Pump-priming is a useful technique but longer term investment is sometimes required if the innovation is to be truly grafted on to the educational system. I believe the new technology will require attention on at least two fronts, if it is to grow and endure. The first is an on-going commitment to teacher training and re-training. The second concerns the realities of software production. If I am correct in believing that teachers want, and will use most of all, educational "utilities", teaching 'tools' and materials which assist the development of concepts rather than merely support the factual side of learning, present evidence suggests that publishers are unlikely to find this side of their work very profitable. How

then will the output be maintained? It would be a pity if the uses of the micro in the classroom were eventually to wither or at best never get beyond a cosmetic gloss on more traditional approaches to learning, because the cost of adequate soft ware support proved to be too high, but it is a problem which sooner or later will have to be faced and solved.

22. As we approach the year 2000, amongst the many statements of educational objectives I have come across, which may be appropriate for the 21st, century , I find the following particularly appealing. They are global objectives of course, within which will be found those detailed, pragmatic requirements all school curricula must ultimately provide, - in basic skills, science, humanities and so forth. But for me, they sum up in a powerful way, the goals which are now understood and accepted by both professional teachers and by the members of the communities which they serve :

the school curriculum must be designed to develop within all pupils,
(a) the ability to think
(b) the ability to communicate
(c) the ability to co-operate
(d) the ability to make decisions

In helping us to attain these objectives, the wise use of microcomputers and other new technologies have a valuable part to play.

New Information Technologies and Youth Education: Problems Facing the Third World Countries

HENRI HOGBE-NLEND
Department of Mathematics, University of Bordeau, Talence, France

May I first of all convey my sincere attitude to the Organizing Committee of this conference for having invited me to present the point of view of the developing countries at the plenary session.

To begin with, I would like to draw your attention to several facts. Firstly, the Third World is very diverse, and the countries forming part of it have different levels of technological development. Obviously, countries like e.g. Brazil, India and some countries in South-East Asia possess a more advanced level of New Information Technologies (N.I.T.) than the majority of the African countries. Still, most of the so-called developing countries are faced with a certain number of common problems. It is these problems that I shall discuss in my statement.

Secondly: The Third World has had very short experience of N.I.T in education. If one studies this experience, one will see more problems than positive solutions.

Thirdly: The "computer-education" issue is closely related to the general issue of "computer-society", i.e. to the introduction of N.I.T. in society. This is particularly valid for those countries which are now making their first steps in this direction; therefore, as far as the developing countries are concerned, priority is now being given to the general issue of "computer-society".

Fourthly, the New Information Technologies were introduced into the developing countries mainly for management purposes - in the economics, banking, administration, transport and communications, and so on - and mainly by way of the transnational companies. Hence, the problem is not whether the Third World can or cannot stop the process of computerization but how it can control and master it in order to make it a useful ally in the economic, social and cultural development of our countries.

In my statement I shall focus on some considerations concerning the efforts of the developing countries to control the powerful tool of N.I.T. and to use it for the purpose of development.

In the first place, we believe that the computer can be a powerful tool for the promotion of our economic, social and cultural development. We believe this is so because:

° The computer increases man's intellectual potential and his creative abilities, unlike all the other technological inventions of mankind, which have so far only increased man's physical power and the potential of machines.

° The computer is essentially universal. It is within the "reach" of machines, and has an enormous simulation ability. Hence, it can be adapted to any culture, and to any civilization; the underdeveloped countries will not need any special N.I.T.

° The computer can be used in looking for integral solutions to problems with many parameters (equations with many unknowns) which is particularly appropriate for the problems of development, since they are multi-variable and interdisciplinary.

° The computer is the antidote to a dispersed culture.

° The computer - and the personal computer in particular - with which man can communicate will make it possible for illiterates to become integrated into the social life of the Third World countries. In the industrial societies of today he who "cannot read or write" becomes an outsider. The information era will promote the renaissance of oral culture and the knowledge and skills of oral communication. With a fifth generation personal computer one will not need to write in order to make oneself useful, or to take up a job, or to transfer knowledge from one generation to another.

° The personal computer will promote the development of an individual, decentralized educational system, which will become particularly important for the transfer of knowledge to remote villages or settlements.

° The personal computer will create a closer link between education and life, employment and leisure; there will be a definite rejection of the concept that teaching and learning can take place only in the classroom.

° The computer will make life-long education possible. "One never stops learning"; this will be the guiding principle for education and training in the information age.

° Finally, the personal computer will lay the foundations for a real revolution by putting an end to the industrial age, and outlining the beginning of "a new world civilization".

In studying the main tendences of this new civilization, a factor emerges which seems paradoxical in itself: the future civilization will in some way bear resemblance to the agrarian civilizations typical of the developing countries. This becomes apparent in examining, for example, the future civilization's energy resources: the future sources of energy, like those of "the past", will be renewable, decentralized, and diversified; they will not be fossilized sources of the present. Other examples can also be found such as, for example, the future economic structure based on decentralization and on the reestablishment of the invisible economy; the new cultural values which will govern the society of the future, such as the harmonious relationship between man and nature; the new concept of working hours and employment free from the principle of synchronization; etc.

This overlapping between the agrarian civilization's strong points, and the information era's elements, is closely related to a concept in which we believe: the concept of "leap-frogging", according to which the Third World countries can cut out the classic conventional stages of industrial development characteristic of the Euro-American "sample", and head directly for the information age.

The underdeveloped countries of today are those which missed the 19th century industrial revolution. We, of the Third World, should not forget this.

This is why we have started working to enable our countries to participate in this great revolution of our century. To this end, we have identified a certain number of principles to be observed, on the basis of an analysis of our countries' development over the past two or three decades (since the acquisition of interdependence).

The guiding principles are:

° Breaking away from the strategy of "imitation". We no longer believe in the existence of universal models to follow or to imitate. Computerization of the Third World must be original and creative.

° Relying on the fundamental values of our culture.

° Opening-up to the outside world by studying and assimilating foreign experience.

° Prospect: A clear, long-term strategy to be worked out concerning N.I.T. and our societies.

° Dispensing with micro-nationalism, and promoting regional cooperation, to allow for the formation of the indispensible "critical mass".

These guiding principles have become the basis for different actions being undertaken at present in our countries, mainly in the form of pilot projects.

The most topical and most urgent objective is the "education of educators" through courses, practicals and seminars organized by national, regional or international centres. Regional and international cooperation is being undertaken within the framework of professional (computer science) associations, networks, and regional vocational training institutes (for example, the African Institute of Informatics in Libreville, Gabon). At national level, computer science departments are being set up at the universities. In many countries, computer centres have been established for management purposes.

While taking a keen interest in the educational aspects of N.I.T., we are forced by circumstances to consider also the applications of computers in agriculture and in health care. In these fields, experiments are carried out in a number of countries.

There is no doubt that in this giant task of introducing the New Information Technologies into our societies and schools, we face numerous difficulties. Among the major ones are, for example, the acute shortage of trained specialists, financial difficulties, the relatively low level of "technological literacy" of society which engenders inert thinking and mistrust, N.I.T.'s short-term effect on employment, the fear of a stronger dependency on the multi-nationals and on foreign powers.

In spite of these difficulties, the Third World is determined to progress along the path of modernization by mastering the new information technologies. Our principle is: "No escape in the future, no escape in the past". We rely on international solidarity to reinforce our own efforts at national and regional level.

Computers in Education. A Critical View

STEEN LARSEN
Denmarks Laererhoejskole, Emdrupvej 101, DK-2400 Kopenhagen NV, Denmark

Technology is tool-using and a fundamental part of human culture and civilization. If we consider technology as the prolongation and expansion of human capabilities, we must realize that without technology there would be no society.

But just because it is a societal construction, a tool can never be defined solely by its natural appearance and immediate characteristics. From a "natural" point of view, a stone axe is a piece of sharpened flint mounted on a handle of wood. But the most important characteristic, and what actually turns the elaborated piece of flint into a tool, is not defined by its actual characteristics, but by the intentions in the mind of its creator. Thus tools are defined by the expectations of what can be achieved through their use. They are never neutral, but create a culture of tool users who must use them on the tool's terms.

The computer is such a tool, and the discussion of its use in education must thus take its point of departure not in the quality of hardware and software, but in the quality of educational intentions behind its use. For this reason the question: "What can we use the computer for in education?", represents a less qualified way of thinking compared to the question: "What tools do we need to attain our educational aims?".

What educational intentions do we have? When this question is raised among people working with computers in education, a frequent reply is that computers can teach children to think. Let us examine this argument more closely. What are we referring to, when we use the word 'think', and how does children's thinking develop?

Some of the greatest contributors to the understanding of the development of children's thinking are Jean Piaget and Lev Vygotsky. Both Piaget and Vygotsky have shown that the child's outer perception and inner imagination is based on preceding motor activity. To be able to imagine things which are not immediately present, the child relies heavily on the sensations and experiences which it has encountered earlier in actually manipulating these things. If we ask a child to think of a ball, the evocation in younger children would be of a solely visual character, but would also draw on tactile and motor experiences encountered earlier in practical activity. In accordance with this view, Wolff & Levin (13) 1972 investigated the relationship between practical manipulation and imagination. They constructed a sort of "house" from a cardboard box, 20 inches long, 10 inches wide, and 12 inches deep, to provide a way in which the children could manipulate toys without simultaneous visual inspection. The lower half of the front of the box was removed and replaced by a cloth curtain. The back of the box was also removed so that the experimenter could observe the children's actions. They selected common toys which were handed in pairs to the children, who then had to try to establish which toys belonged to the same pair. In all 40 children, 20 from kindergarten and 20 from first grade, were included. These children were divided into two groups, each of which had to try to pair the toys under different conditions:

1. The imagination group, where the children were "told to look at each pair of toys and then take them into the house, one in each hand, and imagine the toys playing." These children were not allowed to move their hands once the toys were inside the house.

2. The manipulation group, where the children were told "to take the toys into the house and make them play together, while trying to make up a picture in their heads of whatever the toys were doing."

When all the pairs had been presented, one toy from each pair was arranged in front of the child and the remaining toys were displayed one at a time. The child was now required to hand the matching toys to the experimenter, who recorded the correctness of the response and returned the selected toy to its position in the arrangement.

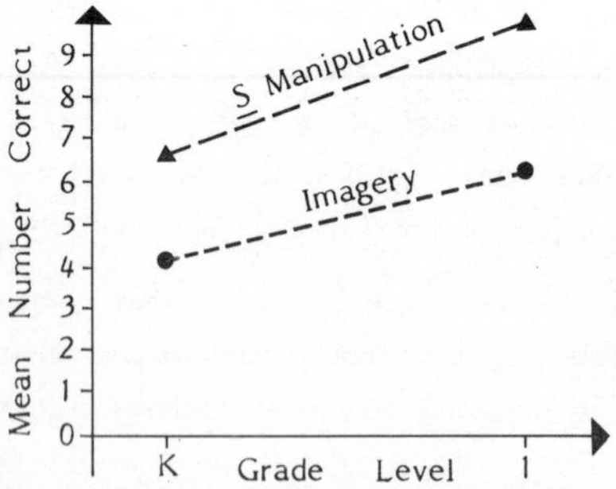

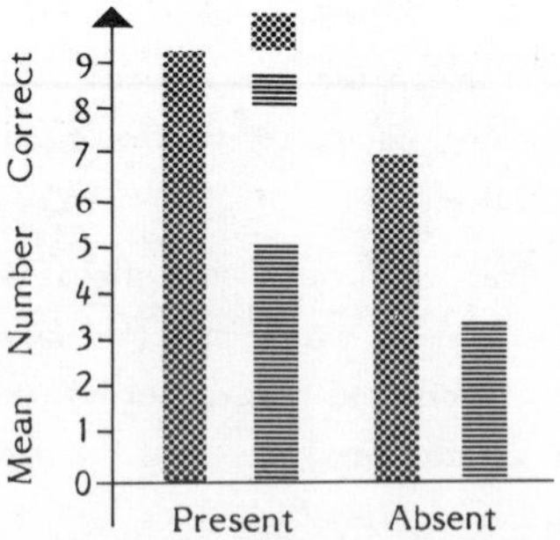

Fig.1. Mean number of correct responses (out of 12) in Imagery and "invisible" Manipulation conditions for kindergarten and first grade children (Experiment II).
Fig.2. Mean recognition scores for Manipulation and Control conditions.

Columns A and B show the number of correct responses when the children were able to see the toys while they were manipulating them (1), and when they just imagined that the toys "played together" (2). The columns 3 and 4 show the same two activities, but now hidden behind the curtain of the "house". As can be seen, practical manipulation was most effective both in the overt visual situation and in the non-visual situation where the manipulations were carried out behind the curtain.

A number of other investigations have supported these findings that practical manipulation facilitates learning. Thus Wolff (12) 1969 found that children from 4 to 7 years of age who voluntarily traced two-dimensional nonsense forms with their hands did better in an immediate recognition task compared to children who did not trace. This degree of facilitation by practical manipulation tended to decrease with age.

Saltz and Dixon (6) 1982 examined the role of practical activity in relation to memory for sentences and words. They presented a number of sentences to children and adults which could be acted out in practice, for example 'The workman was digging a hole in the ground', or 'The teacher pointed a finger at the blackboard'. The subjects were 64 children from the first and second grades and 64 adults. In the Act situation these subjects were told to "act out" such sentence immediately after they had repeated it. In the No-Act situation they were instructed just to repeat the sentence twice without any enactment. The results showed that a very consistent facilitation of recall was produced by motor enactment not only in the children, but, what is perhaps surprising, also in the adult group, were motor enactment almost doubled the recall.

This evidence suggests that learning is apparently more effective if the child is able to manipulate the material in a certain task. However, this phenomenon seems to be most pronounced in younger children, where tactile and motor sensations may be assumed to complement visual perception. During development, this complementary relationship is changed, and the perceptual and cognitive functions of the child come to depend less on overt practical manipulation. Piaget terms this process "internalization". But, nevertheless, the higher-level cognitive skills originally derive both in children and adults from sensory-motor actions. As Piaget states:

"From the most elementary sensory-motor actions...to the most sophisticated intellectual operations, which are internalized actions, carried out mentally...., knowledge is constantly linked to actions or operations...". (5).

When the question of computers in education is considered, it is important to distinguish between the possible impact on younger children up to kindergarten level, and that on older children. In the majority of present systems, the interaction between child and computer is very restricted with regard to the variety of practical manipulations. Extensive use of computers in the education of pre-school children, and children in first grade, might possibly lead to the development of restricted conceptualization and imagination, due to the fact that experiences based on computer presentation lack the tactile and motor dimensions. These dimensions are apparently not so important in older children whose basic conceptual abilities have been established. But in young children, however, where tactile and motor sensations to some degree still complement visual perception, exclusion of these sensations may be critical.

It is not possible at present to determine how serious this argument might be, since there is no relevant empirical evidence in existence. However, Cayler, Lynn and Stein (1) 1973 have published an investigation which might perhaps have some degree of relevance to the present question. Their point of departure was that "because functional or innocent heart murmurs are frequent in children, and because these murmurs are often wrongly diagnosed as due to cardiac defects, many infants and children are incorrectly considered heart disease". Such children with cardiac "non-disease" are frequently restricted from normal physical activities both at home and at school. The authors examined intellectual and perceptual motor development in children with such mis-diagnosis of heart disease. The study included three groups of children between 7 and 11 years:

Group 1 was the restricted group containing 9 children whose practical activity had been restricted due to a false diagnosis of heart disease.

Group 2 was the unrestricted group containing 25 children with false diagnosis of heart disease, but whose practical activity had not been restricted.

Group 3 was the control group containing 31 normal children of comparable age and racial and socioeconomic backgrounds.

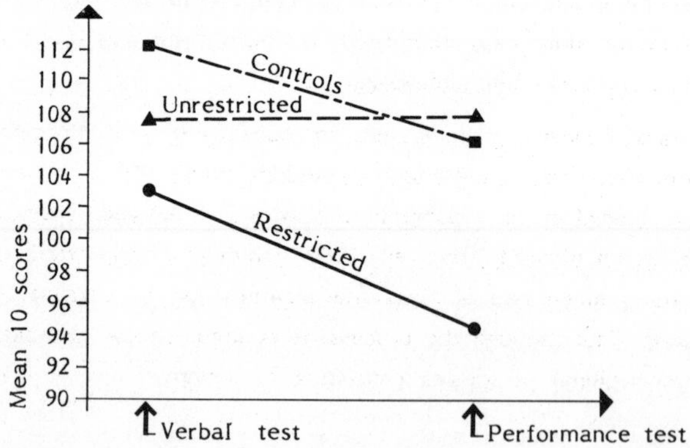

Fig.3. Mean verbal performance IQ scores on WISC for the restricted, nonstricted, and control groups.

Perceptual and intellectual development in these children was determined by the Wechler intelligence test which contains both verbal and performance subtests. A comparison of the three groups revealed that the scores of the restricted children were significantly lower on both verbal and performance tasks compared with the two other groups.

This result should not, for many reasons, be regarded as scientific proof. But it indicates nevertheless that the possible impact of restricted practical activity on the perceptual and intellectual development of young children cannot be ruled out. By the same token, the possibility that restriction of sensory-motor experiences, due to the use of computer-based instruction as a general tool in primary education, could have a negative impact on the children's perceptual and intellectual development should also not be ruled out.

However, computers are not characterized solely by their lack of tactile and motor dimensions. Experiences derived from books also lack these dimensions. This criticism of computers in the education of young children could thus be applied equally to text books. But who today would recommend that young children's early experience and knowledge about the surrounding world should be based primarily on textbooks? According to Piaget and Vygotsky, modern education of young children emphasizes the importance of self-regulated practical experience as a necessary basis for later more text-related kinds of education in school. As far as sensory-motor experience is concerned, computer programs are comparable to textbooks, even if there is no text displayed on the screen.

Thus the construction of a certain figure on the computer screen is just as ideational and theoretical as thinking of it or reading about it. Th process seems to be more practical and concrete on the screen, but actually it is not. The tactile movements on the keyboard needed to type a program that makes a square on the screen, contain no sensory-motor experiences about squares. Similarly, neither do the eye-movements, while reading about squares, contain any sensory-motor experiences related to them. In this way, the child is merely informed about squares, but achieves no direct sensory-motor knowledge of them.

In discussions concerning computers in education, a distinction between the concepts 'information' and 'knowledge' is seldom made. This, in my opinion, is a serious mistake. Indeed it is important to distinguish between 'personal knowledge' and 'knowledge communicated'. The very root 'common' of the word 'communication' implies that to communicate involves the transposition of personal knowledge into common formulae. Thus through the process of communication, personal knowledge is turned into informational structures consisting of separate and defined units, which may be more or less organized or even unrelated. An illustrative parallel to the transition from personal to common information might be the direct and personal experience of a face compared to this same face built up in HR-graphics on the computer screen. From an immediate glance in would appear to be the same face, but a closer look reveals that he computerized face on the screen actually consists of isolated points, whose position and colour each represents individual bits of information.

However, through the transition from personal knowledge into public information something disappears. How can we describe this 'something'? In the psychology of perception we speak of 'gestalts' and define them as integrated wholes that contain more than the mere summation of their units or parts. In accordance with this definition we can say that knowledge is organized like gestalts always containing something more than the mere summation of the information that can be communicated.

In education it is important to understand this difference between gestalts of knowledge and informational facts, because they each represent indispensable dimensions of the educational process. Education is not solely a matter of absorbing as much information as possible on a certain subject, but also a question of establishing a coherent gestalt of knowledge relating to this subject. To simplify this a little, we could say that knowledge of a certain subject is what you have left when all information has been forgotten. And a result of your gestalt of knowledge, the necessary information can easily be searched for when it is needed in a certain situation. To concentrate on giving information to children in an information age, does not therefore constitute a wise educational strategy. Or, as it is set out by Whitehead:

"Culture is activity of thought and receptiveness to beauty and humane feeling. Scraps of information have nothing to do with it. A merely well-informed man is the most useless bore on God's Earth". (11).

The fact that information consists of separate units makes it possible to establish so-called computer-based expert systems, which already exist in various scientific disciplines like, for example, medicine and engineering. Such regularly updated expert systems have also been proposed in educational settings. Dr. Sidney Fernbach, previous leader of the Lowrence Livermore Laboratory's Computation Center, which is one of the largest computation establishments in the world, describes the idea of expert systems in science and education as follows:

"The scientist experiences and learns to understand physical phenomena throughout his entire life, but his most active years for thought are relatively few. The experiences of large numbers of scientists can be put into the data banks of computer systems, and the computers can then be programmed to sort through all this information and come up with "original" ideas... a reasoning system stocked with all the scientific knowledge in the world. This latter system should not be restricted to science alone. Our educational facilities in general need to have the information... at the fingertips of teachers and students. This could be the greatest educational tool in the world". (10).

However, if we return to the distinction between the gestalt of knowledge and the system of public information, an important question now emerges: Has the person who operates a certain expert system an already established gestalt of knowledge in the area concerned? In education this question becomes crucial. Access to information of any kind will continue to accelerate creating a new problem that the amount of information will be overwhelming. As for children in an information age, this is one of tomorrow's problems which must be anticipated in today's education. The educational goal of today must, therefore, be to create the personal gestalts of knowledge which are necessary preconditions for selective and effective use of a boundless mass of information.

But what is actually understood by personal gestalts of knowledge? I have already defined the concepts 'gestalt' and 'knowledge', so let us take a closer look at the term 'personal' and the difference between artificial and natural languages.

The reason for the construction of artificial languages for computer programming is that natural language in a number of respects is insufficient for this purpose. For instance, natural language contains a high variability with regard to word order in the same sentence, isolated words are often very ambigious and, most important, natural language is very context-dependent. From a programmer's point of view, these characteristics are seen as weaknesses which are counteracted by the construction of artificial languages. However, when considering the conceptual development of the child, the very same characteristics can be regarded as valuable qualities which determine the richness and expressiveness of natural language.

If we analyze the process of concept formation in the child, we will recognize that concepts can be established in different ways. Take for instance the concept 'dog'. In its daily activities the child frequently encounters a phenomenon which the adults call 'dog'. These 'dogs' may be very different but are still called by the same word. The child's problem is to overcome these authentic differences, to abstract the common characteristics and to establish it as a general linguistic category.

The cardinal point is, however, to what degree this process of concept formation is based on authentic experiences or on semantic and lexical derivations from already established concepts. If, for example, the child has established the concept 'dog', it is possible, through purely linguistic explanation, to derive the concept 'cow' by modifying the old concept. 'A cow is an animal like a dog. It is bigger, has two horns and you get milk from it'.

Fig.4.

It is important to realize that the differences between authentic and derived concepts are not at the overt level. Both types of concepts can work efficiently on the surface level of the child's language. In the linguistic development of the child, attention is generally directed towards pronounciation, syntax and other overt features, but the question is, nevertheless, if not one of the most important factors, how deeply the concepts are rooted in authentic life experiences derived from concrete episodes.

Episodes, yes. It is precisely the importance of concrete episodes which has occupied memory research in the past decade. In 1972 the Canadian psychologist Tulving (8) proposed a distinction between personal knowledge and public information. Thus episodic memory is derived from "temporally dated episodes and events, and temporal-spatial relations among these events...always stored in terms of its autobiographical reference". (p.385).

On the other hand, semantic memory refers to organized structures of facts and concepts, information about "verbal symbols, their meaning and referents, about relations among them, and about rules, formulas and algorithms for the manipulation of these symbols, concepts, and relations". (p.386).

Summary of differences between episodic and semantic memory

Diagnostic feature	Episodic	Semantic
Information		
Source	° Sensation	° Comprehension
Units	° Events: episodes	° Facts: ideas ; concepts
Organization	° Temporal	° Conceptual
Reference	° Self	° Universe
Veridicality	Personal belief	Social agreement

Summary of differences between episodic and semantic memory (continued)

Operations		
Registration	Experiential	Symbolic
Temporal coding	Present: direct	Absent: indirect
Affect	More important	Less important
Inferential capability	Limited	Rich
Context dependency	More pronounced	Less pronounced
Vulnerability	Great	Small
Access	Deliberate	Automatic
Retrieval queries	Time? Place?	What?
Retrieval consequences	Change system	System unchanged
Retrieval mechanisms	Synergy	Unfolding
Recollective experience	Remembered past	Actualized knowledge
Retrieval report	Remember	Know
Developmental sequence	° Late	° Early
Childhood amnesia	Affected	Unaffected

Fig.5. contains a number of different characteristics between episodic and semantic memory. The characteristics of episodic memory are listed in the second column and the corresponding characteristics of semantic memory in the third column. As you will see, episodic memory is based on sensation, while semantic memory is based on comprehension, episodic memory on events....

Let us illustrate the difference between episodic and semantic memory by an example: One day I meet a friend in the street. He tells me about a certain meeting he has attended recently. While listening, I simultaneously experience the situation on two different levels: the semantic content of his description of the meeting he has attended, which I am now publicly informed about, and the immediate circumstances in which description is made, which constitute an episode in my life. Looking back later I can remember the description of that particular meeting which he had attended, stored as semantic information, and I can also recollect it as a certain episode where I met a friend at a certain place at a certain time. If I were not able to recollect the episodic knowledge, I would still be able to refer to the meeting he had told me about, but would no longer be able to ascertain whether I had attended it myself or whether somebody had just informed me about it. Much like my belief that I was born on a Thursday, I cannot remember, but I am sure I must have been there.

In developmental psychology the memory of concrete episodes is frequently regarded as an early developmental basis for later generalized knowledge. Thus, for example, Kintsch (3) states that the fundamental question of development is "how general knowledge develops on the basis of specific experiences".

Or to use the presentc oncepts: "how semantic memory develops on the basis of concrete episodes."

But is this true? According to Tulving it is not. According to him the relationship is the direct reverse, on the acquisition of skills, where the traditional view has been that beginners start with specific cases and, as they become more proficient, abstract and internalize more and more sophisticated rules. But it might turn out that such processes move in just the opposite direction: from abstract rules to particular cases (2).

Vygotsky's research on egocentric speech supports this view. When faced with a task where the children cannot make direct use of already established skills, their emotional use of language increases as well as their efforts to achieve a less automatic and more analytical solution. Through semantic strategies they search verbally for a new plan, and their utterances reveal the close connection between egocentric and socialized speech (9). However, just at this stage, the child does not work like an expert, but as a beginner using explicit rules and facts just like the programmed computer. But with experience and practice the beginner can turn into an expert who intuitively sees what to do without applying general principles and rules.

Because memory fundamentally implies the existence of some semantic structures, semantic memory is similarly thought to develop earlier as a necessary precondition for the establishment of episodic memory, which must be regarded as a more advanced kind of knowledge. To put it more simply: to have learned general principles is fine, but to have learned to see the general principle in a specific situation is better.

Why do most people recollect almost nothing about the first three years of life? It could be because this period is prior to the establishment of effective semantic memory, the result being that the child is not yet able to integrate experience from concrete episodes of its life into conceptual categories. Thus semantic memory can be compared to the computerized data-bases. The child has an internalized, mental data-base of general semantic information about the world.

In nearly every textbook of linguistics it is stated that the main purpose of language is communication. But there are, nevertheless, two main purposes of language: one to communicate and one to organize the endless chaos of everyday subjective experiences. According to Vygotsky (9) children's egocentric speech should be regarded as the transitional form between external communication and internal speech. In the present terminology we could say that egocentric speech is the transitional form where public semantic information is assimilated and transformed into gestalts of personal knowledge. But to what extent are computers, owing to their function as processors of semantic information, counterproductive to this transformation? This is one of the most important questions to be raised in the discussion of computers in education.

Thus for what reason after all do we educate our children? If we regard education as an end in itself, we will concentrate on letting the child learn to think in general and to give the child an opportunity to gather as much information about the world as possible. From this point of view, education is a matter of training in formal logic and establishing and expanding the child's semantic information systems on various sunjects. For these purposes, a computer will be a very effective instrument. Thus artificial languages like Logo are supposed to develop the child's general ability to think and with programs like Plato the child can gather the necessary amount of semantic information. Indeed, the name Plato is very appropriate for such educational systems. Plato himself wrote over his entrance door:

"Let only geometers enter". According to Plato, all knowledge must be stateable in explicit instructions. If this could not be done, that is if knowing h o w could not be converted into knowing t h a t, it was simply not knowledge, but mere belief. According to Plato, cooks for example, who proceed by taste, and craftsmen who use non-declarative and automatic processing based partly on intuition, have no knowledge. What they do does not involve understanding and cannot be understood or taught. True knowledge is rule-governed and can be taught by making the rules explicit. What cannot be stated explicitly in precise instructions is relegated by Plato to some kind of arbitrary fumbling (2).

If, on the other hand, education is n o t regarded as a general object in itself, but as a personal tool by which I become capable of handling my own life and taking part in the further development of my society, thinking must be m y way of thinking and semantic information must be turned into my own gestalts of knowledge. From this point of view, semantic memory and information established by means of computer-based instruction is no longer sufficient, owing to its lack of auto-biographical reference.

Furthermore, it would appear that this lack can lead to an almost authoritarian relationship between the student and the machine. For example, researchers at the University of Missouri programmed their machines to make systematically increasing errors in computing, giving answers that were from 10 to 50 percent above the correct answer. Testing nearly 1,200 students from grades seven through twelve and adults, they found that even the brightest students and adults tended to take the word of the machine over their own good sense, even when their own rough estimates were correct and the machine was out by as much as 50 percent. (7).

This does not mean, however, that semantic information should in any way be avoided. This would be impossible. But it implies that because of the lack of auto-biographical references, computers should not be used as the children's main source of information or as a sparring partner in general thinking. The programmed micro-worlds have been described by Minsky and Papert (4) as "fairyland(s) in which things are so simplified that almost every statement about them would be literally false if asserted about the real world".

If education is considered to be a process by which one becomes capable of handling everyday situations, this is a crucial point. Because the semantic micro-worlds are built up of separated information, they are ill-adapted to the elusive, shifting world of everyday episodes. Our everyday expertise does not consist of explicit facts and rules, but of our episodic memories of past situations already successfully resolved. If the learner was acquiring still more sophisticated rules and principles, then the episodic aspects could be disregarded and the semantic micro-worlds could gradually increase in complexity as the child developed. But if the child is to be able to see the general principles as aspects of concrete episodes of every-day life, then keeping the learner in a micro-world can actually be counterproductive.

This problem can be illustrated by the terms 'lexicon' and 'biography'. The semantic memory can be compared to the lexicon and the episodic memory to the biography. The question how is how far these faculties of mind are dissociated. Do they constitute different libraries into which the student places new memory records, or is the lexical information turned into coherent personal knowledge as a result of the presence of auto-biographical references?

The interaction with the computer is cyclic. Even if the semantic content of this interaction changes from situation to situation, the educational circumstances remain unchanged: the screen is the same, the starting procedures, the commands of the programs and the actual surroundings are the same. The educational situations cannot be separated and recollected as different episodes of life, even if their lexical content can be reproduced. In fact, this means that the auto-biographical reference is suspended in such educational settings.

Let me conclude by drawing attention to the fact that computers were not originally constructed for educational purposes. To ask what computers can be used for in education can easily lead to an instrumental and superficial approach, where the introduction of various kinds of information technology becomes an aim in itself. This is not an argument against computers as such, but against considering them to be a fundamental and dominant part of educational technology.

As far as primary education is concerned, the absence of sensory-motor dimensions disqualifies computer-based instruction as a general instrument of learning.

Furthermore, the difference between knowledge and information must be considered. Today these concepts are used almost as synonyms, but the rapid development of information technology makes it necessary to devise much more detailed distinctions between such concepts. More or less universal access to information will thus force us to examine and define what knowledge actually is. And as it has been proposed here, knowledge is considered to be something more than mere structure of information. This "more" refers to the auto-biographical references that turn public information into gestalts of personal knowledge. Computers are constructed to work by strictly controlled and self-referring procedures, and their processing goes on unaffected by the surrounding context. Because of this, information obtained from computer-based expert systems and data-bases will be non-episodic and lacking auto-biographical references.

If education is considered as a matter of developing gestalts of personal knowledge, the use of such computer-based systems as the child's main sources of information about the world might turn out to be counterproductive. Instead of achieving the necessary balance between what has been termed the child's direct and derived concepts, the result might be the establishment of isolated lexicons unintegrated with the child's everyday experiences and biography.

Our children should be experts in many fields. But as I have stated, real experts do not, in real life, work according to explicit rules or facts. True experts have advanced beyond the stage of formal logic and semantic self-regulation and work more automatically, guided by experience and intuition. Computer-based instruction used as a general educational instrument might possibly be an obstacle to this development, keeping the child on the level of formal logic and explicit control of new and more complicated areas.

As regards children in an information age, one of the most important problems is to realize that new technology demands correspondingly fresh educational thinking. However, the risk is that educational theory is subjected to gradual and unconscious change until it meets the special needs of computer technology. Tomorrow's problem today is to avoid this, by considering the computer as a possible tool for certain educational purposes, and not as an end in itself.

REFERENCES

(1) Cayler,G.C., Lynn,D.B. and Stein,E.M. 1973. Effect of cardiac 'nondisease' on intellectual and perceptual motor development. British Heart Journal, 35, 543-547.

(2) Dreyfus,H.L. and Dreyfus,S.E. 1984. Putting computers in their proper place: Analysis versus intuition in the classroom. Teachers College Record, 85, 578-601.

(3) Kintsch,W. 1974. The representation of meaning in memory. Hillsdale, N.J.: Lawrence Erlbaum Associates.

(4) Minsky,M. & Papert,S. 1970. Draft of a proposal to ARPA for Research on Artificial Intelligence at M.I.T., p. 39. (Here quoted from Dreyfus and Dreyfus, 1984).

(5) Piaget,J. 1983. Piaget's theory. In P.H.Mussen (Ed.), Handbook of Child Psychology. New York: John Wiley.

(6) Saltz,E. and Dixon,D. 1982. Journal of Experimental Child Psychology, 34, 77-92.

(7) Timnick,L. 1982. Electronic Bullies. Psychology Today, 16, 10-15.

(8) Tulving,E. and Donaldson,W. 1972. Organization of memory. New York: Academic Press.

(9) Vygotsky,L.S. 1978. Mind in society. The development of higher psychological processes. London.

(10) Weinzenbaum,J. 1979. Once more: The computer revolution. In M.L.Dertouzos and J.Moses (Eds.), The computer age: A twenty-year view. Massachusetts: The M.I.T. Press.

(11) Whitehead,A.N. 1950. The aims of education. London: Ernest Benn.

(12) Wolff,P. 1969. The effect of nonocular activity on children's perception. Unpublished doctorial dissertation. University of Michigan.

(13) Wolff,P. and Levin,J.R. 1972. The role of activity in children's imagery production. Child Development, 43, 537-547.

(14) Wolff,P., Levin,J.R. and Longobardi,E.T. 1972. Motoric mediation in children's paired-associate learning: Effects of visual and tactual contact. Journal of Experimental Child Technology, 14, 176-183.

Principles for the Design of an Integrated Computational Environment for Education

ANDREA A. diSESSA
Laboratory for Computer Science, MIT, Cambridge, MA 02139, USA

> Our purpose is not to understand history or predict the future, but to change the course of history and make the future.-- paraphrase

While the aphorism that heads this paper might overstate the case, I am struck at how much time and effort is spent at these very early stages of the penetration of computers into education looking back at what has been done, classifying, looking for the "best" way to use computers, and predicting the future. This much like trying to pick the best fruit just as the sapling tree emerges from the ground.Even worse, such activities seem to assume a kind of inevitable working out of the processes what we currently see in action, without any respect for our own wills and capability of invention.

I wish to take a different tack, looking not so much to what we have,what we might expect or even what we fear, but, instead, toward what we really might like to see happen. I would like to set a project based at MIT to develop a new computational environment for educational purpose in the context of the educational goals that motivate it, and in the context of the means we have at our disposal for getting to those goals. The goals are clearly more important than any single project, and we hope the means will also transcend our local context.

We have already been through the process once. By "we" I mean the Logo Project which produced the computer language LOGO and images of uses of computers that were not at all "in the wind" when the project got its start. On the contrary, our first implementation of LOGO was on a machine that , in today's terms, cost about $ 1,000,000, and many thought the project would never be brought to any practical consequences. Today one can buy a computer that runs a respectable Logo for $150, and as a style of using computers in education, Logo has inspired substantial efforts as indicted by the hundreds of books and articles published about it all over the world. Looking at the continuing decline of cost in computer hardware alone, our imaginations are again challenged to look toward the future. What should we do beyond Logo and other present educational uses of computers with the increment of power that will come at affordable prices within the next 5 years or so?

Before I give our image of the future, I would like to look at goals and means phrased as principles of design.

The Principle of Agency-- I could start theoretically with Piaget or Dewey in describing the importance of active engagement, of agency in education.But to be brief I would like to retell a little anecdote that Eleanor Duckworth relates with great compassion in her article "The Having of Wonderful Ideas." She describes a small boy who was working with some materials designed to teach about electricity, materials consisting of batteries, light bulbs ,wire,etc. The boy was posed the problem of figuring out what electrical object was contained in a "black box" only by connecting things to the terminals that emerged from the box . Although he was captured by the problem and managed to determine that the box contained something that conducted current, the boy was unable to figure out how to distinguish among the materials that conducted. Finally, he had an inspiration, if it was a light bulb in the box, he knew that it would burn out if he put enough current through it. In great excitement the boy went to his teacher with the idea. After debating with herself for some time about whether she should allow him to destroy some materials to follow through on his idea,she told him to go ahead. To his great delight, he managed to burn out the bulb , and solve the riddle of the black box.

From this little story, I would like to draw two morals that I shall merely state, not try to prove in any general sense. First is the importance of personal events. When I think back over my own education, the most memorable experiences were inevitably those that I had some strong personal commitment to, and none were the result of any standard school exercise or lecture. It is easy to underestimate the power of having a wonderful idea of your very own,particularly since such events are exceedingly hard to design into the educational system. But there is a good reason to believe that such events might have powerful influence over the education career of a student. Feelings of achievement and personal satisfaction that flow form such rare events can establish the whole stance that any individual brings to subjects or, indeed, to the whole educational process. It is hard for me to believe that someone who never had such wonderful, personal experiences could care enough about learning to really achieve.

The other moral is the difficulty that the educational system has in designing for such events, in being patient during the time spent leading up to them, and even in accepting them when they happen. Burning out a light bulb is a small price to pay, but it is not easy for teachers to accept personal acts, particularly if some "damage" is done. The damage need not be physical, but it is just as difficult to deal with in more subtle forms, such as the disruption of the routine and expected practic. To make the point more sharply, I would propose the principle of significant corruptibility, that educational materials and practice will leave out essential and irreplaceable elements of learning if students or, indeed, teachers cannot do things with those materials substantially beyond what the designer had in mind. I am waiting for the day when I will see a clear case of a CAI program "branching to my personal insight" rather than to the next problem or to explanatory text that satisfies the designers goals, but almost certainly not satisfying any immediate, personal excitement.

Logo was designed with the principle of agency firmly in mind, and our new design will be in pursuit of this goal with equal vigour.

The Principle of Utility--Let me approach the second major principle through a problem I have noted with Logo. We have found almost all students respond in personal terms to the possibilities of drawing presented by turtle graphics. Sometimes it is a new sense of precision and power through mechanization, sometimes it is a fascination with computational possibilities (iteration,recursion),sometimes it comes from geometric discoveries such as emergent patterns, or building curves with short,straight lines.

But teachers often have not reacted in the same way. In fact most teachers learn Logo "for their students", not for themselves. As a result,many students achieve proficiency with Logo much more quickly and thoroughly than their teachers. I think the reason for this is not difficult to spot. Logo really serves the goals of student much better than those of teachers, at least during early stages of use. In many ways, teachers must either have a prior technical interest in computation,or an extraordinary motivation to get to the level of skill that allows them to build their own materials in Logo, to master the language to the point that teaching it is just a natural extension of their own personal feeling of mastery rather than a duty.

The situation could and should be different. For example, text processing for purposes ranging from keeping personal notes to preparing written materials for students is one of the first things that, I beilieve, teachers would appreciate. Yet the Logo editor is tuned only to preparing programs. Keeping small data bases,for example, keeping notes on student activities or grades, is another area with which teachers would undoubtedly appreciate help. This is not to say that teachers do not see the capabilities of Logo for engaging children, and even engaging themselves in scientific mathematical and aesthetic exploration. But the point is that a computational environment that serves directly some more commonplace and even mental needs would be appropriated with more enthusiasm and less effort than is the case now.

Thus we propose the principle of utility-- that a computational environment will be appropriated in significant measure according to the immediately perceivable value of using it. There is no particular reason Logo limits itself to being a programming environment rather than a more generally useful computational tool, excepting the limitations of present hardware mainly in terms of memory and speed and excepting the effort needed to design those capabilities into the system.Utility is one of the fundamental motivations for the design of our new computational system-- to combine a much broader array of functionality into the same box.To be more explicit, what we have in mind is a system which combines in a simple well-integrated form the following functionalities:

- Text processing, including structured filing.
- Using and modifying prewritten programs.
- Programming from scratch, as is done in many instances with Logo.
- Data base capability, largely in terms of informal databases such as journals, etc.
- A rich, programmable graphics capability to support all of the above.

The intention is not so much just to increase the usefulness of a programming environment by adding features, but to produce a genuinely new medium-- a reconstructable, interactive medium. We want a medium which will be only a little more complex than Logo (and, indeed, easier to learn at early stages), but which will do far more. The breadth of applicability means also that the environment can be learned in increments according to the particular needs of the beginner or novice. A child can still start with turtle graphics (or the extension to turtle graphics that we are also anxious to try out other introductions to computation, such as those based on building, exploring and analyzing data-rich worlds. A teacher may choose to start his own experience with text processing or data base building or browsing. Yeat each path into the system can easily be extended since the environment is truly integrated, not a collection of separate subsystems. In sections below we will also provide examples of kinds of things that can be done in an integrated environment that depend crucially on the synergy that can be obtained by combining all these functionalities into the same product.

Readers should read "reconstructable, interactive medium" in the context of an advance over such well-established media as the written word. The role of programming is crucial here. It provides the capability for interaction far beyong static media of the past. But it is perhaps more important that programming is a generally accessible means for constructing in the medium. Unlike such media as films, where the technology of production is too complex and expensive for a child to regularly use as part of his own personal means of expression,programming can be made accessible to everyone , more like the typwriter, or better , the pencil, so that the medium truly becomes a personal tool for intelectual development. And programming need not have the finality of producing a film-- it is corruptible.To be sure, virtuoso professional programmers will produce untouchable masterpieces like the great authors of history, but that will not keep every student from expressing himself and exploring ideas with programming in the way every child learns the same written language as the masters.

Programming will need to change its image and character to fill this role. It will need to be easier to do than with present languages. It will have to be adapted to doing relatively simple things trivially, more than to doing long and complex things flawlessly. Interaction will need to become a much more prominent part of the language, since the pont of an interactive medium is to have responsive entitles, not the silent invisible algorithms toward which current programming languages are aimed. Our conviction is that this change in the meaning of programming can be accomplished.

INSTRUMENTAL PRINCIPLES

I need to say something about the means we are employing to make the system easy to understand, easy to learn and use. Utility, as I implied above,must be understood as value received in proportion to effort expended. Very useful things that can be done will not contribute to the utility of the system unless it is relatively easy to achieve them. Readers should be aware that this is the most technical section of the paper, aimed primarily at sophisticated users and designers.

The Principle of Multiple Models -- At this historical stage in our understanding of "understanding", I believe some of our preconceptions are beginning to unravel. One of the most insidious of these preconceptions is that simplicity is a simple concept. Indeed, some analysis of what makes computer languages or systems easy to understand has shown surprising results. In particular, the notion that a system having a single uniform structure (a structural model) is necessarily easy to understand is a notion whose time has past. One would like to make systems that have such models for purposes of the uniformity that aids some aspects of learning. (It particularly aids recall after the system has initially been largely learned, and some aspects of interaction, particularly debugging, where one must be very careful to track down mistakes that might well be based on reasonable, but incorrect assumptions about the collective behaviour of a set of commands). But having a simple structural model is not nearly enough to assure a learnable system. Now is not the time for a complete review (see [diSessa 85]), but we can very briefly point to two other kinds of understanding that probably are at least as important as structural models in term of making a system that is perceived as simple by beginners as well as by experts.

In many instances, one learns about elements of a language according to the function they perform.Variables are learned to be information repositories as much as they are simply associations between names and objects. Variables also perform certain common functions in stereotypical concert with other commands. A counting loop is such a case. Studies of expert programmers show that an important part of of their knowledge of a programming system is in terms of functional fragments, little plans or sketches of how to get things done, rather than simply a complete understanding of how each command works. So it is not only the beginner that benefits from functional models.

Functional models seem problematic in that they are often relatively ad hoc and one cannot expect to have a complete and uniform understanding of a system in terms of functional models alone. Yet thinking about early experience with a language especially for non-computer experienced people should help convince that learning instances of getting things done can be a powerful wedge into understanding the whole system. It should be no surprise that it is not only beginners who maintain and develop functional ways of understanding a system. After all, getting things done is always one of the most prominent and important parts of a computational experience.

Stepping even farther from the mathematical simplicity of the abstract structure of a system, one often sees people remembering, predicting and "understanding" aspects of the system on the basis of things like visual metaphors or rationalizations that may not even be correct, but allow the user to generalize properly for some length of time. For example, the syntax for the definition of a procedure seems to be much more learnable if it matches the visual presentation of the invocation of a procedure. Experience with several languages, including Logo, have verified this.Note similarities between the definition line, TO..., and the recursive call of SQUARE in the following Logo definition.

```
TO SQUARE  : SIDE
FORWARD : SIDE
RIGHT 90
SQUARE : SIDE
END
```

Along the same lines, most Logo users think the parameters in a procedure definition have a : in front of them (which in Logo denotes the value of a variable) because they are variables. In fact, to be consistent with Logo's conventions for handling symbols,input variables should be marked with a quotation mark. Instead, they are idiosyncratically marked with : simply so beginners can remember the syntax through the rationalization that " inputs are variables". These kinds of fragmentary, sometimes inconsistent ways of understanding a system I call distributed models.

The general design principle that emerges from these considerations is that one must be aware that people spontaneously construct many kinds of meaning in using a computational system. We must design to whatever kind of model is appropriate for the thing that we want to teach and appropriate to the level of expertise that the user can be expected to have when he encounters that aspect of the system. Though I will not have time to comment in detail at how the principle of multiple models has impacted out design to date, some of this should be evident in the descriptions I will give of the system.

The Principle of Re-using Intuitive Knowledge -- One of the simplest but most profound principles of learning is that all learning take place at the edge of what is already known. Thus in order to build an understandable system, it is important to examine the kinds of things peopled already know about and to see if that knowledge can be modified and reapplied to the computational system.

With our new system, we are attempting to apply this principle in two related ways. First, we are attempting to design a system so that users can adopt an attitude of "naive realism." That is, the user should be able to pretend that the system is what he sees on his monitor. In contrast, essentially all present systems rely on sending commands off into an invisible system, which might, in return, present a reply. Many previous proposals for simplifying systems have in fact been the opposite of this notion of naive realism and, for example, suggest that users should only see a part of the system chosen to be less complex than the whole. Naive realism means we must accept the responsibility to make the system truly simple so that a user will not be inundated by complexity in looking at it or, as with the hiding principle, so that a user will not be unpleasantly surprised at a later time by aspects of the system initially hidden from him.

Naive realism means that users can apply all of their perceptual powers to analyze the appearance of the system, and that that analysis can be translated directly into an understanding of the system, rather than into an understanding of some idiosyncratic configuration of text and other things that happen to appear on the screen at a given time. Window systems are popular with experts, but windows are structure entirely outside the main computational semantics -- they do not simplify understanding, but only provide some increased flexibility for comprehending users in terms of use of the area of the monitor screen.

The second sub-principle of the principle of reuse of intuitive knowledge is specifically to use geometric and spatial commonsense knowledge to make system structures understandable. Thus, "the spatial metaphor" requires us to use placement as seen on the screen, more particularly, adjacency and containment, to represent important structural relations in the system. Once more, this is nearly the opposite of techniques such as windowing.

It is time to begin to apply these principles and describe a bit of the system we are in the process of designing.

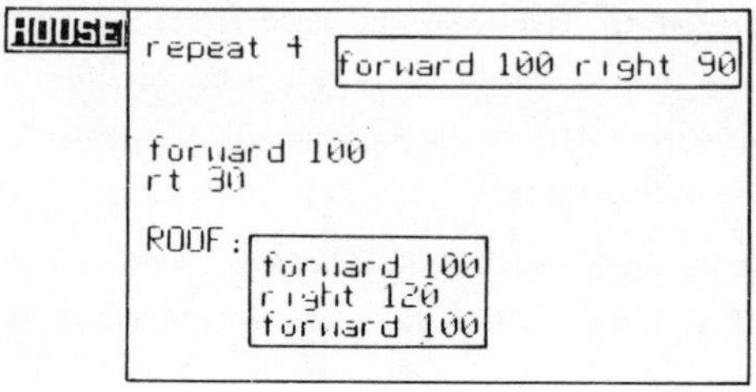

Figure 1. A program definition, HOUSE, with a subprogram,ROOF,written in place.

Figure 1 shows a simple program in Boxer. Boxes are the principle means of denoting and structuring things in the system, as the name Boxer is meant to imply. Here we see a subprocedure, ROOF, written directly into place as part of a major procedure. In order to create this program, all one has to do is assemble elements into the visible pattern. Thus, if one tried out a series of commands one after another-- say, the commands constituting ROOF-- one can turn those into a program merely by pointing to them and pressing a "make-box" key. In this case that program is mnemonically labeled with ROOF:. Since it is intended for a one-time use, it was not turned into a definition. Any box can be turned into a definition. Thenceforth, the object may be referenced by name.

Note the use of the spatial metaphor; the subprogram occurs directly in place of use. In Logo and many other languages, that cannot be done. Also, naive realism implies that to change any part of the program, all one has to do is move to the place where one wants to make a change and type in the change. (The easiest method for moving is to use the "mouse"-- a hand-held device which moves the cursor on the monitor when it is moved over the desk top.). Thus in Boxer, one uses always -available editing commands to move around and change the system directly. A separate procedure definition mode does not exist. One can also use or try out pieces of a program simply by moving to them, and pressing the doit-key, which causes the line on which the cursor resides to be executed. Thus one could move into the HOUSE definition, point to and execute a part of the definition such as the ROOF. Indeed, one could point to and execute each line of the definition, one at a time, for the purpose of careful debugging.

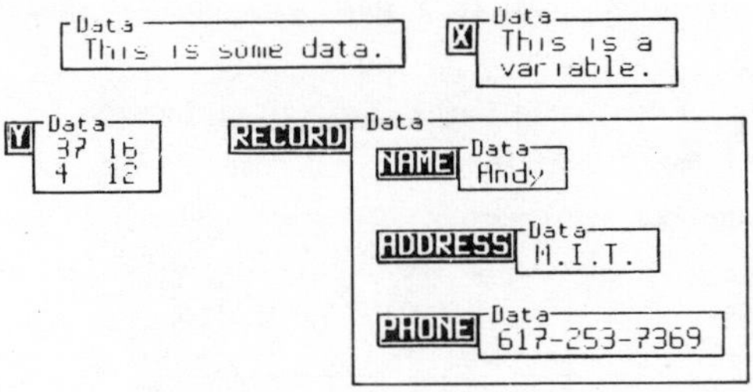

Figure 2. Data boxes and variables.

Figure 2 shows a data box, which is different from the kind of box, the "doit" box, shown in Figure 1. The distinction between "things to be done," and "things that serve as data" (information to be passed around and modified by the system) is a functional distinction that is relatively simple for beginners to make. Data boxes are not only the universal data type in the system, but, when named with a name tab, are the visible representation of variables. Note that creating a variable is almost identical visually to creating a named program.

Whenever a program changes a variable, that change will appear on the screen. Alternatively, one can simply use an editor function to change the contents of a box hence the data associated with the variable name will be changed. These are direct implications of naive realism.

The variable called RECORD in FIgure 2 shows that nested boxes are useful for data objects and variables as well as with procedures (doit bxoes). Nested data boxes create the functionality of records, with independently named subparts. RECORD.NAME fetches the part of RECORD with the name tab NAME. Pieces of any data box may be accessed or changed in a number of ways, by item number (counting left to right, top to bottom), by row number, by row and column (as a matrix), and in some other ways as well.

Data boxes are generally useful containers of information far beyond what one might expect of a variable. They might contain a paper typed in with the editor; they might contain some subboxes in a standard format (hence become a data base); or they might contain some subboxes which are papers of places that special programs are expected to be run. In the last case, the hierarchical structure of boxes becomes a file system. We intend users to construct or reconstruct their whole computational world out of boxes, and indeed, we expect that one of a beginner's first activities might well be to wander around in some previously created system of boxes.

In the role of environments or of a file system that one may want to wander around in, it is particularly important to be able to suppress detail when one wishes to. So boxes can be shrunk down to a small grey box with the touch of "shrink" button on the mouse. One touch of an "expand" button opens the box for inspection, and a second touch of the same button expands the box to full-screen, suppressing the context of the box, and effectively entering the box as a sub-environment. Figure 3 shows some shrunken boxes.

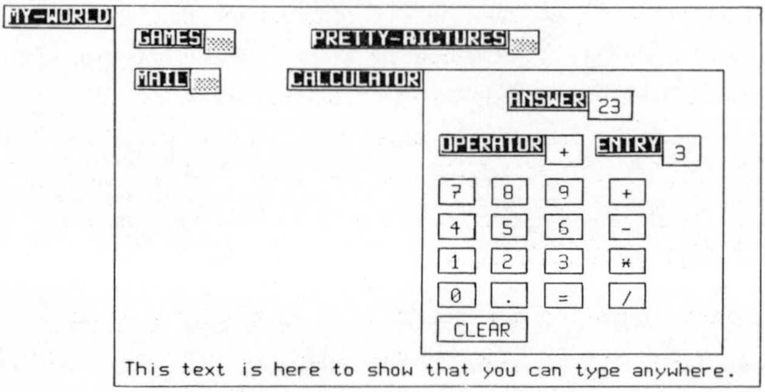

Figure 3. A personal environment in Boxer.

In order to play the role of an environment that has special capabilities, one needs a means to localize these capabilities and keep them from interfering with the rest of the system. Special capabilities will in general simply be definitions made in a box, whether data definitions -- variables, or named files, or whatever are all the same thing in Boxer -- or procedure deifinitions. Localization is accomplished by having all definitions accessible only within the box in which the definition appears. Outside of it, the names of the definitions are not understood unless specific reference is made to the box in which they are defined. This fact, that containment implies inheritance of definitions, is one of the principle uses of the spatial metaphor in Boxer. Incidentally, note that one can also take advantage of the capability of defining new things within any box to define sub-procedures inside the procedure that uses them, a practice that makes large systems of procedures easier to understand.

Environment, that is boxes with special defintiions and other things aimed toward a particular purpose, are very important to Boxer. They allow to become a universe of microworlds, places where particular object and actions are available for students to play with, modify and recombine in an unconstrained manner. Boxer can provide as much structure as the teacher wishes in a microworld, but that structure is always available for the student to inspect, change or rebuild.

Figure 3 shows a personal computational environment organized by boxes. If a user wants to do some things with mail -- sent,receive or look at or reorganize past messages -- he simply opens the MAIL box and conducts his activities.This contrasts to the usual way of doing similar activities in present systems, which is to start up a special program whose every keystroke might be different than for the editor or programming environment. In Boxer, almost all activities will happen in places that behave in the same way as each other, but that have specialized pieces of data,text or procedures that distinguish their use. The calculator that appears in that figure is an example of a simple " information appliance " to use a phrase of Steve Draper Its buttons can be pressed by pointing and clicking mouse buttons. Such appliances, which include simplified versions of spread sheet programs, etc., are very easy to build in Boxer. We expect that collections of these that are particularly useful to teachers or interesting for students will find their way into the culture surrounding Boxer, and into almost everyone's box world.

The graphics system we are designing to extend turtle graphics of Logo has generalized graphical objects, called sprites, that live inside of graphics boxes. Like turtles, sprites can move and turn; their shape can be set to be that described by any turtle program; and their size can also be adjusted separately.

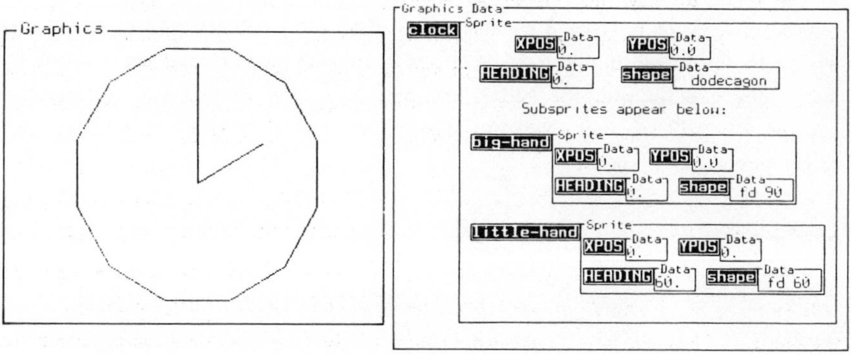

Figure 4. A graphical object, a clock, and the data that defines it.

Sprites can have sub-sprites, for example, the sprite in Figure 4 has two sub-sprites which are hands of the clock. One can move the clock as a whole, TELL CLOCK FORWARD 100; or one talk to the subparts, for example, TELL BIG-HAND RIGHT 6, to turn the hands of the clock. Sprites are sensitive to the cursor in that they highlight themselves when the cursor moves over them. In that case, pressing mouse buttons causes user-defined procedures to be activated in the sprite. This means it is very easy to create information appliances that work using only the mouse, much as Macintosh and similar software often does. Special commands like FOLLOW-THE-MOUSE extend the functionality of mouse operations on sprites.Sprites can draw with a pen, like turtle; they can stamp their shape on background in their graphics box; and they are sensitive to other sprite's touch, which simplifies writing many kinds of programs involving interacting objects.

Graphics boxes actually have two forms. The primary form is purely graphicsl, as they are mostly intended to be used. But in order that every part of the system be visible and manipulable in the same way,graphics boxes can also be turned into graphics-data boxes, in which case the sprites contained in the graphics box have the usual box structure that is Boxer's hallmark. In this form, graphics boxes and sprites can be named and manipulated with the editor in the same way as all other kinds of boxes. The second box in Figure 4 is the same graphics box turned into its "data" form. Note the sub-sprites that appear inside the clock sprite. The spatial relation of containment means "part of" for graphical objects. In the data form, one can see the position coordinates of the sprites, and one can see other attributes (boxes) that are either built-in to all sprites (like HEADING) or have been added. Naturally,when a sprite is given a command like FORWARD 100, its position coordinates change on the screen if the graphics box is in its data form. And if one changes the coordinates directly with the editor, the position of the sprite in the graphics box changes. One will see that change as soon as one returns the graphics data box back to its purely graphic form.

CONCLUSION

Boxer is a system designed to be the first genuine example of a reconstructable, interactive medium for non-computer specialists, combining all sorts of useful computational capabilities -- programming, text manipulation, data base and computer graphics activities-- into a uniform,easy-to-learn system. Above all, we wish to make sure that such an environment serves the individuals that use it, that their personal agency to change and build as they see fit is given first priority. We are trying to use such principles as deliberately designing to multiple models and reusing intuitive knowledge about objects and space to insure perceived simplicity.

Boxer already exists in prototype form on a Symbolics 3600 Lisp Machine. Though such machines are in the $ 100,000 class right now, it will not be long before that kind of power reaches the range of affordability for individuals and school systems. Over the next three years, we will be finishing Boxer's design, making a new implementation for a less expensive machine, and exploring the educational possibilities that are opened through such a system.

REFERENCES

[diSessa 85]

diSessa,A.A.

A Principled Design for an Integrated Computational Environment. Human-Computer Interaction 1(1):1-57,1985

[diSessa 86]

diSessa,A.A.

Notes on the Future of Programming: Breaking the Utility Barrier, in User Centered System Design: New Perspectives on Human-Computer Interaction. D.Norman and S.Draper (eds). Hillsdale, N.J.:Erlbaum, expected 1986.

[Lay, Klotz and Neves 85]

Lay, E.,Klotz,L.and Neves,D.

Boxer Manual.

M.I.T. Laboratory for COmputer Science, Educational Computating Group,1985.

[Roschelle 85]

Roschelle, Jeremy.

The Design of a Graphics Subsystem for Boxer.

B.S.thesis, Massachusetts Institute of Technology, June,1985

Department of Electrical Engineering and Computer Science.

ATEE's Proposal for a Teacher Education Syllabus "Literacy in Information Technology"

PETER GORNY

Angewandte Informatik, Universität Oldenburg, P.O. Box 2503, D-2900 Oldenburg, Federal Republic of Germany

1. What is ATEE?

The Association for Teacher Education in Europe (ATEE) is an international association, founded in 1976 by European institutions and individuals whose aims embrace both the academic and the practical aspects of education. Its members, from approx. 20 European countries, are engaged in teacher education at preservice as well as at inservice levels. A large number of colleges and universities offering teacher education courses are institutional members.

2. ATTEE's work in New Information Technology (NIT)

ATEE has established a Working Group on New Information Technologies (Chairman: Rhys Gwyn, Manchester Polytechnic, Manchester UK). This group has been engaged in a series of comparative studies of the objectives and approaches which have been chosen in the different countries to introduce computers and informatics into the educational systems. The results have been published in several reports ([1]-[6]) and conference proceedings ([7]-[9]).

Another problem examined was the issue of programming languages for teaching informatics in secondary schools (approx. age 13-18 years). The resulting recommendation was a promotion of structured languages such as PASCAL and COMAL.

In cooperation with other ATEE working groups the topics of computer-aided special education, the influence of NIT on sex equality in school and audio-visual teaching/learning methods are also being investigated ([7]-[9]).

The main outcome of the Working Group on NIT, however, was the group's conviction that the educational system should provide for literacy in information technology for a l l children. The reasons for this conviction need not be discussed here, but they are founded on the belief that information technology is changing or influencing practically all professions, is a medium for handling information in the private sphere and as a 'tool for thinking with'. Thus it will strongly influence the development of society in almost every imaginable aspect. For these reasons all pupils should be able to acquire some fundamental knowledge about the new information technologies and attain a reasonable and balanced attitude to them.

3. NIT in Teacher Education

If (and when) all children have to acquire some literacy in information technology, it is necessary to educate teachers appropriately. Therefore the Working Group has destined a syllabus "Literacy in Information Technology for All Teachers". The first part of the proposal was published in 1984 [10], the second part is in preparation [11] and will be published for the annual ATEE conference, held in 1985 at Tilburg, The Netherlands.

The syllabus which the ATEE Working Group proposes, is necessarily not very detailed: an adaptation to a broad variety of cultural traditions, educational systems and national educational policies should be possible; it may be transformed into curricula for pre-service or for in-service teacher education; last but not least, it does not rely on the state of the art of microcomputers and programming as applied in school today, but has to be open to new concepts and developments in the field of education and school-oriented hardware and software products.

ATEE refrains similarly from recommending a set length or organizational framework for a course in 3IT-Literacy for Teachers", because teacher education systems differ widely from country to country.

4. The Objectives of the Syllabus

Where a political decision has been taken to expose all children to some form of teaching about information technology, it still has to be decided what goals should be pursued and what content and methodology would be appropriate to these. In respect of the school curriculum, the ATEE Working Group has stated:

> "The central need in the teaching of literacy in information technology is to create insights which enable the pupils to develop a reasonable and balanced attitude towards information technology, and which enable them furthermore to react appropriately to situations in which contact with automated systems takes place." [10,p.9]

This means in practice, that the curriculum designer can draw a conceptual line from environment to machine for the following areas:

(a) Social impact:

The gathering, protection and integrity of data; information systems (use and evaluation); changing methods and quality of work; changing employment; influence on individuals and their cooperation; influence on organizations.

(b) Use of application systems:

e.g. text processing, spreadsheets, information systems, data bases, graphics programs, simulations, process control, educational applications such as drill and practice or tutorial programs.

(c) Problem solving by algorithmic methods:

Methods of problem analysis and problem solving; principles of programming.

(d) Principles of software and machine architecture:

Functional models of complex systems for information processing.

For a curriculum in teacher education the areas "social impact" and "use of application systems" will have to include discussion of the impact of IT on education and school and a close investigation of the application of IT in the teaching/learning process. Beyond that there is also a need for a methodology of teaching IT.

Thus the objectives for teacher education have to centre on enabling the teachers to develop a reasonable and balanced attitude towards:

- IT in general,
- the application of IT as a medium and a tool in the teaching/learning process,
- IT as a subject in school (whatever label it might have: e.g. informatics, computer science, data processing, programming etc.).

Since only a few teachers will have to teach the subject and need a sound knowledge of informatics and its methodology, the syllabus for a l l teachers has to focus on the areas (a), (b) and (c) in order to achieve the desired level of competence. In other words: ATEE neither proposes to train all teachers as informaticians, programmers or system designers nor to reduce the literacy course to a mere course in "computer awareness for teachers".

Figure 1 gives an overview of the components which the Working Group proposes for the syllabus.

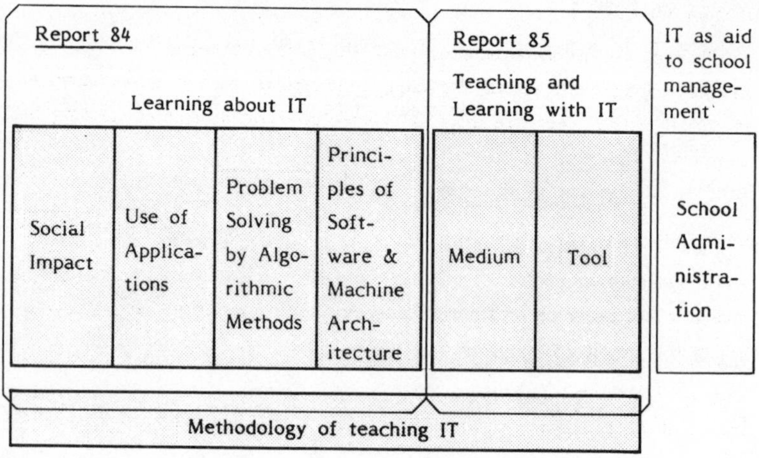

Fig.1: Literacy in Information Technology for all Teachers - Course Areas.

5. Course Areas

In the following section, substantial parts of the report [10,pp.16-21] will be quoted directly. But the reservation made there is also important: the ideas presented in the report are in no sense intended to be prescriptive; this would in fact be contrary to the philosophy of ATEE.

Course Area: Information Technology and Society

"Aims

The central issue in teaching "Literacy in Information Technology" is to bring about insights which enable (future) teachers to develop and present a reasonable and balanced attitude towards information technology. Students should gain insight into the value and the importance of information technology for society generally, and into the consequences this technology may have for society, especially where educational applications of information technology are concerned.

A further aim of the course is to help students to develop a basic understanding of the ways and means of teaching about information technology and society.

The following is an i l l u s t r a t i v e outline of contents.

Content

° Information and society

information processing, the importance of information technology, the Information Society.

- Automation of information processing and process control
  In the management sector (including simulation), in the administrative sector, in the industrial sector and in the home (in devices such as washing machines, watches, TV-games).
- Influence of information technology on
  daily life, privacy aspects, upholding individuality, interhuman relationship.
- Work and study
  changing the working methods, changing employment, quality of work, human-machine interface (ergonomic aspects), interhuman relationship and cooperation.
- Organizations (especially educational organizations)
  forms of organization, structure of decision making, balance of power/working relations.
- Democratic and social structures
  structure of decision making, balance of power.
- International relations
  balance of power, control of multinational organizations.
- The sector of information technology
  organization of information industry, functions in relation to information technology, interests, social "responsibility".

Changes brought about by information technology should be viewed as part of a process of change. This process has a past, a present state and a future. In order to be able to understand this process it is essential that reasons for, and implications of these changes be clarified. In this judgement, values, norms and responsibility play a role.

Presentation

The content should preferably be treated in as concrete a manner as possible, for example by working out relevant applications through games, case studies or projects. A too theoretical approach should be avoided. Special attention should be given to the transfer of the body of knowledge covered in a classroom situation from teachers to pupils."

Course Area: Practical Work with Application Software

"Aims

The central aim is to acquaint future teachers with the range and use of application software. This includes analysis and assessment of the introduction of these application systems in existing organizations.

Content

Applications such as the following should be included:

- text processing
- information systems (e.g. the use of databases)
- computing
- financial analysis (e.g. the use of spreadsheets)
- process control

and applications such as Computer Aided Learning (CAL) and Computer Managed Instruction (CMI). The analysis and assessment of the application of NIT should also apply to their to their introduction into the school as an organization.

In respect of each application, students need to see

- its use in practice
- possibilities for presenting (simplified) versions to pupils
- use as aids/means to learning
- possibilities for teacher contribution to design and maintenance.

Presentation

Practical work with application software is an integral part of the course. In this practical work the possibilities and limitations of the use of application software in school should be highlighted rather than the technical possibilities. Furthermore, invariant aspects of the application software should be explored; details of the software actually used may be ignored."

Course Area: Introduction to Problem Analysis and Systematic Problem Solving by Algorithmic Means

"Aims

The aim of this course area is to give teachers a first introduction to problem analysis, systematic design of algorithms and simple data structures, and to the realization of these algorithms in a higher programming language.

Content

- General concepts: algorithm, object.
- Notation: basic control structures, expressions, procedures, parameters, data structures.
- Top-down design of algorithms: problem analysis, formulation of a solution strategy, top-down design by refinement, levels of abstraction.

- Design of typical algorithms
  screen control, e.g. screen editor, pupil/machine interfacing.
- Realization of algorithms in a concrete programming language, syntax and semantics, implementation aspects, aids (tools) for the programming process.

Presentation

In the presentation of the course materials the top-down design of algorithms should be the central focus and n o t the details of the programming language or the implementation."

Course Area: Introduction to the Architecture of Information Technology

"Aims

In introducing the architecture of Information Technology the main issue is to present students (teachers) with a functional model of IT systems including fundamental concepts such as:

- process,
- object (data),
- process description (i.e. algorithm),
- interface,
- protocol.

Content

The lower levels of programmed systems structure, starting with the level of integrated circuits, should be treated briefly. This treatment should be aimed at the reduction of the "mystery" of information processing. As an example, the principles of the memory function may be discussed.

The levels of the conventional machine and of the assembly language should only be treated insofar as necessary to give a grasp of what goes on inside a programmed system and should not involve assembly language programming.

The level of the operating system should be discussed from a user's point of view: what functions are implemented and how these are used.

The level of interpreters and compilers should also be treated from the user's point of view and in relation to the operating system level.

The level of data base systems should once again be discussed from the view point of what one can or cannot do when using such a system. The relationship of this level with the previous one is of importance. The same applies to the level of application software.

Finally the treatment of the level of network architecture should give users a grasp of what goes on in a network.

Presentation

The presentation of the content should be as concrete as possible and involve practical work. The students have to see that their functional model "works", and it allows them to think and speak about programmed IT systems in a down to earth, functional manner without any mistification.3

Course Area: Didactics of Information Technology

"It is clear that, in teacher education, the study of a given subject area calls also for the complementary study of the appropriate teaching methodologies. This is true of NIT as it is of any other area. Admittedly the subject matter is new, but its methodologies are becoming progressively clear, as is the matter itself.

What we must emphasize here, however is, that we are concerned **in this document** with the general framework of understanding of NIT required by **all** teachers. It is implicit in our adoption of this perspective that we see the methodological implications of NIT **in the context of the teacher's own subject area.** NIT has already generated, in many subject areas, new ways of teaching and of learning, and we consider it more useful to deal with these separately in the contributions planned to follow in this series. These will deal, as we have indicated, with the potential of NIT as both an aid to teaching/learning and as a means.

The other implication of our adopted perspective is that the treatment of the teaching methodology of NIT sui generis more properly belongs to an analysis of the training needs of NIT specialist teachers, and it is in this context (again in a later publication) that we propose to deal fully with the topic. ..."

Here we close the quotation from the first report, though it is necessary to point out that the Working Group found it extremely difficult to find a common denominator for the different approaches to methodology adopted in the different countries. In preparing the report, for example, there were long debates about the various connotations of the words "methodology" and "didactics" the extent to which the phrase "teaching methodology" in English covers the area typically called "didactics" in other European languages.

Course Areas: Teaching and Learning with IT

In the second, forthcoming report [11] the ATEE-Working Group investigates the course areas "Learning and teaching with IT" which in other publications bear the labels "Learning with IT" and "Learning by means of IT" or "IT as medium" and "IT as tool". Since there is no sharp dividing line between medium and tool and since the same information technology may often be interpreted as an educational medium as well as an educational tool (e.g. dictionary=tool, book=medium; filmed animal life=tool, film=medium), the report shapes the categories not so much from the technical side but from the respective viewpoints of the pupil ("learning with IT") and the teacher ("teaching with IT").

Before we go into more detail in this question, it is important to distinguish between two broad categories of computer software:

- programs and application systems which have been constructed specifically for an educational purpose,
- application systems which were not necessarily conceived for educational purposes, but which are extremely usable in education.

These two initial categories distinguish software from the point of view of software designers and software buyers and are of importance when evaluating the user surface of a given piece of software and the educational limitations resulting from its non-educational purpose.

The following classification, however, is based on the **educational intentions and effects** of software systems and allows six major categories of educationally relevant software to be identified:

1. **"Tools for thinking with"**

   These include languages such as LOGO and PROLOG which offer the user an extensive potential for exploring and building a variety of concepts and included procedural, relational, functional and object-oriented approaches. Systems not yet available or affordable for schools have also to be considered here, such as SMALLTALK and BOXER.

2. **"Tools for organizing knowledge"**

   This refers to application systems largely drawn from business and technical practice; these include databases, word- and text-processing, spreadsheets, and pictorial representation of information.

3. **"Guided discovery learning"**

   This category includes simulations and educational games which have intentional educational aims but which nonetheless allow users (teachers and pupils) considerable flexibility.

4. **"Resources for teaching/learning"**

   This refers to the "electronic blackboard" material which, because it is interactive and/or dynamic, extend the range of teaching and learning resources currently available. The (video) transfer of information from the teacher's master screen to all the pupils' screens and the connection of all workstations in a classroom to a local area network are also other aspects of this category.

5. **"Tutorial software"**

Programs in this group are those which are designed to instruct, i.e. to transfer knowledge to the pupil.

6. **"Drill and Practice"**

In this final category we include programs whose function is to reinforce knowledge and skills already acquired to test knowledge (and often to keep a record of the pupil's performance, - also called "Computer Managed Instruction").

Figure 2 represents schematically, the pattern described in the six categories. It is instructive to look at it from a variety of standpoints. It already contains the balance:

Learning tool <-->Teaching tool

(1) (2) (3) (4) (5) (6)

We can also see it in terms of open-endedness:

Open-ended approach <-------------------------> Closed, finite goals

(1) (2) (3) (4) (5) (6)

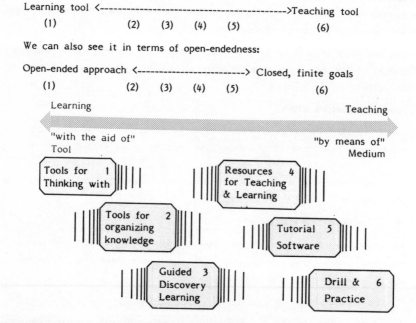

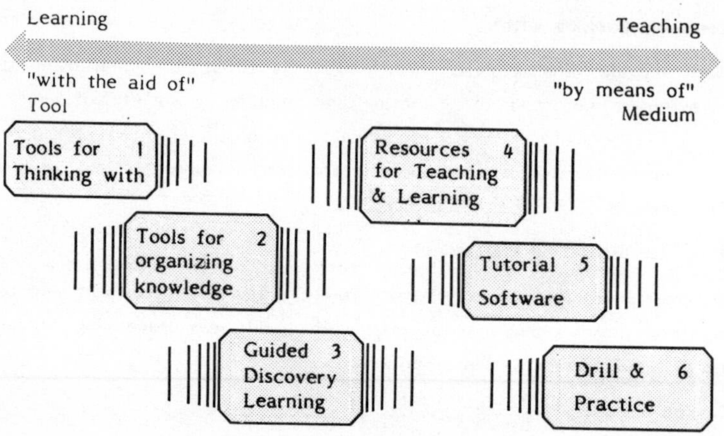

Fig.2: Teaching and Learning with Information Technology.

or, interestingly, in terms of teacher involvement:

High-involvement required (clear grasp of teaching possibilities) <------------------------> Low involvement required (Program takes over)

(1) (2) (3) (4) (5) (6)

In the forthcoming report the Working Group will present its ideas on the different topics listed above and describe in more detail where the advantages and limitations of the six categories of educational software are emphasized.

6. Transfer to National Policies

Since this presentation of the efforts of ATEE in the field of Information Technology is part of the conference working session on National Educational Policies, we would like to close by mentioning that in at least three countries the syllabus is at present being implemented on an experimental basis: in Denmark there is a series of short courses on the lines described; in the Federal Republic of Germany, where an in-service course for teachers of approx. 300 hrs. on fundamental informatics, including all course areas described here, is being tried out for the first time, and in the Netherlands, where the educational authorities are preparing a corresponding repeatable education program for teachers. The organizational conditions for the courses in these three countries differ widely, but it will be interesting to follow the progress of these efforts and compare the results.

ATEE will be very proud, if it has been able to construct a useful framework for developmental discussion, and perhaps also to contribute one more brick towards the construction of the curricula for this most challenging educational phenomenon called New Information Technologies.

References:

[1] E. Oldham: The New Information Technologies. Implications for Teacher Education. Country Study: Ireland. ATEE Brussels 1981.

[2] R. Gwyn: The New Information Technologies and Education: Implications for Teacher Education. ATEE Brussels 1981.

[3] R. Gwyn: Information Technology and Teacher Education: Perspective on Development. ATEE Brussels 1982.

[4] P. Gorny: The New Information Technologies and Education. Implications for Teacher Education. Country Report 2: Federal Republic of Germany. ATEE Brussels 1982.

[5] T. A. Jensen: New Information Technologies and Education in Denmark. (Implications for Teacher Education) Country Report 3: Denmark. ATEE Brussels 1982 - unpublished manuscript - also in [6].

[6] L. Cerych (Ed.): Computers in Education. National Policy Perspectives. With articles: P. Gorny, F. R. Germany; R. Gwyn: England, Wales and Northern Ireland; J. Morris: Scotland; T. Jensen: Denmark; A. Zucker: USA; J. Acker-

mans/T. Plomp: The Netherlands; L. Cerych: Major problems and key policy options. Special Theme issue of European Journal of Education, vol. 17 no. 4 (1982).

[7] Teacher Training and the New Information Technologies. Papers presented at the 7th Annual ATEE Conference at Birmingham 1982. ATEE Brussels 1983.

[8] F. Busch/K. Spelling (Ed.): Schulleben heute - School life today - La vie à l'école aujourd'hui. Material of the 8th Annual ATEE Conference at Alborg 1983. Oldenburg. Kobenhavn 1984. Especially with articles: K. Spelling: Equality and School; R. Gwyn: The new information technologies and the role of the teacher; M. Fauquet: L'école d'aujourd'hui face aux Mass Media.

[9] F. Buchberger/H. Seel (Ed.): Lehrerbildung für die Schulreform - Teacher Education and the Changing School - La formation des enseignants et l'école en transition. Proc. 9th Annual ATEE Conference at Linz 1984. Especially with articles: R. Gwyn: New Information Technologies and Education: the Search for Policies; D. Harris: Knowledge is Power: Social Aspects of the New Technologies of Information in Teacher Education; M. Fauquet/E. Presker: L'utilisation de nouvelles technologies dans le travail de formation; M. Fauquet: Nécessité d'une formation à la maîtrise des formes médiatisées de communication.

[10] T. van Weert (Ed.): A Model Syllabus for Literacy in Information Technology for all Teachers. ATEE Brussels 1984.
In German: P. Gorny/I. Wanke (Uebers.): Modell-Lehrplan "Informatische Grundkenntnisse für alle Lehrer. LOG IN vol. 4 no. 4 (1984), pp. 36-43.

[11] R. Gwyn: (Ed.): A Model Syllabus for Literacy in Information Technology for all Teachers. ATEE Brussels (in preparation).

The UK Microelectronics Education Programme 1981–1985. A Record of Achievement

MIKE ASTON
National Co-ordinator for Computer Based Learning, Microelectronics Education Programme, UK

STRATEGY

Introduction

1.The aim of the Programme is to help schools to prepare children for life in a society in which devices and systems based on microelectronics are commonplace and pervasive.These technologies are likely to alter the relationships between one individual and another and between individuals and their work; and people will need to be aware that the speed of change is accelerating and that their future careers may well include many retraining stages as they adjust to new technological developments.

2.In developing a strategy for the Programme it has been assumed that:

(i) schools should be encouraged to respond to these changes by amending the content and approach of individual subjects in the curriculum and,in some cases, by developing new topics;

(ii)with the dual aim of enriching the study of individual subjects and of familiarizing pupils with the use of the microcomputer itself,methods of teaching and learning should make use of the microcomputer and other equipment using microprocessors: this may be expected to add new and rewarding dimensions to the relationship between teacher and class or teacher and pupil;

(iii)for those children with physical handicaps, new devices should be used to help them to adjust to their environment while those with mental handicaps should be encouraged and supported by computer programs and other learning systems which make use of the new technologies.

The Scope of the Programme

3.The Programme is concerned with microelectronics applications in schools and in non-vocational courses courses for 16-19 year olds in further education.

4.It may be helpful to distinguish between the two main areas which are covered by the Programme. The first covers the investigation of the most appropriate ways of using the computer as an aid to teaching and learning, as a guide to the individual child, as a learning aid for small groups of children, or as a system which involves the whole class. In principle, software can be developed for computer-based learning across the curriculum, but the Programme gives priority to applications in mathematics, the sciences, craft/design technology,geography and courses related to business or clerical occupations. Some attention is given to careers education,languages and the humanities.As mentioned above,children with learning difficulties and special education needs also benefit from materials for use with microcomputers as a teaching and learning aid and the Programme assists appropriate developments in remedial and special education.

5.The second area with which the Programme is concerned , is the introduction of new topics in the curriculum, either as separate disciplines or as new elements of existing subjects. The new topics,(which may of course be taught at varying levels of specialization), will include :

(i) microelectronics in control technology;
(ii) electronics and its applications in particular systems;
(iii) computer studies;
(iv) computer - linked studies,including computer-aided design, data logging and data processing
(v) wordprocessing and other 'electronic office' techniques;
(vi) use of the computer as a means of information handling;
(vii) use of the computer as an intelligent terminal in a communications network;

6. The main focus of interest in both areas is on the secondary school curriculum, but the Programme is concerned to assist appropriate developments in primary and middle schools.

Programme Activities

Work is supported under three headings:

A.Curriculum development;

B.Teacher education and progessional development;

C.Resource organization and support;

CURRICUMLUM DEVELOPMENT

New materials for teaching and learning are needed to meet the following needs:

(i) materials which make use of microcomputers and other devices based on microprocessors to asist with the teaching of 'traditional' subjects;

(ii)materials which support the teaching of and learning of new topics;

(iii)supporting documentation which will help teachers make the most effective use of the new equipment and its associated curriculum materials.

Such resources are developed on national,regional or local bases. Examples of such existing 'national projects' are the 'Computers in the Curriculum' project at Chelsea College and the work of organizations such as the Geographical Association Package Exchange.Projects already serving schools in more than one LEA include certain LEA centres for computer-based learning, such as the Advisory Unit for Computer Based Education at Hatfield and organizations and units in institutions of higher education drawing support from a number of neighbouring authorities. These generate valuable resources which can be suitable for general use. Locally based projects generated by individual schools, teachers and user groups are developing materials for their own needs or amending nationally available materials to reflect their own styles.

It is important to give access to materials from all these sources.The commercial publication of materials is developing at present, but the Programme may need to make increasing use of a variety of other methods of dissemination.

In the longer term it is necessary to consider how the introduction of new topics in the curriculum should be reflected in examination syllabuses.

TEACHER TRAINING

Teachers require both information about microelectronics and professional skills to apply the technology effectively in the classroom. The training of teachers both in-service and pre-service,must therefore be organized in such a way as to support curriculum change. Training has been provided at a number of levels :

(i) courses aimed at improving general awareness and familiarization (of 1-3 days'duration or their part-time equivalent), for teachers of all kinds, but in particular for headteachers and their deputies and for teachers of subjects such as languages and the humanities where microelectronics applications may be less apparent, and for careers teachers;

(ii)short specialist familiarization courses, (of up to one week's duration or its part-time equivalent), for teachers who have been enthused by the awareness courses and for those wishing to modify their subject teaching to include new topics, for example teachers of commerce requiring knowledge of wordprocessing and biology teachers requiring knowledge of data logging.

(iii)longer specialist courses, (of up to three months' duration or the part-time equivalent), aimed at teachers requiring additional training in particular fields: examples include science or craft/design teachers wishing to expand their knowledge of electronics, and teachers wishing to acquire the skills needed to develop computer-based learning materials;

(iv)for these courses to be effective, resources have been devoted to the training of trainers and to refresher courses for LEA advisers;

(v)the Programme is also concerned with the advise which should be given in agencies wishing to design longer diploma and degree courses in micro-electronics, (eg.of one year's duration or its part-time equivalent).

Regional Centres of In-Service Training

MEP has offered pump-priming support for the establishment of a regional network of in-service training centres which arrange for the provision of a variety of subject courses. The location of these centres is a matter for agreement with the local education authorities whose teachers they serve. The object of the exercise is to enable groups of authorities to coordinate their resources for in-service training and the centres provide a focus for developing and evaluating different methods and materials.

It is necessary to:

(i) to identify appropriate centres and trainers;

(ii)provide,where necessary, a small amount of supplementary equipment for training in computing or electronics;

(iii)provide some teaching and learning materials, and, in some cases, arrange for their production;

(iv)identify needs for new teaching and learning materials and ensure their preparation;

(v) evaluate the work of the centres and, where appropriate, negotiate their continuation as local problem-solving and referral organizations for teachers in the region.

To qualify for support, regional training centres need to have adequate staffing at an appropriate level of expertise and be suitably equipped. They must also offer a reference and support service to teachers who have taken the courses and those sufficiently qualified not to require them.

In the case of the courses which it supports, the Programme contributes towards the salary costs of tutors and the cost of teaching materials and may also assist with the cost of equipment and software. As far as possible, the Programme tries to ensure that courses bear no cost to those attending, and some money is set aside for their travelling expenses. However, LEAs are encouraged to meet part of these and other incidental costs which would otherwise fall on trainees and it is normal Programme policy to contribute towards the cost of replacing teachers who attend the courses.

FOUR DOMAINS

MEP has defined the scope of the teacher education element of the Programme within four domains which should be catered for within each region. The four domains are electronics and control technology, the computer as an instrument computer-based learning, and communications and information systems.

(i) ELECTRONICS AND CONTROL TECHNOLOGY

This domain is concerned with all aspects of the teaching of electronics in schools. Electronics appears as a single subject at all levels of the examined curriculum and is included as part of many syllabuses such as control technology, craft design and technology, engineering science,physics,computer studies. Syllabuses containing electronics as a whole or in part are continually evolving and the number of pupils studying electronics is increasing rapidly. Few teachers have been given initial training in this subject and it is essential that teachers are given opportunities for in-service training to enable them to teach these subjects competently and to appreciate the significance of new developments in the subject and their application.

(ii) COMPUTER AS A DEVICE (Computer Studies)

Computer studies is part of the curriculum of a large number of secondary schools.Most courses are directed towards external examination such as CSE or O-or A- level. All the examination boards have madde arrangements for examinations in computer studies or computer science.

(iii) COMPUTER-BASED LEARNING

Computer-based learning is taken to cover any activity in the curriculum where a computer has the possibility of enhancing the learning process. It is recognized that teacher-centred, machine-centred and child-centred systems all have a part to play in this activity and that computer-managed learning and computer-based information handling systems will feature more and more in the curriculum as teachers become aware of their potential. he domain is not primarily concerned itself with the teaching of electronics technology or about the computer as a device, but recognizes that CBL models can be used in these subjects with equal opportunity for learning. Cross-fertilization between the domains has taken place as MEP strategies have developed.

(iv) COMMUNICATION AND INFORMATION SYSTEMS

CAIS (communication and information systems), encompasses all aspects of microcomputer applications that involve the generation,storage,retrieval, communications processes and systems,rather than the computer processes required to accomplish these tasks. CAIS includes both the cognitive and manual skills required for information-handling in all areas of teaching and learning, and in the curriculum area of business studies.

Information is an intangible concept but an all- pervasive one, forming a substantial part of teaching and learning both in terms of content and process. Acquiring knowledge implies the acquisition and handling of information; education implies some form of knowledge communication. CAIS has, therefore, applications across the curriculum and across the school. The acquisition of knowledge itself, and the acquisition of the cognitive and manual skills for its handling and communication, form the core of the learning and teaching process and are at the heart of everyday classroom experiences.

Primary education provision is catered for within the National Primary Project

Three levels

The different skills levels in teacher training are identified in three increasing depths of competence: 'familiarization' (basic), 'understanding' (intermediate), and 'applications' (advanced). When applied to teacher training under MEP the first two different levels of need for training are distinguished:

(i) 'awareness training',which must take as its aim the elementary introduction of the existence and impact of the technology to a wide audience with the aim that they be familiar with it; and

(ii) 'expertise training', which is a second-level course building on the basic awareness to provide users with a deeper appreciation and understanding. This should include the skills needed to apply and adapt the technology effectively in the classroom.

At the third stage, applications of the technology to teaching are more often new developments, and the skills involved are needed by the leaders of innovation.

In reality, those engaging in 'expertise traning' will simultaneously be initiating new applications and will be engaged in development activities, as well as completing the cycle by initiating further awareness training for others.Thus learning and doing become indistinguisable.

The MEP strategy paper states that teachers require both information about microelectronics and professional skills to apply the technology effectively in the classroom. The training of teachers, both in-service and pre-service, is therefore organized in such a way as to support the curriculum changes envisaged by MEP. Tranining is required at a number of levels, including:

(i) courses aimed at improving general awareness and familiarization (of 1-3 days's duration or their part-time equivalent), and needed for teachers of all kinds :

(ii) short specialist expertise courses (of up to one week's duration or its part-time equivalent), designed for teachers who have been enthused by the awareness courses and for those wishing to modify their subject teaching to include new topics.

As an example of a domain philosophy we look in detail at:

COMPUTER - BASED LEARNING

Domain priorities

Within the curriculum we have concentrated on subjects which have generated 'good' software. The policy has been to identify that which has a proven quality and to weave it into INSET modules.

The fields in Phase 1 were physics and chemistry, i.e. earth sciences; biology and home economics, i.e. life sciences; mathematics and statistics, i.e. numerical sciences ; geography,art and graphics, careers education.

Phase 2 subjects : music,history; English and modern languages; which are currently receiving considerable attention.

Domain levels

Familiarization - awareness level

The target audience at this level consists of secondary school teachers in any discipline, who have a computer facility in their school, but as yet, have not been made aware of its relevance in the classrooms. They probably see it as a resource for computer studies and mathematics but will have heard somewhere about its use in their subjects. They are interested enough to investigate further but worried by 'experts' and problems of actually getting time on the system for (a) hands-on experience and (b) use in their classrooms.

Understanding-intermediate level

The target audience here consists of secondary-school teachers, advisers , inspectors with subject responsibilities who have attended an INPUT course, (an induction course for teachers qualifying under the U.K. Department of Trade and

and Industry Micros in Schools scheme) or similar familiarization course. They have probably seen one or two programs or computer-based packages which are relevant to their disciplines but are not able to judge whether they are 'sound', robust and worth using in the classroom. They are motivated to find out more, prepared to try new materials in their schools, but not necessarily to be involved in a curriculum development group. They have few programming skills, beyond understanding the structure of the programs they are using.

Application-advanced level

At this level are teachers, advisers, etc. who have used CBL materials in the classroom, feel the need for more resources in their own subject and are prepared to collaborate with others to generate subject-based or inter-disciplinary packages with software support. They are sufficiently motivated and skilled to look objectively at new material and report back on its educational effectiveness and the quality of the user interface,documentation and any other criteria outlined by an evaluation group. They will probably have simple programming skills, i.e. sufficient to alter data statements, user messages, etc. and at least enough knowledge to specify their developmental ideas in terms that a programmer can understand.

N.B. At all levels of experience it must be recognized that using CBL is not an easy option. Teachers with inadequate skills or little experience in traditional teaching methods should not be encouraged to experiment with new technologies unless a clear advantage in the classroom can be identified.

Summary

The Microelectronics Education Programme is scheduled to cease in March 1986. A lot has been achieved in a remarkably short time. The greate debate about learning and information technology is probably just beginning. Teachers and local education authorities are faced with the greatest challenge since 1944. MEP is just the beginning, the pump primer, the catalyst, the lever, or whatever else history might refer to in the annals of education. The future holds a great opportunity for us all.

Bibliography

* FOTHERGILL R, ANDERSON J.S.A. et al, Microelectronics Education Programme Policy and Guidelines London :CET,1983, ISBN 0 86184-114-X

APPENDIX I

Regional Patterns in MEP Teacher Education, 1981-March 1984

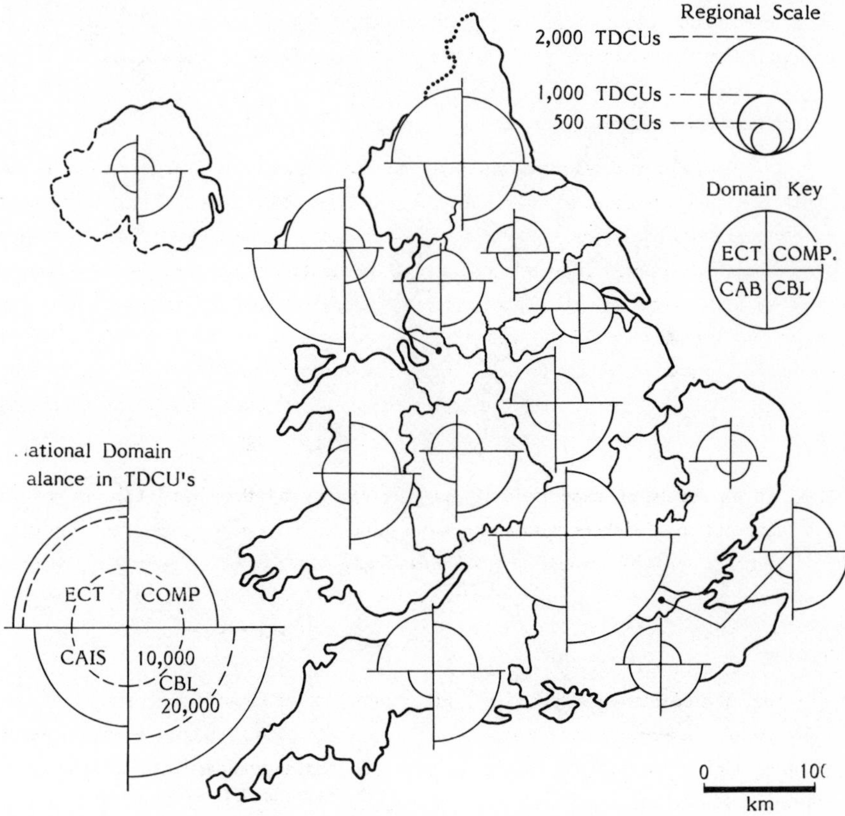

Notes:

A The radius of the symbols is proportional to the TDCUs (Teacher Day Course Units) returned for that domain.

B Cross domain TDCUs are not included in this diagram.

APPENDIX II

Distribution of MEP Regional Curriculum Development Projects and National Units-January 1981 to November 1984.

Note: The larger Regional Project symbols in London, Birmingham and Doncaster represent six projects at a single location.

The map shows mainstream regional and all national projects in excess of £ 1,000 per anum.

It does not cover projects under the Small Regional Projects scheme or small projects supported by the Directorate.

APPENDIX III

MEP Curriculum Development Projects

Numbers of funded projects within different curriculum areas

Art	(2)	XX
Business Studies	(1)	X
CDT	(3)	XXX
Computer Studies	(14)	XXXXXXXXXXXXXX
ECT	(24)	XXXXXXXXXXXXXXXXXXXXXXXX
English	(4)	XXXX
Geography	(9)	XXXXXXXXX
History	(5)	XXXXX
Home Economics	(2)	XX
Life Skills	(2)	XX
Mathematics	(13)	XXXXXXXXXXXXX
Mix	(6)	XXXXXX
Modern Languages	(1)	X
Music	(1)	X
Primary	(9)	XXXXXXXXX
Science	(16)	XXXXXXXXXXXXXXXX

The Use of the Microcalculator in Junior Schools

V. BOLTIANSKI
VNIISI, Ryleeva Str. 29, Moscow 119034, USSR

Before we know it, people will stop doing sums in columns on paper. The extent to which a person is accustomed to working on a microcalculator will become one of the most important characteristics of his readiness for practical activity.

These forecasts have a direct bearing on school education. The slide rule will lose its function completely as a counting instrument, and it will consequently no longer be necessary to learn how to use it. The same is true of logarithms and other tables.

We should also emphasize that the calculations connected with the estimation of solutions of polynomials and other functions will be simplified which will significantly affect graphplotting, the approximate solution of equations and so forth.

All this, however, refers to upper forms. But what about mathematics in the 1st-5th forms where the development of counting skills, in particular, the techniques of mental arithmetic, is seen as one of the main tasks? Is the use of microcalculators in this age-group advantageous or, on the contrary, harmful ?

There is a widely held view among school teachers, specialists in educational methods and also among parents that the spontaneous intrusion of microcalculators into junior school should be firmly resisted and schoolchildren should be forbidden to bring these devices into school and use them for calculations. The main argument in support of this view is that "children will forget how to count".

On the contrary, as the experience* , described in this article shows, when microcalculators are used rationally in junior school and there is a correct balance

* In two Yerevan schools N°35 and N° 68.

between mental arithmetic exercises and use of a microcalculator, as was the case in our experimental class, schoolchildren show better results in mental arithmetic than those in the neighbouring control form. What is more, they acquire better understanding of the logical techniques involved in solving various problems and better habits of mathematical thinking.

The reassuring results are explained by the fact that soundly based theoretical principles and methods were developed for this experiment. Here are some of them.

Let us first of all consider the solution of textual problems. The main requirement for this is to learn how to establish the functional connections between the values given in the statement of the problem. This applies mainly to problems solved in one operation, where the terms used are "sum", "difference", "greater by" "less than", and so forth. It is precisely the combination of these which produces more difficult problems. When the children solve a problem in written form most of their time is spent on writing (for children write slowly) and on counting, while the logic of the solution, the process of establishing connections between the given and the target values, that is, the most essential thing that the children should gain from this part of the lesson, takes up a mere one tenth of the time, if not less. Whereas if the problem is solved by an individual pupil at the blackboard a large number of the children remain passive and inattentive, no matter how hard the teacher urges them to listen to his answers.

A microcalculator allows this type of work to be conducted promptly and with the active participation of the entire class. The main form here is mathematical dictation. The teacher reads the text of the problem slowly, telling the children not to write anything down but to listen attentively and think how the problem should be approached for the correct solution. Then he reads what is given a second and, if necessary, a third time, after which the pupils perform the required calculation on the microcalculator.

In this way the pupils in the experimental classes solved up to 8-10 problems in the course of 15-20 minutes. The teacher then used the remaining part of the lesson for traditional tasks, for mental arithmetic exercises, solution of examples in columns and so on. The advantages here are obvious: the pupils are not distracted by the necessity to write things down or by the calculations as such, but are concerned solely with the logic of the solution.

All this is sufficient for anyone to see clearly that when such methods are used the microcalculator becomes an integral part of the lesson as a technical means of education which opens up new, progressive opportunities for obtaining knowledge, skills and practices. Moreover, the microcalculator performs here the function of an important ergonomic means of education which allows work in class to be organized on a scientific basis, when the amount of numerical and logical information assimilated by the children during the lesson increases 1,5-2 times. And if we add to this the factor of an increasing interest in mathematics (the children wait for the moment when voltage is applied to the microcalculators as a regard for their good performance during the previous part of the lesson), it becomes clear why the pupils in the experimental form demonstrated better grounding both in mental arithmetic and in logical thinking as such.

There is also another important teaching device which we refer to as the mathematical practicum. We shall try to explain what it is based on the material of the textbook now used in the 4th form. This textbook contains several hundred exercises on calculations with whole numbers and decimal fractions; their difficulty increases towards the end of the course: the number of figures in the written examples reaches seven, and one or even two brackets are used. All the exercises are intended for counting in columns, a job which requires all of several dozen hours. The pupils in the experimental form were given two such problems to solve at home, while the rest were treated as material for the mathematical practicum. They were solved in class with the help of the microcalculator, with wide use being made of its storage register.

This method, as the experiment showed, did not lead to a reduction in counting skills and saved a great deal of teaching time.

The most important thing in solving difficult examples is to decide on the order of operations with insight and understanding. But this element of mental activity remains even when pupils work with microcalculators. When solving the problem "by hand", so to speak children spend 90% of the overall time entering the operations in columns, meticulously spelling out one digit after another. Microcalculators free them of these time-consuming actions and shift the main emphasis onto their comprehension of the exercise as a whole. In short, the creative element remains, while the purely mechanical, unthinking use of counting algorithms is no longer necessary.

It is clear from what has been said that if the time freed by the use of the microcalculator is devoted to mental arithmetic with a set of exercises, the result will be a better feel for numbers and better skills in mental arithmetic than in the case of traditional teaching.

We recommended introducing microcalculators from the very first lessons or to be more precise, from the second week of studies in the 1st form.

As a first step, the pupils should get used to the equipment and learn how to use it at the simplest level : how to fill in the display with numbers and read them on the display.

After that it is expedient to combine mental arithmetic with work on the microcalculator. For instance, the pupils press the buttons for 3+2 and discuss what the result should be. Then the teacher suggests that they push the button for "=" and see for themselves that the result they expected is confirmed.This kind of work is repeated many times over, which helps the children to memorize the addition table.

In the 1st form approximately 1/3 of the exercises in the textbook (those chosen by the teacher) are to be done with the help of the microcalculator; the rest are to be done mentally, without it.

The material on the commutative law of addition allows the first use of the microcalculator for a mathematical experiment. The teacher writes on the blackboard what is given :

1 + 4 =	3 + 4 =	3 + 2 =	5 + 4 =
4 + 1 =	4 + 3 =	2 + 3 =	4 + 5 =

and so on. Then he tells the children to do these sums with the help of micro - calculator : Gayane adds up 1+4 and 4+1, Karen adds up 3+4 and 4+3,etc. The teacher writes down the answers as given by the children. A collective discussion of the results of the calculations will give the pupils a vivid picture of the quality of interchangeability and it will be imprinted on their memory. This type of work is quite difficult without a microcalculator, for children count slowly; while they do the sums and the teacher checks the results and corrects the mistakes, the pupils might forget the main point of what they are doing.

Junior schoolchildren have great difficulty in learning the techniques of the order of mathematical operations, of how brackets should be opened, how to add up numbers with the sum exceeding ten, which is connected with the associative law of addition. But for the microcalculator it does not matter in the least whether during the addition ten is exceeded or not- it counts practically instantaneously. From the point of view of method, this gives children the opportunity to learn the addition table and gradually know it by heart as something ready-made, that exists in the calculator, instead of constructing it on their own. After all, an adult (or a senior pupil) does not have to apply the rule for exceeding ten, but remembers the whole addition table of one-digit numbers.

In junior school, children learn by rote a large number of different rules of addition and subtraction. These rules are in fact concrete examples of the general rules for opening brackets which the pupils will come across in the fifth form. Instead of this multitude of rules it would be easier to teach them one rule for opening brackets, which also corresponds to the school program for senior forms.

In our experiment the general rule for opening brackets was taught in the 1st form.

The most simple way of teaching this rule is as follows:

The teacher formulates the rule and to test it writes on the blackboard unfinished examples like this:

5 + (7 + 2) = 5	7	2	
9 - (6 - 3) = 9	6	3	
(16+9) + (21+14) = 16	9	21	14
(7+5) - (3+4) = 7	5	3	4
(16-9) - (5-2) = 16	9	5	2

The pupils are asked to insert the correct signs in the first part in order to understand how the rule as formulated should be applied. Then, with the aid of the microcalculator, the children are convinced of the correctness of the equations written.

At a more advanced stage examples on the opening of brackets are solved on the microcalculator in the following way. The pupil pushes the button with the first number, then, having determined (in his head) the next sign, he presses the button with this sign as well as the second number; he then again determines the next sign mentally and pushes the button with this symbol and the third number,etc

Apart from that, the apparatus can be used for checking the results of the calculations. In particular, it would be useful to solve the equations in the traditional way using established mathematical processes, and to check the results with the help of the microcalculator.

The method of using the microcalculator for division with remainder is also of interest. Say we have to divide 50 by 8. We can try different numbers in the set, multiplying 8 successively by 4,5,6,7. We shall then see that the incomplete quotient is 6, for 6 is less than we need and 7 is greater; we then establish the remainder by subtraction : 50 - 48 = 2. Thus, 50:8 = 6 (remainder 2). The other method lies in direct division. Pressing the buttons for the operation 50 : 8 = , we obtain 6,25 on the display. The teacher then explains that if a number does not divide without a remainder, then the number before the comma on the display is the incomplete quotient, and as for the digits to the right of the comma, they will be discussed later, in senior school. For instance, coming out of the operation 82 : 29 we obtain 2,8275862 on the display. This means that the incomplete quotient is 2, i.e. 82 contains the number 29 two times and there is also a remainder left. In order to establish the remainder we should multiply 29, by 2 and then subtract 82-58. The answer is 82 : 29 = 2 (remainder 24).

The microcalculator is used according to the same principles in the 3rd-5th forms.In this age-group the mathematical practicum is used systematically instead of counting in columns (which has been discussed above). Apart from that it is advisable from the 3rd from, onwards to use the storage register during calculations.

Let us also analyse the solution of equations in the form of mathematical dictation. The teacher writes out the given equation on the blackboard, and the pupils look at it and decide mentally how it should be solved. Then, without writing anything down in their notebooks, they establish value of the unknown quantity, performing the calculations on their calculators, while the teacher walks betwen the desks, watching them.

In conclusion we shall touch upon one of the specific features of mental arithmetic, so as to demonstrate more vividly the advantage of using microcalculators as opposed to counting in columns.

In assessing the general aptititude for mental arithmetic we pay great attention to the ability to make rough estimates. For instance, if we multiply 375 . 2219 we round off the cofactors ($4 . 10^2$) . ($2 . 10^3$) and we get the approximate result of 8.10^5 , i.e., something of the order of eight hundred thousand When adding up 3452 + 4791 we see that the sum of the numbers in the thousands column is 7 (thousand), we get another thousand and something when we add up the hundreds, i.e., the approximate result is 8000.

We can see from those examples that the rough estimates are made by taking into account the digits to the left, while the algorithms of addition and multiplication in columns are done from the right. Thus, doing regular calculations in columns hinders the development of ability to make rough estimates. As to this latter ability, it must be said that an aptitude for rough estimates is very important for an engineer, physicist and economist, as well as for people of many other professions. The habit of checking the result of calculations with the help of rough estimates testifies to the high level of counting standards.

Rough estimates were regularly used in our experiment in the addition of two-digit numbers. For instance, the children were asked to make a rough estimate for the example 25 + 57. Their answer was : "Adding up the decimals we get 70, we get approximately ten after adding up the units; the total is 80 (and something)." The experiment convinced us that the development of an aptitude for rough estimates helps in mental arithmetic. It is sufficient, to ask the pupil one more question: "And what is that something, what should be added to make the result exact ?" and after looking at the last digits, he quickly produces the final result : 25 + 57 = 82.

It was only possible to pay adequate attention to the development of an aptitude for rough estimates as a result of saving time through the use of microcalculators. We referred the development of basic skills in making rough estimates in the addition and subtraction of two-digit numbers to the program for the 1st form Consequently, in the 2nd form children learned quickly and without difficulty how to estimate mentally the exact sums and difference of two-digit numbers.

The time thus freed was used in the 3rd-5th forms not only for exercises in mental arithmetic but also for mathematical games at the end of some of the lessons. In our experiment the teachers were given corresponding instructions relating to methods. Special attention was paid to those mathematical games where it is appropriate to use microcalculators.

It is clear from what has been said, that we consider the microcalculator not only as means of conducting rapid calculations, but also as means of developing intellectual activity and mathematical thinking. Moreover, the microcalculator in our experiment performs the function of an important ergonomic tool allowing classroom work to be organized on a scientific basis. We consider that type of work in junior schools as an essential aspect of the use of computers for educational purposes. This is a good introduction to computers in education because the children develop a logical way of thinking and early programming skills, including wide use of the storage register. Moreover, using microcomputers in junior schools in this way enables about one year of teaching time to be saved, which is essential if a place is to be found for new and important school-subjects such as informatics.

The Open University Approach to Computer Education

M. A. NEWTON
The Open University, Walton Hall, Milton Keynes, MK7 6AA, UK

1. INTRODUCTION

The Open University is based on teaching at a distance and this particular form of education affects the way various aspects of computing can be taught. The purpose of this paper is to review the development of a number of Open Univeristy computing courses and to report on the resulting needs for educational software and hardware.

It is necessary to initially be aware of some of the features of teaching at a distance. There are many forms occurring in different countries but generally characterised by a student having some learning materials to be studied at home. While it is not seen as the main means of providing education in any sector, there are a significant gaps in the availability and appropriateness of conventional education that makes learning at a distance the choice for many students. Some of their reasons for this choice are :

. remoteness from facilities
. constraints of employment
. personal restrictions of family or handicap
. barriers in conventional education of age or qualifications.

It may be noted that such independent learning is particularly appropriate for teachers because for many types of educational course they can immediately relate their studies to the classroom situation. They also avoid the possible embarassment when any limitations may be exposed in a conventional course with their peers.

The Open University presented its first courses in 1971 and currently has over 65,000 undergraduate students registered on one or more of over 120 courses. Such courses contribute either a half or one credit to the total needed for a degree- six for an ordinary degree and eight for an honours degree. There is also a continuing education. programme which has developed various types of special interest courses and study packs. Over 25,000 associate students are currently registered for one year to study either an undergraduate course or a continuing education course. The study packs are sold as a learning resource and the University does not register any student enrolment- the purchaser is free to use the resource as required.

2. UNDERGRADUATE COMPUTING

All Open University courses have a number of components, the most important of which is the correspondence text- the equivalent of lecture notes in conventional teaching. This is supported by locally organised face-to-face tutorials and assessed by regular assignments and a final examination. Further optional components include set books, television programmes (sometimes made available to students on video cassettes), radio programmes or audio cassettes, experimental kits, summer schools and computer-based activities. These latter activities are part of the work for nearly half the student population and are supported by the Open University educational network- over 200 terminals around the country with access to one of the three DEC System 20 machines.

Before considering computer education, it is appropriate to comment briefly on the general use of this educational network by many courses. There are a wide variety of different types of computing activity, from CAL to calculation, and there is no single style of program which predominates. However, two important features may be noted. First, our students are working on their own, with no form of educational assistance (there is a telephone advisary service on equipment operation) nor even fellow students to talk to in most cases. Thus it is essential that programs are both robust enough to cope with student mistakes and can provide help and guidance for understanding. Second,each program, is developed after careful analysis of the particular educational requirements of a course by experienced programmer /analysts who are familiar with our teaching environment.

Apart from such efforts to provide quality educational software, the educational network is not satisfactory for many students in several respects. Having chosen hard-copy terminals so that students can have a copy of their work to study, this places a limit on speed of a dialogue and any graphics. Also, the student has to take time to travel to the terminal location, which are generally hosted by agreement in some local college or similar organisation. Finally, the availability of the terminals for students is restricted both by the size of the student population and by time constraints on their use by the host location. However, the Open University is very conscious of these problems and has considered alternative ways of providing computing facilities for students in a distance learning situation.The main need for computing facilities arises from computing courses so it is appropriate to review the way that these courses are supported.

There are two introductory computing courses, both with over 2,500 students currently enrolled and many more having applied but in each case the limit of resources prevented any more being accepted. One course, Computing and Computers, involves a significant amount of programming in Pascal and for this the students need access to large machines on the University's educational network. The other introductory course, The Digital Computer, involves some study of hardware architecture, machine code, assembler and BASIC programming so it was considered essential that students have a computer at home to study in detail. The full requirements of this course could not be met by any of the commercially available home computers so the University developed its own educational computer called HEKTOR because it was provided as a Home Experiment Kit. While HEKTOR has been very successful for its specific course needs, it is not an appropriate computer for general home use though it has been enhanced to provide terminal emulation capabilities for other educational purposes.

There are two advanced computing courses, one established in 1980 and the other currently being completed for students in 1986. The older course, Computer-based Information Systems, uses the educational network to access the various types of database system included in the practical work. Home-based computing was not feasible at the time this course was developed. The new course, Programming and Programming Languages, involves practical work in Pascal and Prolog. For this, the University is providing students with a commercially available home computer which has the capability of linking, via a telephone, to the educational network.

This latter provision is for one year only, for evaluation purposes, because the University is now faced with some difficult choices if students are to have improved computing facilities at home.The major choice is whether the University continues to supply all the capabilities required for each course or the student is expected to purchase some or all of the equipment, as currently practised in some universities of the USA. Both the initial costs and the continued overheads of supplying equipment to students for each course studied argue against the University being able to provide complete support on an adequate scale- which is for many thousands. However, it is not clear that students can or want to pay for the increased benefits of doing their computing at home.

A second issue is whether the home computer should provide all necessary facilities as an independent machine or use a communications link to the educational network for part of the students work. Currently the power and storage available on home computers seem to indicate that some courses still need the additional capabilities of mainframes, so communication is essential.

A further issue is whether a special educational computer, such as HEKTOR, should be chosen or a widely available home computer be recommended, which can also be used for other purposes. General opinion indicates that a purely educational system is not likely to appeal to students if they are expected to purchase it .

As a final comment on some of the experience of distance teaching of computing, it can be noted that we do not consider the exploratory, open-ended style of working with computers as appropriate for our students. With time limited by resources or other commitments of part-time students, it is essential that any practical computing activities are focussed on the educational objectives of the course and this is explained to the student for motivation to complete the work. Thus students are not just required to sit using a computer, but any task starts with preliminary exercises to ensure that the problem is understood, followed by detailed planning of what the computing task involves. During a practical session, there needs to be supporting software which limits the student contribution to that required for the purpose of the activity. For example, there should be no need to construct large programs, because of time and irrelevant errors that may be introduced, but students should be able to run modules which can be embedded in provided test-bed software. Again, there is a need for careful analysis of the educational requirements of the software and to ensure that it is robust and cannot introduce errors hidden from the student.

3. CONTINUING EDUCATION

The continuing education programme has developed a wide range of different types of learning materials. In computing, this varies from a collection of post-graduate courses which are part of a Masters programme. The Industrial Applications of computers, to a set of study packs produced by the University's Micros in Schools Project. These latter packs are each an independent collection of learning materials intended for in-service training of teachers and are the focus of this section.

The Micros in Schools Project was established in 1981,initially funded by the national Microelectronics Education Programme to produce an "awareness" self-study pack for teachers. This followed government schemes to encourage every school to have at least one microcomputer, and the subsequent realisation that many schools did not know how to use them effectively. In some cases it would be the children rather than the teacher who took the initiative in using these new facilities, not always with satisfactory educational aims. Thus the first study materials, Micros: An Awareness Pack, are intended for teachers who have no experience of using any computer. The overall aim of the pack is to give an appreciation of the role of microcomputers in education and to evaluate their potential.One component supporting the educational role describes various case studies of classroom situations, backed up by video-tapes. Another major component is the practical work, with the objective of giving teachers basic skills in using educational hardware and software.

In developing this practical component of the pack, it had to be assumed that teachers had access to some microcomputer of their own or in school. However, in order to give detailed descriptions, and pictures, showing exactly how to set up and operate a machine, it was necessary to select five computers commonly available to teachers and prepare separate introductory booklets for each one. A number of educational programs were also chosen with the main objectives of demonstrating a variety of features in such software and giving teachers confidence in using it.

Each program was implemented on the five different types of computer, so that there were five versions of the pack, with each version containing the operating instructions and programs appropriate to one machine. Careful programming, using BASIC but derived from an independent specification, limited the differences between the implementations to mainly screen effects. Thus there was only need for one version of the program descriptions and activities using them.

The final part of the awareness pack shows how various features of programs can be assessed, with the intent of increasing appreciation of the many aspects of educational software. Particular features considered are the mode of use, i.e. for individual, group or teacher, the style of interaction, i.e. menu, command, etc, program personality, handling of errors, educational role and the contributory factors to cost, such as robustness, documentation and flexibility.

The other four packs can be studied in any sequence because these are quite independent, only assuming the basic knowledge and experience equivalent to the awareness pack. They are:

Learning about Microelectronics
Inside Microcomputers
Micros in Action in the Classroom
Educational Software.

Both of the first two packs use a small microcomputer kit known as DESMOND-Digital Electronics System made Of Nifty Devices, specially developed for this project by the Open University. DESMOND is a battery-driven single board- and that is all - containing microprocessor, memory,keyboard,display and many devices such as clocks, switches, sensors, lamps, buzzer and motor. For the first pack, the emhasis is on the electronic components and the design and logic of circuits. This is supported by practical work using DESCOND's built-in-program which enables simple specification and operation of circuits involving any of the various components. The second pack is concerned with computers and programs so the practical work with DESMOND enables machine code and assembly language instructions to be input and executed. The various activities include controlling the different devices and while program size is very limited there is overall a good grounding in the principles applicable to larger microcomputers.

The third pack is based on a number of case studies describing the experience of teachers in using microcomputers in various ways, but also includes some practical activities involving programs used in the case study situations. In particular this involves work using LOGO, aiming to give some experience and appreciation of the potential of this language for classroom use. This course is similar to the awareness pack in assuming that teachers have access to some microcomputer, but the requirement for LOGO led the University to develop its own LOGO system for one popular computer.

The final pack, Educational Software, aims to provide insight into the nature of programs which are appropriate for use in the classroom. This does not include programming skills but does involve practical activities, again using LOGO, intended to demonstrate the problems involved in developing software. One of the main objectives is to help teachers evaluate educational software so that sensible purchasing decisions can be made, which has to occur before assessment in a classroom situation is possible. Detailed selection criteria are provided as a basis for this evaluation.

The five packs of the Micros in Schools Project together provide a range of learning materials which can encourage teachers and give them confidence to begin investigations of the potential of using microcomputers in their own classroom.

4. CONCLUSION

In the above descriptions of Open University courses, a number of aspects of educational hardware and software were considered but it is important to appreciate the particular requirements of distance teaching in assessing these views.

The University has considerable experience in developing specialised hardware appropriate for particular educational needs. These developments are justified by the numbers of students taking our courses, but it should be noted that for general purpose requirements of a home microcomputer the University considers that a commercially available system is most appropriate.

As for educational software, teachers or lecturers should not have to be responsible for producing it but do need to understand it to the extent of being able to contribute to program specification and design, and be able to evaluate the finished product. Since, in general, programmers do not appreciate educational requirements, the solution appears to be the creation of a role of educational analyst. Such people need to be able to analyse educational needs so that computer systems can support teaching rather that distort.

Using the Microcomputer as a Teaching Tool for Handicapped Children with Learning Disabilities in Italian

GIANNA DOTTI MARTINENGO
DIDAEL, Via Lamarmora, 3/A, 20100 Milano, Italy

INTRODUCTION

One of the most important developments in the field of education is the possibility of using the microcomputer to produce assisted teaching systems. The ability of the computer to memorize and store exercises and data allows a vast amount of material to be drawn on for diagnosing, teaching and assessing a large number of pupils with different needs and with regard to various subjects. Those pupils who derive a limited benefit from verbal channels are aided in learning by the possibility which exists of using sound and graphics and their flexibility. In this way the computer becomes a new and essential tool,provided for the teacher and educator by modern technology,which allows him to achieve the objective of a form of teaching directed at the individual.

There are different individual aspects to each pupil, which must be taken into account for teaching to be effective:

- different learning speeds ;
- different mental development among pupils of the same age and in the same class;
- varying ability of individuals to retain information ;
- the privileged channels through which information arrives.

If these differentiating elements are found in pupils of normal ability, then they are even more prevalent in the case of handicapped or disadvantaged children who must rely on planned intervention specific to individuals, including the analysis of specific needs and elaboration of a support and catch-up programme for each individual.

It is easy to see that individual-specific teaching is impossible using traditional aids,since the mass of exercises, data, its collection and assessment would require an immense amount of work and time, certainly beyond the capability of any human being. Although it is not a miracle solution for all problems, in some cases the computer is an indispensable support for the pupil and the teacher,whose efforts can be multiplied and more effectively multiplied.

Some of the most significant ways of applying the computer are :

- objectively detecting the existence of knowledge and ability and learning levels ;
- systematic recording of results ;
- measuring progress in achieving objectives ;
- logical -perceptive organisation of learning material and activities ;
- the very high number of activities gradually selected in the form of presentation and structure suited to each individual ;
- immediate response analysis ;
- multisensory approaches to learning and presentation of lessons.

Individual-specific teaching is achieved in practice by giving each pupil the possibility to work at his own pace in continuous interaction with the machine and actively involved in the teaching/learning process.The features which account for the uniqueness and originality of this process are those which provide pupils, in need of constant and continuing help, a large number of exercises and patient systematic repetition of ideas, with the possibility of assimilating information and acquiring skills at different stages and through privileged channels.

The computer tackles the needs of subjects with learning difficulties not only from the operational, but also from the psychological point of view; it functions not only as a learning instrument, but also as a learning stimulus which pays constant attention and assists memorizing. It is a patient instrument, which produces invariable, precise and simple instructions, so that the pupil is able to concentrate all his attention, grow in self-confidence and be remote from external variables which may influence the quality of his response. The computer reacts immediately and never with a value judgement, but rather systematically and objectively measuring the pupil's progress and difficulties. With the aid of the machine the teacher can use teaching time to greater effect, make the most of the pupil's span of concentration, plan and put into practice integrated curricula, check the achievement of objectives and have a means of communicating with subjects lacking dexterity and deprived of verbal communication.

The first experiment in the use of microcomputers for teaching Basic Italian to handicapped children.

During the 1983-84 school year an experiment was undertaken in the use of the computer for individual-specific learning of basic Italian intended for handicapped pupils.

This experimental project involved the contribution of resources and skills from different sources. Those collaborating were the psycho-medical section of the Pro Juventute Foundation, the Education Office and a group of 33 primary and secondary school teachers at State School units under the Foundation, DIDA.EL with its course in Basic Italian and with 700 hours of technical-teaching assistance by the co-ordinatiors who directed all the stages of the experiment, Olivetti with an M20 microcomputer and lastly S.I.V.A.

The course in Basic Italiasn is the result of the combined efforts of a team of Italian researchers at DIDA.EL, who for several years have been researching into the use of the computer in education, with particular emphasis on learning difficulties.

The course (1), aimed at pupils with linguistic or general learning problems, is divided into 44 programmes and processes 25,000 exercises, beginning with the elements which make up the word and the sentence and proceeding to more and more complex and articulated syntheses. The skills required for mastering the verbal code are singled out and presented in gradual succession. Due to its flexibility and capacity for continuing adaptation to each pupil's learning pace and reports, the course is suitable for insertion into an educational project and for integrating into curriculum-type programming.

It draws on the most widespread theories about learning, paying special attention to those in the cognitive field. Concepts and methods have been called from linguistic, psycholinguistic and neuroliguistic theories which are used, by means of the potential offered by the computer, on condition that they produce adequate results which help to achieve the objectives of the course. Basic Italian is part of a general project for which other programmes are envisaged: one relating to the prerequisites for writing and reading and another to text comprehension, communication and reflection on language.

The experimental project consisted of a series of stages,each with specific objectives related to different fields.

At the learning/teaching level objectives were formulated with regard to the areas of cognitive development, emotional motivation and work organization.

The psycho-medical educational team chose the 20 subjects for the experiment from among primary and secondary school pupils with learning difficulties resulting from different kinds and degrees of multiple neuromotor and psycho-sensory problems. They established the starting level in relation to knowledge and skills and formlated the medium and long-term objectives.

The data, collected systematically at each session (15 minutes a day for five months), were evaluated collectively at regular intervals. At the end of the experiment assessment cards were compiled corresponding to the specific objectives (App.2).

We will now take a sample of 14 primary school children who took part in the experiment and seee what conclusion we can draw from their assessment cards.

Cognitive objectives:14 pupils out of 14 achieved the objectives set in the field of knowledge and 11 finished in a shorter time than expected.Their curriculum was thus enriched by a series of new stages with a positive conclusion.

It was possible to detect that use of the computer had enabled learning times to be reduced in somes cases.

One teacher remarked, "the systematic way in which the exercises are presented reduces explanation time and , once he has mastered the procedures, the pupil knows how to organize and get on with his own work... his attention is more sustained and his memory is helped by multisensory presentation (in this type of activity, visual and auditory perception, motor skill and listening-reading aloud by the pupil or teacher- are in fact brought into play) and interaction (in as much as the pupil directs his own path of learning which constantly adapts to his logical-perceptive capacity, learning pace and needs)."

Another teacher, having observed that a pupil was learning more quickly than expected, wrote on the card for test 1: "Relatively short response times and a limited number of attempts were programmed in. L.willingly accepts it as a contest and as a matter of fact often asks for this type of procedure. He/She derives great satisfaction from successfully overcoming problems of increasing difficulty and difficulty and feels stimulated to do better. He/She can achieve a high performance level with a very small margin of error."

ATTENTION

In the area of mental operations necessary for learning, both long-term and selective attention, that is, the type of attention which discriminates, unifies, organizes and classifies, were analysed and tested. This skill was reinforced by three pupils, nine showed and improvement and two a change in terms of learning.

The starting level of B. was recorded by the team as follows: "poor ability to pay attention, only willing to do so when externally stimulated and, in any case always for a short time." After the first test the teachers observed, "He/She is very attentive, concentrating to the extent of even being able to control his/her head movement very well." After the second test, "B's attention is constant, because he/she has identified in an operational way the criteria and procedures needed to be able to use the course and complete the task, that is, "he/she knows how", feels satisfied, confident and motivated to learn."

Similarly, this observation was made about a second child after test 1: sustained attention not only helps to improve the quality of performance (ability to analyse the stimulus and make a synthesis), but also increases speed of task completion. The printouts for the exercises show continually increasing percentages for accuracy and an increase in the number of exercises completed at each session."

At the start, "inability to pay attention and easily distracted" was emphasized with regard to pupil M. After test 1 the teacher noted that M. "directed his/her attention at the screen without having to be encouraged."; after test 2 "the ability to concentrate his/her attention throughout the entire session is improving... this behaviour is now constant enough to state that it is becoming a way of operating."

Referring to L., said to have a satisfactory capacity for sustained attention, the following observation was made after test 1:

"He/She fixes his/her attention and explores with the aim of understanding the mechanism by which words are formed." In other words, "selective attention" is used in a way, which aims at task completion, to analyse the stimulus,explore, experiment and become aware of all the elements in the situation and their possible combinations. Attention is used to follow the various stages of the task achievement project; and finally he/she concentrates on checking the results and planning any adjustments (error management).

MEMORY

With regard to the objective of memorizing forms, meanings and relationships between meanings, it was possible to ascertain that nine subjects reinforced their mnemonic ability in the field examined, four improved it and for one this type of ability was not an objective.

Reinforcement of long-term memory was observed in G. "He/She stopped for two weeks for health reasons and after returning to school and renewing participation in the course, it was sufficient for him/her to look at the first exercise to be able to start studying again according to methods and procedures learnt previously and to show that he/she had internalised content and skills in a lasting manner.

For B. who had difficulty in spatial-temporal organisation and laterality, especially when writing, it was possible to ascertain after test I that "he/she easily memorizes what is seen on the screen, particularly the letters p,b,d and q... Before writing them in his/her exercise-book, he/she recalls on what side the line and the round section were located on the video."

PERCEPTION

Given the type of neuromotor problem from which all the subjects were suffering to a greater or lesser extent, the objective of Perceptual-spatial (of forms and directions, change in direction and lateralization) and Perceptual-temporal (sequence,contemporaneity and pressure). Discrimination was of primary importance for all the subjects examined and involved not only the perceptual aspects associated with writing, but also the use of the directional keys (right and left, up and down), regulating the pressure on them, eye-hand co-ordination and the ability to keep in mind and operationally combine several perceptual and motor skills at the same time, by grasping the Cause /Effect relationship.

In this field, the results showed particularly that the Course and the computer function combined to produce significant results in a short time.

Positive performance levels, often much greater than expected, were attained by all the subjects.

SYMBOLIZATION

The objective relating to ability to symbolize was planned for only seven pupils, three of whom reinforced this type of skill, three showed an improvement and one learnt for the first time to associate verbal signifier and the signified.

This objective was formulated for some of the pupils only after the first or the second test, when the achievement of planned objective had been permanently acquired and entry tests had indicated the possibility of using new units, through which the objective could be achieved.

The initial objective for B. was "recognition of letters and syllables." The objectives achieved were "word reconstruction,agreement of terms within the syntagm,sentence reading and reconstruction. At the end of the school year B. was able to produce orally and write on her own well-structured sentences without spelling mistakes."

The child's starting level showed "difficulties in spatial-temporal organization and laterality, and poor ability to symbolize."

LOGICAL THINKING

The objective relating to the acquisition of a type of learning based on understanding and use of mechanisms, rules and procedures and on the formation of increasingly integrated reference schemes was achieved by all the pupils.

The following was entered in O.'s assessment card: "... O has acquired a system of selective links which allow him/her to analyse the essential aspects of the stimulus,select the secondary ones, unify (synthesize) the basic aspects and make generalizations which enable objects (letters, syllables and words) to be placed in their respective categories (classification)." This pupil had been presented as adult-dependent, with erratic and weak motivation, and lacking interest in assessment and academic success", as a result of which his learning activity lacked cohesion and his knowledge seemed poorly integrated.

WORK ORGANIZATION

The ability to use procedures and to take charge of the organization and operational direction of their own tasks is a desirable objective, but difficult to achieve for subjects with often considerable motor problems and many difficulties with laterality.

This objective was not set for four pupils, seriously handicapped in the use of their upper limbs; three subjects showed an improvement in this field and it was possible to note skill acquisition for seven of them.

Some uncertainty was detected with regard to C. in using the four keys ↑ → ← ↓ on the keyboard to co-ordinate the action of pressing with that of observing.For about 15 days he/she found it somewhat awkward to relate pressure and control of the video and to use the keys for specific purpose by regulating direction and applying pressure at intervals. By the third test the teacher noted a considerable improvement in motor skill:" C. is able to organize a series of different interventions, calculate how many times the key must be pressed to produce the chosen syllable or letter... then he/she carries out the operations, directly controlling what is happening on the screen (he/she discovered by experiment an economic and functional way of solving the problem in the shortest possible time with maximum efficiency)."

EMOTIONAL MOTIVATION

Examination of the subjects' starting levels showed that many of them were low in self-esteem, as well as in learning motivation and interest in academic assessment.

Faced with failure, especially if repeated, many of them abandon the task and their behaviour is characterized by anxiety and refusal.

The results of the final test indicated reinforced selfesteem for 2 subjects and improved self-esteem for 11. Learning motivation was reinforced for 7 subjects and improved in 7 cases. 4 pupils learnt to react to failure and manage error, 7 displayed noticeable improvement, 2 reinforced already positive behaviour and in only one case was the objective not achieved.

We can read that at the starting level C. "... alternates between low self-esteem and an attitutde of wanting to do more than he is really capable of." Already after the first test it was possible to detect some acquisition of self-confidence, a satisfaction linked to the relationship between belief in one's own capabilities and commitment.

The realization fo knowing how to do something, of being able to check immediately the results of one's own performance leads to satisfaction, mobilizes commitment and activates attention. "When an error is committed, S. does not feel uneasy, because he/she knows that the error can be corrected immediately afterwards and a positive result achieved."

(It should be pointed out that the Course adapts itself very flexibly to the logical-perceptive capabilities of each subject and gently follows his/her learning speed. Consequently, the margin of error is considerably reduced).

M. generally displayed indifference towards assessment and academic satisfaction. At the first test the teacher observed "... M does not wish to commit any errors. He/she attaches great importance to succeeding and checks the error percentages to see the difference compared with his/her performances in the previous sittings. He/She is competing with him/herself. He/She is satisfied by the activity carried out, because he/she can direct it and achieve success."

ERROR MANAGEMENT AND REACTION TO FAILURE

Error management represents a very important objective for the purpose of learning and reaction to failure. The possibility of repeating a test after an error, mastering the criteria for completing a task and the steps necessary for arriving at the solution to a problem and having immediate confirmation of the correctness of the procedures used and of a positive result are the fundamental aspects which have led to the achievement of truly encouraging results in such a sensitive field as learning.

When P. sees his mistake, "he acts in a critical manner", that is, he repeats all the operations and steps necessary for achieving a positive result. "he is calm because he has understood that the test can be repeated and knows how to arrive at the solution, since the logical-operative tools for altering the situation are in his possession." The following was recorded for the starting level of this child:

"... he does not know how to adapt to new situations and will not accept his own mistakes, nor the remarks made about him by others." The important thing is for the required performance to correspond to his capabilities. In fact, "by increasing the degree of difficulty too much, P. is less willing to accept failure." Faced with this situation the teacher uses entry tests to check the pupil's ability to follow a predetermined set of steps, presets long response times, takes advantage of the reinforcement modules and allows many attempts at doing the exercises. The flexibility of the course allows the tests to be regulated and graded according to the pupil's actual capabilities, by asking for types of performance appropriate to the given responses.

AUTONOMY

In general, the subject in the experiment were presented by the teachers in the following way: "... adult-dependent in their acitivity and learning, they constantly ask for confirmation and outside intervention. Faced with a difficulty they are stuck and go no further, until guided by the teacher in the direction of the solution." In this field, the results of the experiment showed 3 cases of change in behaviour the acquisition of operational autonomy being such as to allow the children to choose and preset the procedures in cooperation with the teacher, and to ask by themselves for " a lower number of attempts or reduced times for each exercise", work the printer and carry out other operations.

" A.'s behaviour is totally adult-dependent." "...A acts more and more depending , and is able to correct him/herself when he/she makes a mistake." He/She also knows how to take initiatives: "... I have recently noted that A. shows a marked interest in the written word. A. wants the words on the video to be read out to him/her.../.

SOCIAL INTERACTION SKILL

Concerning the objective of forming relationships, by accepting the presence of others during the sessions, having respect for the work of others, making and accepting contributions to group work, and referring and communicating one's own experiences to the computer, there was an improvement in 6 of the subjects with difficulties in social interaction. The others showed no problems in this field and one of the children failed totally to reach the objective.

CONCLUSIONS

Today, after many years of research and experiment, the question is still being asked as to what benefits and advantages can be obtained from applying new technologies to the education of handicapped pupils. We maintain that the experience gained leads to the conclusion that not only are there no disadvantages in using the computer (provided, of course, educationally valid and suitable software is used), but that the benefits to be gained from its use are, on the contrary quite clear, and capable of being increased to an as yet inconceivable extent.

Therefore, work and especially means and resources must be channeled in this direction, on the understanding that it is the only way of opening up a new and better future for the less fortunate.

APPENDIX 1

CONTENT OF CURRICULUM : BASIC ITALIAN

INSTRUCTIONAL BLOCKS

Blocks are divided into units.

Each unit contains a series of exercises in the same skill area. Letter identification, syllable identification and reconstruction word pattern, structural analysis, syntagm and sentence.

The level of difficulty in each unit increases gradually.

Withing a session the number and quality allotted for each instructional unit is adjusted individually for every student taking the course, the volume of exercises is based on each student's strength and weaknesses. A student's progress through the curriculum will depend on the mastery of skill objectives associated with each strand.

Exercises in the units are divided into classes of six exercises each. As students work on exercises that constitute a class in one of the instructional strand, the computer makes a judgement about whether the student is prepared to move on the next class, return to the preceding class or repeat exercises in the current class .

The computer can provide the teacher with reports of the student's progress at any time. The Course Report gives a summary of each student's work in the course. The Session reports a summary of each student's work in the session.Reports can be printed or automatically entered on individual disks.

The reports give detailed information about:

student's identification number, number of placement test, date of the session number of items represented in the last session, number of items corrected in the last session, number of tries, number of time-outs, cumulative time spent working on this course.

APPENDIX 2

14 STUDENTS			
LANGUAGE- COGNITIVE SYSTEM			
COGNITIVE OBJECTIVES	have achieved the objectives set		14 students
	have achieved further objectives		14 students
	ATTENDING SKILLS	reinforced	3 students
		improved	9 students
		changed	2 students
	MEMORY	reinforced	9 students
		improved	4 students
		not an objective	1 student
	PERCEPTION	reinforced	7 students
		improved	7 students
	CAUSE-EFFECT	reinforced	5 students
		improved	9 students
	SYMBOLIZATION	reinforced	3 students
		improved	3 students
		changed	1 student
		not an objective	7 students
	LOGICAL THINKING	reinforced	1 student
		improved	8 students
		changed	5 students
	TRANSFER OF KNOWLEDGE AND SKILLS	improved	3 students
		changed	1 student
		not an objective	10 students
WORK ORGANIZATION			
		improved	4 students
		changed	7 students
		not an objective	3 students

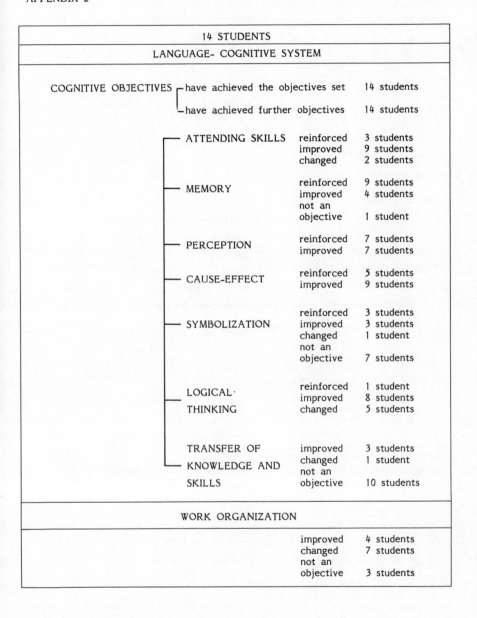

APPENDIX 2

EMOTIONAL MOTIVATION		
SELF-ESTEEM	reinforced	2 students
	improved	11 students
	not an objective	1 student
ACHIEVEMENT MOTIVATION	reinforced	7 students
	improved	7 students
REACTION TO FAILURE ERROR MANAGEMENT	reinforced	2 students
	reinforced	2 students
	improved	7 students
	changed	4 students
	objective not reached	1 student
AUTONOMY	reinforced	1 student
	improved	7 students
	changed	3 students
	not an objective	3 students
SOCIAL INTERACTION SKILL	reinforced	6 students
	not an objective	7 students
	objective partially reached	1 student

APPENDIX 3

BIBLIOGRAPHY

1. SUPPES P.,FLETCHER I.D., ZANOTTI M., Models of individual trajectories.In Computer-assisted instruction for deaf students, October 31,1973. Institute for Mathematical Studies in SOcial Sciences. Tecr.Report 214, Stanford University.

2. SUPPES P. ZANOTTI M. et al., Evaluation of Computer-Assisted Instruction in Elementary mathematics for Hearing-Impaired Students. Institute for Mathematics for Hearing-Impared Students. Institute for Mathematical Studies in Social Science.Tech.Report 200, Stanford University,17,March,1973.

3. SUPPES P., A Survey of Cognition in Handicapped Children in " Review of Educational Research", 1974,44.

4. CHARROW V.R.,FLETCHER J.D., English as the Second Language of Deaf Students, Tech.Report 208, Stanford University, 20,July,1973.

5. SEARLE B.W., LORTON P., SUPPES P., Structural Variables Affecting CAL. Performance on Arithmetic World Problems of Disadvantaged and Deaf Student. Tech.Report 213 IMSS Standford University, 4,September.,1973.

6. MACKEN E., SUPPES P., Evaluation studies of CCC elementary-school curriculum: 1971-1975, in " CC Educational Studies", Summer 1976,21-24.

7. HOFFMEYER D., Computer Assisted Instruction at the Florida School of the Deaf and the Blind , in " A.A.D.",September 1980,ch.35.

8. ARCANIN J., Computer Assisted Instruction at the California School for the Deaf - Past,Present and Future : An Administrator's View, in "American Annal for the Deaf", 124,5, September,1979.

9. MADACHY J., MILLERJ., Gallaudet College,English Department,Washington D.C. personal communication with them regarding status of project 1977.

10. WATSON P.G., The TICCIT System at the Model Secondary School for the Deaf in Journal of the Computer Based Instruction,Spring 1976.

11. RUBINSTEIN,BOLT,BERANEK,NEWMAN, Personal communication regarding the status of this project. Cambridge,Massachusetts, 1977.

12. HERMAN R.B., Testimony to the House Committee on Science and Technology Special Session on the Utilization of Computer in Aiding the Education Handicapped.Washington D.C., October,1977.

13. MANJULA WALDRON, SUSAN ROSE, Educational Software for Problem Solving by the Hearing Impaired Students, in ADCIS proceedings,May 1984

14. HARDING R.H., TIDBALL L.K., A national microccomputer software survey for microcomputer usage in schools for the hearing impaired American Annals for the Deaf, 1983, 127,5,673-683.

15. WITHROW, Auditorily Augmented Interactive Three-Dimensional Television as and Aid to langage Learning Among Deaf and Hearing Impaired Children, in "Proceedings of Association for Development of Computer Based Instructional Systems Conference ", February,1978.

16. KOLOMYJECT W., ROSE S., WALDRON M.B., Computer graphics and creativity/problem solving skills with deaf and severely language disordered students, Part III : Using microcomputer as a creative tool. Proceedings CEC National Conference on Special Education. Nazzro (Ed.) ERIC/CEC,Reston,VA.,1983.

17. AESCHLEMAN S.R., TAWNEY J.W., Interacting : A Computer-Based Telecommunications System for Educating Several handicapped Pre-schoolers in their Homes in "Educational Technology", October,1978.

18. TAWNEY J.W., AESCHLEMAN S.R. et al., Using Telecmmunication Technology to Instruct Rural Severely Handicapped Children, in "Exceptional Children" October,1979.

19. CHIANG A., STAUFFER C., CANNARA A., Demonstration of the Use of Computer Assisted Instruction with handicapped CHildren, final report, RMC Research Corp. Arlington, Virginia,September,1978.

20. KNUTSON J.M., PROCHNOW R.R., Computer Assisted Instruction For Vocational Reabilitation of the Mentally Retarded, Monograph 2, The University of Texas, At Austin College of Education Rehabilitation Research and Training Center in mental Retardation, August,1970.

21. PAPERT, MINDSTROMS S., New York: Basic Books, 1980

22. WEIR S., RUSSEL S., VALENTE J., LOGO, An Approach to educating Disabled Children, September 1982, Byte.

23. HOWES JIM, Teaching Handicapped CHildren to Read A C.B. Approach, in Computers in Education - North Holland Publishing COmpany IFIP. 1981 p.½433. etc.

24. OSIN L., Computer-Assisted Instruction in Arithmetic in Israeli Disadvantaged Elemenary Schools, in COmputers in Education- North Holland Publishing Company IFIP, 1981, p.469, etc.

25. DOTTI MARTINENGO G., PERTICI MAGI G., Sperimentare un course-ware Compuscuola, Ottobre 1984.

Conceptual Processing for the Casual User: Perspectives in Educational Technologies from the Artificial Intelligence Viewpoint

STEFANO A. CERRI

Artificial Intelligence Laboratory, Department of Informatics, University of Pisa, Corso Italia, 40, 56100 Pisa, Italy

ABSTRACT

In this paper I highlight some of the requirements that knowledge-based systems should satisfy in order to offer both the expressive power and the cognitive simplicity needed for the design, development and use of effective automated assistants in many learning activities, both in an institutional and in a personal environment.

INTRODUCTION

The emerging technologies of knowledge-based systems in all their diverse aspects may generate a wide spectrum of reactions- including indifference- particularly when they are proposed for institutional or personal learning and teaching applications.

From the long and contradictory experience of the use of computers in educations, especially when the computer has been designed for simulating the teacher in Computer Assisted Instruction programs, we should have learned the lesson that success and failure in the field are not primarily due to the available technology **per se** but to the use of that technology in a particular setting. The most relevant factor instead is the educational theory chosen as it directs the design choices which underly the construction of the application software.

Unfortunately, the large, time shared systems mostly used in the 70-ties did not provide the resources (hardware and software) needed by the interactive and unskilled user, such as a student, and required a heavy financial commitment. The availability of small and cheap personal machines at the end of the 70-ties allowed a more widespread familiarity with the computer as a teacher or as a learning environment, but did not offer any relevant improvement concerning the cooperativeness of the software. The phylosophy underlying most of the educational softwar for these machines was too often bound to the Skinnerian attitude which considers the learner as a feedback-driven mechanistic system and proposes consequently "branching programs" for teaching.

Remarkable exceptions to this view were simulation programs and powerful learning environments such as LOGO (Papert, 1980).

The first direction of investigation did not emerge for the specific purpose of teaching, but was an application of state of the art computer technologies to education.

The second one, instead, addressed successfully many educational problems in a **"revolutionary"** way (O'Shea & Self, 1983 provide an insightful, critical review of these issues). The learning paradigm of LOGO was the first comprehensive attempt to consider the learner as an autonomous individual which needs to be stimulated in order to build his own conceptual structures and skills.

The research towards the identification of basic concepts to be embodied in environments for learning by programming has continued with the BOXER project (di Sessa , 1985) and within the SMALLTALK community (Goldberg and Ross, 1981). The key issue of these endeavours is to offer a computing environment for novices powerful enough to express computationally complex notions- such as the satisfaction of constraint relations between objects (cfr. THINGLAB, Borning, 1981)- and simple enough to be naturally understood and mastered by a novice- therefore based on metaphores, simulations and sophisticated input-output interfaces

The educational success of the design choices made for these systems is certainly worth to be evaluated empirically. However,we need to invest resources not only in emprical research for the evaluation of the existing ideas and systems but also in fundamental research for developing new environments, as we are far from having identified what is conceptually simple as a metaphore for learning problem solving in general and learning programming in particular. Further, these research directions may have an impact not only for their applications in education, but also for the construction of the next generations of computers.

Unfortunately, not **every type** of learning can take place by means of an interaction with an environment such as BOXER or THINGLAB. The reason is not simply technological, but more fundamental. **Learning by discovery** (e.g. interacting with LOGO) and **learning by doing (e.g. using the simulations available in a THINGLAB environment suitably equippped with simulation modules)** seem to be insufficient as a paradigm for many important learning (and teaching) activities. For instance, descriptive knowledge cannot be modelled by simulations- or at least : we have not yet discovered metaphores suitable for embodying many fields of expertise where the competence is primarily represented by descriptions of concepts and their relations.

Further, one of the most relevant components of any teaching-learning interaction is the diagnosis and remedial of misconceptions underlying the student's bugs (see Sleeman and Brown, 1982, for a collection of Intelligent Tutoring Systems developed in the 70-ties). Therefore, our view is that **tutoring dialogues are and will remain** an important paradigm for learning.

The failure of most of the traditional, **frame-based (*)** tutoring dialogues conducted by CAI branching programs has been attributed to the scarcity and inadequateness of computational tools and (perhaps consequently) to the choice of simplistic educational theory inspiring the programmed dialogues.

In this paper I present a few fragments of dialogue between a student and a computer-based tutor in order to relate the advanced, knowledge-based computational methods and tools available now with the opportunity offered of exploring new and promising tutoring paradigms.

The aim of the paper is primarily to convince that sophisticated technologies are on the one site a necessary but by no means a sufficient condition for the development of software managing effective tutoring dialogues. Instead, the real difficulties arise from the lack of explicit indications about the " educational competence" that these systems should embody.

Provided there is an active awareness of the expressive power of these advanced computational methods and techniques, we believe that the challenge of making the computer-based learning assistants of the future is open to many institutions and idividuals, and is not restricted to the ones who have produced the technological tools.

Our insights are based on the experience gathered in building prototypes of tutoring systems by means of representing the educational competence in the form of chunks of descriptive **and control** knowledge. The knowledge-based approach adopted in building these systems needs some further justification before specific examples cna be appreciated.

(*) The term frame refers here to a unit of information to be presented to the student, as it is common in the CAI literature, not to Minsky's stereotyped description of a chunk of information.

CONCEPTUAL PROCESSING

As Artificial Intelligence has now become popular , one is tempted to consider it uncritically as the key to the solution of any "difficult" problem, i.e. a problem such that its global solution is not clear beforehand. This attitude may be misleading for many reasons. We will not be able to present here our position with respect to the correct use of AI, but simply stress two point we believe to be relevant in the context of the use of AI in Education.

First, AI is an instrument and perhaps a methodology for representing the principles guiding an "intelligent" tutoring dialogue, but **the actual choices in the design of such a dialogue are left to the AI user.** As there are no general algorithms or recipes for guiding the user in these choices, it is wise to envision the possible solutions and then select the AI tools (or extend the ones available) instead of vice versa.

Second, within AI we can discriminate between two approaches **the power-based** and **the knowledge-based approach** (Steels, 1984). As the descriptive and control knowledge relevant for managing a sensible tutorial dialogue is complex, approximate and contradictory, the real power of the successful systems must be based on the adequateness of the representation of the competence that they will embody, not (simply) on the efficiency of their computational engines or on the completeness and consistency of their knowledge.

We maintain that a programming system can be called adequate if it provides both expressive power and cognitive simplicity for the user.Mathematically elegant but conceptually rigid programming tools and languages- such as PROLOG- do not seem to be adequate for representing and using the sophisticated knowledge structures needed for an "inteligent" tutor in a dialogue with a real student in a real domain (*). The claim of simplicity for the structures of these languages is better to be related to the language design and implementation than to the language use in representing problem solving strategies in complex domains.

For this reason, we called **conceptual processing** the **kind of** AI processing typical of the knowledge based approach.

The major requirement of conceptual processing systems used for managing man-machine dialogues- such as a tutorial dialogue- is that they should include simple representations of (partially) incorrect or incomplete knowledge chunks which are necessary for modelling the user's behaviour.

(*) This does not meant that it is **in principle** not possible to express in PROLOG any kind of knowledge that one can express in a conceptual processing system (see, for instance, Bundy, 1983). The argument here refers to practical-not theoretical-availability of tools with an adequate expressive power and cognitive simplicity.

These components are relevant at two different levels. The "intelligent" automated assistant should have a model of its user- the applicative level- and the "intelligent" system should help the programmer to prevent mistakes and to diagnose and remediate misconceptions during the programming activity itself- the environment level- There are several reasons to believe that the application and the environment level should be **integrated** into an unique framework (cfr. Barstow, Shrobe and Sandewall, 1984).

As the research on **student models** can be considered typical of the stream of developments for making intelligent Tutoring Systems, we propose to consider its achievements as a general need for the next generation of "intelligent" machines.

REPRESENTATION OF KNOWLEDGE RELEVANT TO TUTORING DIALOGUES

We can distinguish at least three modules that must be programmed in order to build an "intelligent" tutor : a module for the **interpretation of the student's message**; a module **planning the search (and construction) of the next tutor message's content**, and a module for the production of **the tutor's message.**

Each of these modules relies on knowledge, in the form of descriptive or control structures. As it will not be possible here to give a complete account of each of the three modules, we will simply provide some examples.

When the student sends a message to the tutor, this may be a request of information or explanation or either it may consist of an answer to a question.In both cases the student may have been correct, but he may have formulated his utterance in an incomplete or ambiguous way. In the second case he may also have been wrong.

DIALOGUES ABOUT GEOGRAPHY

In the following we present a dialogue showing the occurrence of inadequate interpretations of the student's responses by the computer.

(tutor) What is the capital of Belgium ?

(student) Bruxelles

Wrong, the correct answer is: Brussels.

What is the name of the State with London as capital?

England

Wrong, the correct answer is: United Kingdom, or: Great Britain.

What is the seat of the Dutch government?

Amsterdam

Wrong, the correct answer is : The Hague.

While the first student's answer is correct, it should be interpreted in the context of the use of a different (French) denomination for the name of the capital of Belgium, the other answers are incorrect.

However, a skilled tutor should recognize that England is often used for United Kingdom (the part for the whole) and that while the government of the Netherlands is in The Hague, the capital of the Netherlands is Amsterdam, an uncommon situation which might suggest a plausible interpretation of the cause of the mistake. This knowledge should be explicitly represented and guide the tutor's reaction so that a more sensible dialogue would be produced.

For instance, if the student asks an ambiguous question such as:

What is the capital of Holland ?

should be answered by :

If by Holland you mean the province of North Holland, then it is Haarlem, if you mean South Holland, then it is Rotterdam, if you mean The Netherlands, then it is Amsterdam. The seat of the Dutch government is also in The Hague a situation different from most other countries where the seat of the government is in the capital.

The knowledge needed by a tutor for managing correctly dialogues like these might be extremely complex, and can be hardly modelled "locally" as it occurs necessarily in traditional CAI programs. Instead, a description of geographic concepts and of their relations is needed.

For instance, one might define the classes: Nations , States, Capitals, Regions, Provinces, Cities etc. and relate them to specific instances so that instances (or subclasses) of a class inherit properties of the class provided we are not in exceptional cases. While the expected value of the attribute "SeatOfGovernment" could be defined to be equal to the value of the property "Capital for all the instances of State, in the exceptional case of The Netherlands, SeatOfGovernment should evaluate TheHague instead of Amsterdam.

A flat rule-based system (e.g. a PROLOG program not including an explicit [meta]representation guiding its own interpreter's behaviour) would perhaps represent globally all the assertions concerning the Capitals of States and would have a rule stating that for each State X, if the SeatOfGovernment property is required, then the answer is the Capital of the indicated State X, if instead the SeatOfGovernment of TheNetherlands is required, then the answer is TheHague. Let us explicitly represent this knowledge.

```
Capital (Italy, Rome )
Capital ( TheNetherlands, Amsterdam )
SeatOfGovernment ( X,Y, ) : - Capital ( X,Y, )
SeatOfGovernment (TheNetherlands , TheHague )
```

The control knowledge of this representaiton consists of the following (simplified) strategy for guiding correctly the inferences :

If you have to show that property P holds between X and Y, i.e. that P(X,Y) is an explicitly asserted fact or it is deductable from the facts and the rules; try first to match P(X,Y) with the existing facts. If this is the case, exit successfully. Else, try to see if there is a rule such that its left hand side matches P(X,Y), say: P(W,Z): -Q(X,Y,). If this is the case ,substitute the goal of matching P(X,Y) with the goal of matching Q(W,Z) and repeat the procedure.

This control strategy correctly deduces, for instance, that the SeatOf Government of Italy is Rome (because it is the Capital of Italy), and also that the SeatOfGovernment of The Netherlands is TheHague (because the asserted fact is checked before any trial for a matching rule).

If the student answers incorrectly **Amsterdam** to the question **What is the seat of the Dutch government?** the tutor's model of the student's incorrect knowledge could be represented as a deviation of the correct knowledge. There are three possible student models.

1. (false fact)

   Capital (Italy, Rome)

   Capital (TheNetherlands, Amsterdam)

   SeatOfGovernment(X,) :- Capital (X,Y)

   SeatOfGovernment (TheNetherlands, Amsterdam)

The tutor's diagnosis of the student's mistake based on this model can result in a remedial such as: **You believe incorrectly that the seat of the Dutch government is Amsterdam.**

This is a paraphrase of the student's mistake, and therefore does not provide any plausible explanation of the student's behaviour. The same holds for the model

2. (missing fact)

   Capital (Italy,Rome)

   Capital (TheNetherlands, Amsterdam)

   SeatOfGovernment (X,Y):- Capital (X,Y)

where the knowledge about the exceptional Dutch situation is absent. A remedial like: **You do not know that The Hague is the seat of the Dutch government** provides an interpretation of the cause of the mistake which seems to be of little help for the student.

The third model is one which relies on the correct knowledge base, but uses a control strategy which is incorrect:

3. (incorrect control)

If you have to show that property P holds between X and Y, i.e. that P(X,Y) is an explicitly asserted fact or it is deductable from the facts and the rules; try first to see if there is a rule such that its left hand side matches P(X,Y), say: P(W,Z):-Q(X,Y).If this is the case, substitute the goal of matching P(X,Y) with the goal of matching Q(W,Z) and repeat the whole matching cycle. If there is no suitable rule, try to match P(X,Y) with the existing facts.

This **incorrect control** model justifies the student's behaviour, but it is hardly plausible from a cognitive viewpoint. If this model would indeed hold, the same student would also say that dolphins belong to the family of fish or that the British drive on the right hand side of the road, even when he would have been told several times that these situations differ from the norm.

The three models described are also weak, in the sense that they assume a complete search in the knowledge base in order to find a matching fact or rule. Even if the student's neurons would fire at an incredibly high speed, it would] probably be insufficient for scanning the huge knowledge available to a human. Instead, a knowledge base structured in the form of **frames or scripts(*)** seems more plausible.

A reasonable internal interpretation available to a skilled teacher, of the incorrect student's behaviour in the example discussed is described by the following text.

Because the subject of the conversation is the geography of European capitals, [localization of the source of mistake, excluding the over-generalizations to dolphins and roads] **and in the large majority of cases the capital of an European State is also the seat of its government** [look at the default procedure], **it is plausible that a kind of incorrect generalization has taken place; i.e. that the student knows that The Hague is an exception, but has used the default method for deducing that Amsterdam- the capital of The Netherlands-is the seat of the Dutch government.**

(*) These are Minsky's frames and Schank's scripts, i.e.stereotypical descriptions of objects or events in terms of predicates. Their arguments may be dynamically evaluated, i.e. their value may be the result of the run-time application of a procedure. Side effects such as changes of the structure and/or the content of the calling frame are also allowed.

These remarks indicate the need for a model of the student's behaviour such that knowledge is organized (and accessed) in chunks relevant for the subject considered, and that control knowledge is included locally in the representation.

A knowledge-based system, would perhaps represent the knowledge needed for answering the question in the following way:

```
The Netherlands     is-a State
                    Capital  Amsterdam
                    SeatOfGovernment  TheHague
State part-of       Country
      has-part      (Capital,SeatOfGovernment)
SeatOfGovernment    part-of State
     if-needed      (or (SeatOfGovernment (instance-of State))
                        (Capital (instance-of State )))
```

In this representation three aspects are relevant for us. First, predicates-such as Capital, SeatOfGovernment,etc.-appear also as values of other predicates- e.g. has-part-; so that (intuitively) one can express quantification also on predicates. Second, the knowledge representation is strictly co-referential, so that one avoids over-generalizations which are a dangerous source of computational load and may lead to cognitively unplausible models. Third, the control knowledge for inferences is explicityly represented as an "active" value of the declaration.

```
SeatOfGovernment
    if-needed ( or (SeatOfGovernment (instance-of State))
                   (Capital (instance-of State )))
```

In order to answer (correctly) to the question about the seat of the Dutch government, such a system would access first the knowledge concerning the property (and also the concept) SeatOfGovernment, discover there that its value (if needed) is either explicitly stated (in exceptional cases), or deducible (default value); check if there are exceptions valid for the current instance of state, i.e. TheNetherlands , access the knowledge about TheNetherlands; check if its SeatOfGovernment has indeed an(exceptional) value and finally retrieve that value instead of the value of its Capital property.

In a default reasoning system the assertion checking the existence of an exception would not be explicitly represented, so that

SeatOfGovernment if-needed (Capital(instance-of State))

would be sufficient explicit representation of the control knowledge, provided one takes also into account the part of control implicit in the default reasoning strategy adopted by the system.

A model of incorrect behaviour such as the one shown by the preceding dialogue, could consist in this framework of the absence of the check for exceptional cases. An adequate knowledge representation system allows one to express explicitly this (incorrect) control knowledge as valid for this specific class of questions but perhaps not for other cases of default reasoning

SearOfGovernment
if-needed (or (Capital (instance-of State))
(SeatOfGovernment (instance-of State))

A similar description of the control in the student's reasoning process about the concept SeatOfParliament, would justify the answer: **Brussels** to the question: **What is the seat of the European Parliament;** instead of the more correct **Brussels and Strasburg.** On the contrary, if the student's answer is correct in this case, the local model of his reasoning is the default one.

Notice that an adequate concept processing system should not only allow the explicit representation of locally valid deviations from the default control strategy, but also the dynamic modification of it, because the user model has to be **constructed** during the dialogue. This is a very stringent requirement on the flexibility of the system, as it may include the possibility of generating alternative **structures,** not simply the dynamic updating of the existing ones.

For instance, suppose that we wish to allow some acquisiton of knowledge by the system during the dialogue. Suppose that initially the system knows that:

Europe HasSeatOfParliament (Brussels, Strasburg)

and that the student answers to : **What is the seat of the European Parliament?**

with **Brussels** i.e. incorrectly. An interpretation of the mistake could be that he confuses the viewpoint of Brussels as a Capital of Belgium and seat of the Belgian government with the viewpoint of Brussels as a seat of many institutions of the European Community.

Suppose that in a later phase of the dialogue, to the question: **What do you remember about the relations between Brussels and the European Institutions?** the student answers (perhaps among other things): **Brussels is the location of the permanent commissions of the European Parliament.** The model of the system should be modified accordingly, but in a fashion such that it will use the new knowledge appropriately. For instance, a modification such as:

Europe HasSeatOfParliament
(ParliamentaryCommissions Brussels)

seems not to be suited for further use. Suppose the system knows that a Parliament is composed of a GeneralAssembly and a number of ParliamentaryCommissions. A nice idea would be to transform the knowledge about the SeatOfParliament of Europe in the following way:

Transformation #1: (inversion and decomposition of the predicate)
X SeatOfParliament Y -> Y IsASeat (ParliamentOf X)

Strasburg IsASeat ParliamentOf Europe
Brussels IsASeat ParliamentOf Europe

Transformation# 2: (split whole into its exclusive parts)
ParliamentOf->
ParliamentaryCommissionsOf or ParliamentaryGeneralAssemblyOf

Strasburg IsASeat ParliamentaryGeneralAssemblyOf Europe
Brussels IsASeat <?ParliamentaryCommissionsOf> Europe

so that the natural next question of the system is: **Where is the seat of the European General Assembly?** Notice that the transformations indicated allow the system to formulate a **new**, perhaps relevant question from knowledge not directly linked to the topic of conversation.

The difference between the rule-based and the frame-based representation of knowledge and their corresponding control structures may be even better appreciated considering the answer of the tutor to the question: **What is the capital of Holland?**

In the knowledge-based approach, once the description of the concepts to be considered at this point of the dialogue has been accessed - focusing the domain of discourse - all the knowledge (or at least the most relevant part of it) is available for formulating an answer as complex as the one given in the preceding section of this paper. This would be hardly the case of a system with an unstructured architecture.

From the examples given it should be noticed that a flexible representation of specific descriptive and control knowledge about the subject matter more than a general but rigid inference scheme is of fundamental importance for a correct interpretation of the student's messages.

TRANSLATIONS INTO A FOREIGN OR A PROGRAMMING LANGUAGE

In other papers we describe systems for the diagnosis of misconceptions in the task of translation of "difficult" foreign language words (Cerri and Landini, 1985) and in the task of programming (Cerri et al., 1983, 1984). We will not be able to enter here into the details of these systems, but let us simply suggest, by means of an example, what are the requirements for the representation of (incorrect) knowledge in the case of a student's mistake in translating conjunctions.

Suppose that a student translates the Italian **perche** in an indirect interrogative meaning with **because** instead of **why**. As it is not possible, in Italian, to discriminate between the two conceptual meanings on the base of the conjunction used, one cannot be sure if the student makes a mistake because he does not recognize the presence of an (indirect) interrogation or because he confuses the English conjunctions. The first possibility relates the bug to an incomplete awareness of the Italian student about the semantics of interrogative clauses, while the second one indicates an incorrect knowledge of the English language.

The diagnostic dialogue for inferring the specific nature of the second type of misconception can evaluate to one of the following plausible interpretations:

inverted use of the conjunctions with respect to their conceptual meaning,
absorption (i.e: using just one of them in both meanings);
total confusion (i.e: indiscriminate use of both of them).

These misconceptions may be discovered also in many other situations, so that the diagnostic strategy to be applied may be a general one, activated specifically when the student's bug and the representation of the correct knowledge about conjunctions satisfy some general requirements.

The incorrect awareness of the existence of an indirect interrogation, instead, is a misconception specific to this particular class of questions (i.e. about interrogative clauses), and the control knowledge for guiding the diagnostics has to be tuned explicitly for it.

This example should suggest once more that an effective diagnostic strategy for inferring misconceptions from bugs relies on a flexible representation of descriptive and control knowledge, and that this representation can neither consist of simple anticipated answers - as is the case of traditional CAI programs - nor of a globally designed set of assertions and rules.

CONCLUSIONS

Conceptual processing refers to the behaviour of systems based on Artificial Intelligence methods and techniques using the knowledge-based approach. In order to distinguish these from rule-based systems - such as most of the expert systems of the first generation (Mycin, etc.) we call them Conceptual Processing Systems.

In the design of intelligent tutoring systems, the complexity of the interpretation of the student's message, of the control for building a representation of an adequate response and of the production of a "natural" answer from the representation require knowledge to be expressed in the form of concepts, relations among them and explicit control strategies.

The paper did provide exmples of tutorial dialogues in the field of geography and foreign language learning. On the basis of the examples, we presented arguments that support the view that concept processing systems, more than rule-based systems, are adequate for representing the models necessary to build and use tutorial programs.

The definition of "adequateness" of a system for the design of a dialogue manager has been related to its expressive power and cognitive simplicity. Some requirements have been indicated that include the following.

EXPRESSIVE POWER

1. In order to model the student's incorrect behaviour, a Conceptual Processing System should allow to <u>express explicitly its control strategy</u>.
2. <u>Control strategies</u> should be expressible as <u>locally valid</u>.
3. It should be possible to <u>modify dynamically</u> these control strategies.
4. It should be possible, as a result of reasoning on the student's model, that <u>transformations</u> occur both <u>in the content</u> of the knowledge available to the system <u>and</u> also <u>in its structure</u>.
5. Knowledge should be co-referential, so that the <u>access</u> to related items is facilitated once the focus of conversation has been identified.

COGNITIVE SIMPLICITY

1. The representation and the transformations should require a minimal effort in <u>understanding</u> and consequently in designing. One does not have to write a new, specialized interpreter if he needs to describe a new, local control structure modelling the behaviour of the student that results from the analysis of one or more interactions.
2. The Conceptual Processing System should support an integrated set of tools, so that the same flexible and powerful set of user modelling tools should be active within the <u>system's environment</u> and guide the programmer-system dialogue.

As currently Expert Systems have become very popular, there might be the hope (or perhaps the fear?) that it will be possible to produce effective intelligent tutors using these methods and techniques.

Our paper supports that hope, as it argues that traditional Computer Assisted instruction techniques do not offer the basic technology for allowing the system to reason about its own competence and therefore to provide a sensible response to un-anticipated messages of the user.

Further, the examples discussed support the conviction that knowing the methods and tools is necessary but not sufficient for using them effectively for the purpose. What really matters is the expertise embodied in the system's behaviour, and we believe that the task of explicitating that expertise is a challenging goal for the users of these systems. The requirements of expressive power and associated cognitive simplicity should ensure that this is an achievable goal.

Finally, we have suggested that "casual users" should be the target audience for Conceptual Processing Systems. This specification has been indicated in order to focus the attention on the much wider impact of the teaching and learning systems of the future. First, they will not necessarily be used in a traditional, institutional setting, such as the school, but more privately, perhaps in the leisure time. Second, they will not be designed and developed by teams of specialists, as it was often the case for CAI programs. The requirement of cognitive simplicity at the level of the application and at the level of the system environment may justify the forecast that novices in computer technologies will try to transform their ideas about tutoring dialogues into effective programs to be used by a much larger public than it was the case in the past.

ACKNOWLEDGEMENTS

I am grateful to Luc Steels and Marc Eisenstadt for providing comments to an earlier version of this paper.

I am also indebted to the many collaborators of the Artificial Intelligence Laboratory of the Free University of Brussels, who contributed to make inspiring and pleasant the period I have spent at their Lab on leave from Pisa.

REFERENCES

Barstow, D.R.; Shrobe, H.E. and Sandewall, E. (Eds.) (1984)
Interactive Programming Environments
McGraw-Hill

Borning, A. (1981)
The programming language aspects of Thinglab, a constraint-oriented simulation laboratory
ACM Trans. on Progr. Lang. and Systems 3: 353-387

Bundy, A. (1981)
The Computer Modelling of Mathematical Reasoning
Academic Press

Cerri, S.A.; Colombini, C.; Grillo, M. and Mallozzi, R. (1984)
RADAR: Reasoning on ADA Rubbish
In: Proc. ECAI-84: 6th Eur. Conf. on Artificial Intelligence, Pisa: 409-418.
To be published in: O'Shea, T. (Ed.); Advances in Artificial Intelligence, North Holland

Cerri, S.A.; Fabbrizzi, M. and Marsili, G. (1983)
The Rather Intelligent Little LISPer
In: Proc. 1st AISB Conference on Artificial Intelligence and Education, Exeter.
Also in: AISB Quarterly 50: 21-24 (1984)

Cerry, S.A. and Landini, P. (1985)
Misconceptions in Multilingual Translations
In: Proc. 2nd AISB Conference on Artificial Intelligence and Education, Exeter, Sept. 85

DiSessa, A. (1985)
A Principled Design for an Integrated Computational Environment
Human-Computer Interaction 1: 1-47, Lawrence Erlbaum Ass.

Goldberg, A. and Ross, J. (1981)
Is the Smalltalk-80 system for children?
Byte 8, 6: 347-68

O'Shea, T. and Self, J. (1983)
Learning and Teaching with Computers: Artificial Intelligence in Education
The Harvester Press, Brighton, Sussex

Paper, S. (1980)
Mindstorms: Children, Computers and Powerful Ideas
New York: Basic Books

Sleeman, D. and Brown, J.S. (Eds.) (1982)
Intelligent Tutoring Systems
Academic Press

Steels, L. (1984)
Design requirements for knowledge representation systems
In: Laubsch, J. (Ed.) Proc. of GWAI-83. Springer Verlag, Berlin

The National Programme of the People's Republic of Bulgaria for the Introduction of Computers in Secondary Schools

A. PISAREV
Ministry of Education, Sofia, Bulgaria

Scientific and technological progress and, above all, the development of computer technology, have created favourable conditions for the intensification and individualization of the educational process, as well as for a wide application of the creative principle in education. The formation of a universally and harmoniously developed individual, who is an incarnation of the wealth of national and world culture, requires transformation of the usual means and forms of education to comply with the spirit and needs of our times.

Education in Bulgaria has deep-rooted national traditions. Bulgarian education provides numerous examples related to development and spiritual heroism. The education system in the country has achieved indisputable success in all its stages and forms. It has become an important factor in the formation of the social individual and in the training of specialists for the needs of all spheres of the national economy.

In view of this, the education system has always been the object of special attention on the part of all Party and government organs in the country. A special Plenary Session of the Central Committee of the Bulgarian Communist Party was held in 1979 on the problems of education, which defined the basic tasks facing the education system as follows:

- Expansion of general education and its development in accordance with present-day requirements;
- Training of the younger generation and provision of opportunities to acquire professions.

The abovementioned tasks form the basis for the curriculum prepared for the new Bulgarian 12-grade school, and its implementation in practice necessitates a search for new techniques of instruction, as well as new means for reducing the overload on students. Our search was particularly active in the sphere of new techniques of instruction, such as the application of school television, films, tape-recorders, programmed instruction, with the use of computer technology as well. In the 1970's all these experiments did not produce any substantial results. The reasons for this are varied and generally known. We sought new factors which would make it possible to expand the educational process, to attract both teachers and students, and to encourage the creative process. At that moment, microcomputer technology emerged and began to be widely applied in secondary schools. We analyzed the experience of the USSR, Britain, France, Japan and the USA in introducing this technology, and became aware of the need to start using microcomputers in Bulgarian schools as well. In view of the importance and ever-increasing role of the computer in Bulgarian society, the Ministry of Education adopted a number of goal-oriented measures related to the computerization of secondary education, to pre-vocational education and to the acquisition of knowledge, skills and other requirements needed to work with computer equipment.

In order to create the material and technical basis to meet the agreed objectives, the Ministry of Education in 1981, through the Bulgarian Academy of Sciences, commissioned and financed the elaboration of the first series of 200 Bulgarian personal computers, intended mainly for practical use in the education system. In addition, the necessary literature was provided and the training of approximately 80 teachers was organized.

Personal computers entered the new schools as an element of the syllabus and curriculum initially in the 11th and 12th grades and later in the 8th grade as well. The first appropriate computer type has been developed and is being released in series as PRAVETS-82 by the "Instrument-Building and Automation" Association. The technical characteristics of PRAVETS-82 are well known: its software is fully compatible with that of Apple II computers. Naturally, we are aware of the limitations of this type of computer (small memory, the need for standard keyboard, etc.), but at the same time we believe it is very suitable for secondary schools: being simple, inexpensive and widespread, it fully complies with the objectives of secondary education. Moreover, the experiments carried out so far with 1,300 computers introduced in various schools have shown that it complies with the requirements laid down for it. What are the prospects for PRAVETS-82? This computer is already manufactured in series. Secondary schools will receive 6,000 computers in 1985, while by 1990 there will be about 40,000 personal computers of the PRAVETS type with modifications in secondary schools alone. The factory manufacturing the computers has been modernized, which means that its production will improve both qualitatively and quantitatively.

There are consequently many prerequisites for the implementation of computer technology within the secondary education system, namely:

° The solution of the problems related to the material structure, to the supply of computers, and to the modification and development of computing equipment, peripheral devices, etc., produced in Bulgaria;

° The possibility of using the experience and results of the practical implementation of computer technology in the higher educational institutions of the country, and the research potential of the higher institutions, the Academy of Sciences, as well as other institutions and organizations.

Both these are prerequisites for the stable functions, self-renovation and constant improvement of the education system. The procedure for introducing computers into the secondary education system, the relevant stages, objectives and tasks, were part of a complex programme for the implementation of computer technology in secondary schools, worked out and approved by the Higher Council for Education at the Ministry of Education in Bulgaria.

This programme is on a national and long-term scale - until 1990; it guarantees the implementation of the resolutions concerning the introduction of computers into secondary schools and is linked to various programmes at district and regional levels. The social and political significance of the programme lies in the creation of conditions for the creation of multilaterally developed individuals who are familiar with the modern trends towards automation and the extensive use of computer technology.

The following facts were given particular consideration when the programme was being worked out, namely:

1) The wide application of computer technology, particularly microcomputers and microprocessors in education, raises a number of questions related to its study and application as a technical aid for improving the quality of the educational process.

In view of this, the main trends in the implementation of computer technology in Bulgarian secondary schools may be determined as follows:

° Training in the field of computer technology and the basic principles of programming, as an element of general education;

° Application of computer technology (microcomputers and microprocessors) as technical school aids;

° Application of microprocessor and microcomputer equipment as a means of control in such subjects, as automation of production, introduction to cybernetics, automation and computer technology, etc.

2) Computer technology and its study are important for the formation of the students' world outlook, since they create conditions for new trends in thinking, revealing the role of computers in automation and control systems, in changes in the character of labour, and in problems of quality and productivity.

The cultivation of algorithmic thinking is particularly important for the students' development.

The programme has been elaborated with a view to complying with a number of basic needs, namely:

1) The introduction of qualitatively new control systems for different objects and processes and systems of an organizational type raises the problems of training specialists, their pre-vocational education, and the acquisition of knowledge, skills and needs.

2) The control of complex technical devices, equipment and apparatus requires the acquisition of new skills and habits, development of the intellect - combinatory and intellectual thinking - a description of the various objects and systems, and the setting up and use of information facilities.

3) The application of computers makes it possible to intensify and individualize the educational process, the means of individual control and the change in teaching strategy.

4) The introduction of computers in education, particularly in secondary schools, is aimed at creating and pursuing a scientifically substantiated strategy for their implementation, in addition to encouraging research into the educational, psychological, physiological and other problems of computerization.

The main aims of the programme are as follows:

° To provide for both theoretical and practical study of computer technology with the aim of training secondary school graduates in the programming, operation, maintenance and production of computer equipment, i.e. to provide for the particular profession;

° To provide extensive computer education with the aim of imparting a system of knowledge and skills in using computers, i.e. to promote computer literacy;

° To guarantee the effective use of computers as teaching aids, and to create the necessary software for general education;

° To provide the necessary technical facilities and personnel for the introduction of computer technology into secondary schools - training of teachers;

° To provide the necessary hardware and software for the control of the educational process and of the educational institutions.

The complex programme for the introduction of computer technology in the process of instruction and education, as well as in the management of secondary schools, links in with other programmes which are being implemented concerning education in secondary schools, namely:

(a) Complex programme "Teaching and Technical School Aids, and the Training of Teachers for Subjects Forming the Basis of Vocational Training".

(b) Complex programme "Higher Education and Professional Qualification of Teachers of Computer Technology and Programming, and the Application of Microcomputers in the Educational Process and Management".

In accordance with the complex programme "Teaching Aids", the disciplines involved in professional training in the 11th and 12th grades of the Unified Secondary Polytechnical School (mechanical and engineering science, automation of production and computer technology, electronics and electro-technology, should be provided with the necessary teaching and technical school aids, methods and equipment, and steps should be taken to improve and update the professional qualifications of the teachers. The functioning and implementation of this complex programme provides for research, development and production of experimental specimens, technical design of study-halls and laboratories, software, teacher training and the introduction of the necessary school aids to consolidate the foundations of the students' vocational training.

The programme for improving the teachers' qualifications in computer technology and programming is an element of the complex programme and covers the 1985-1990 period. It defines all types of activities related to the pre- and in-service training of teachers.

The main aim is to train the teacher to apply computer technology in the educational and the educational-production process, to provide qualified teachers for theoretical and practical training of students in computer technology and programming, to train educational management staff in the application of computers to the control and management of education, and to provide the material prerequisites for qualification projects.

In the first place, the organization of qualification courses presupposes the existence of a module structure for the courses, which are divided into four levels:

First level - duration of training one week, 36 hours. This course is intended for all teachers and management staff in the education system.

Second level - duration one month, 140 hours. Intended as general introduction in computer technology for nonspecialist teachers.

Third level - duration three months, 440 hours. Intended for teachers who are to teach computer technology and programming in secondary schools.

Fourth level - duration one year, 940 hours. Intended for training specialist teachers After successfully completing this course, they are entitled to teach computer technology and programming.

Teachers trained at the last two levels are appointed deputy headmasters of the schools in which they teach, with the obligation to teach 8 hours per week.

In accordance with the Programme, it is necessary to organize laboratories for the training of teachers, to create the necessary technical and teaching aids, and to provide for the writing of textbooks and manuals. These courses are already functioning and it may be said that the training they provide is not always without problems. In spite of selection procedures, the trainees have different background qualifications and this creates certain difficulties.

The Ministry of Education is working on the problem of introducing computers in secondary education, together with a number of other organizations. The Central Commettee of the Dimitrov Young Communist League plays a major part in this training by organizing dozens of "Computer Clubs" throughout the country. This clubs conduct out-of-class organized activities with the students on various aspects of computer technology, the elaboration of software products, the organization of programming competitions among the schools, etc.

In our opinion, the implementation of the programme will produce the following socio-economic results:

° Satisfaction of the national economy's needs for qualified personnel with secondary education in the programming, operation, maintenance and manufacture of computers;

° Organization of extensive computer education which will make it possible to apply computers in future work; increase in efficiency and promotion of creativity in the work of both teachers and students;

° Intensification of the educational process and individualization of education, change in the character of education, with particular reference to the content of knowledge and the way in which this knowledge is acquired.

We are also aware of the shortcomings which microcomputers will introduce into the school education system. Each school has its own shortcomings. Microcomputers will cure some of them, but may also cause others.

The most important problems awaiting solution are:

° First and foremost, health problems. Serious studies are needed on the effect of computer technology on the health of the younger generation;

° Psychological problems - at the level of both student and teacher, and those concerned with student-teacher interrelationships;

° Social problems related to the role of the computer, to computerized education and to the use of trained specialists in various spheres of the national economy;

° Resource problems - guaranteeing the material structure, i.e. hardware and software for the needs of the educational process. A particularly complicated problem is to provide the necessary software of the required quality in sufficient quantities;

° Methodological problems resulting from the new approach, the new technology of training resulting from the application of microcomputer equipment which requires new syllabuses, new textbooks, a new type of teacher, etc.

Analyzing in turn all the objectives discussed above and included in our complex programme, we are aware of the difficulty of implementing all these tasks in their entirety, as this will require very large resources and will take a lot of time. Nevertheless, we believe that with the joint efforts of all, through the cooperation of UNSECO, a speedier solution will be found to many of these problems.

Issues and Trends on the Use of Computers by Children in an Information Age

SILVIA CHARP
Consultant-Education and Training, 39 Maple Avenue, Upper Darby, PA 19082, USA

We are in an Information Age. This concept has gained acceptance by many, but the implications of being in an Information Age are not always clear, nor has there been much direction to assist our children in preparation for this phenomena.

It is no longer reasonable to expect students to be able to learn even the basic rudiments of what they will need to know in their adult lives to function as competent and productive individuals. The growth and use of new knowledge in present day society is too rapid. Enabling copying skills in information use must be provided. This includes an opportunity to learn individually, an awareness that knowledge is everywhere, always changing and that learning is on-going. This also involves acquiring the technical and conceptual skills needed to process a continuing flow of new information. The use of computers, in particular microcmputers, at the elementary level is growing. Most of the computer acquisition, software development and teacher training that has occurred is the result of the introduction of computer literacy as part of general education of young children. The definition of computer literacy is still not clear but certain trends can be noted. Programming is becoming decreasingly important. Until recently the skills essential to using a computer was the ability to program. Presently the emphasis is how best to use the computer in a variety of applications. Younger students are given an integrated approach in their early schooling.The following objectives are stated:

- All students will have an opportunity to acquire basic knowledge about computers and their impact on society.
- All students will be trained to use and have access to computers.
- A computer science department will be introduced at the high school level which will provide computer courses to as many students as possible.

° Computer education will be integrated into the curriculum.

° Computers will be used to assist in the development of individualized instruction for all students.

° Impact of computers in student education will be reviewed and changes made.

° Staff will be developed to the level necessary.

A school system in the U.S. which has a well developed plan for computer education for all children from 6-18 years of age lists the following objectives for the first 3 years.

OBJECTIVE 1

Students will develop keyboarding skills and learn correct operation of peripheral equipment, including tapes,diskettes, and printers.

° Students will gain manipulative facility with the computer as a by-product of using computer-assisted instruction (CAI) applications packages in music,math, science,social studies, and language arts.

OBJECTIVE 2

Students will study the history of computers and the impact of the Computer Revolution on modern-day society.

° Students will learn ways computers are used in every-day life. Students will identify common tasks which are not suited to computer solution.

OBJECTIVE 3

Students will learn a level of programming consistent with their educational abilities and use this capability to develop logical thinking and strategies for problem solving.

° Students will learn to follow directions.

° Students will use LOGO-Turtle Graphics. LOGO is a system of elementary statements which control the movement of a "turtle" on the CRT. It teaches elementary concepts of "program" and "logical structure" through visual observations of the computer's responses to various program statements. It is recommended that the teaching of LOGO be implemented as an enrichment to the regular course of instruction,possibly in an "after school" type program.

OBJECTIVE 4

Students will study the structure of computer systems, developing suitable vocabulary and understanding the internal operation of the system, including the the interaction of software with hardware components.

° Students will learn what a computer is.

° Students will learn a few basic computer terms.

° Students will learn to identify parts of a computer.

OBJECTIVE 5

Students will gain more information on the subjects they are studying .

° Students will use drill and practice exercise, simulations, data basis, word processing applications and tutorial CAI packages to help them learn their material.

Emphasis is beginning to be placed on problem solving : Information handling and teaching young children how to sort through information provided by computers how to use computers to solve problems and how to communicate problems and solutions to others.

Though courses in "Computer Literacy" are still being given across the U.S., questions are being asked. "What happens after Computer Literacy?" Is education addressing the information environment for all young people?". "What technological and conceptual tools are needed to process a continuing flow of new information?"

The American Federation of Information Societies has been developing curriculum guidelines for a one year course on the technologies of information and computers, for all secondary school students. The stress on information is intended to help prepare students for the world in which they will live and work. Most of the workforce will be employed in information related jobs.

The curriculum of this course consists of material equivalent to 36 weeks (one year). Modules of material are being prepared so they can be used in other courses where they may fit into the curriculum.

General goals for the course include:

° Students will understand the impact of computing and information technology in today's society.
° Students will understand the importance of effective information, both to an individual and to society.
° Students will learn how information is processed: by humans, by computer, by other technologies, and by human/computer systems.
° Students will understand how to obtain and use information for problem solving and decision making.
° Students will understand their roles and responsibilities for living and working in an information age.

This course examines the pervasiveness and importance of information in today's society. The way humans process information is contrasted to the way computers process information

Human/computer interaction demonstrates the use of information technology to enhance human capabilities. Students learn the conditions of information use in problem solving and decision making. They learn how to access and evaluate a variety of computer-based information resources to acquire information at the point of consumption. The course ends with an examination of some of the issues surrounding the new information technologies, possible future careerpaths, and speculations about future changes.

It incorporates interdisciplinary material and an approach that equips today's students to cope with the changes brought about the information technology. A range of assignments and activities are provided to accommodate the needs of the individual student, whatever his or her previous experience and intellectual gifts. The course involves extensive hands-on experience with computers but no prior computing background is required.

The course is not intended as a prerequisite to other courses in computing. Other courses offered will provide students with the opportunity to acquire programming skills.

A number of specific areas and objectives have been identified.They include:

I. Origins and Roles of Information

A. Information Environment

1. To describe the elements/attributes of the information society
2. To understand how we got to the information society
3. To know the difference between data and information
4. To recognize how the availability of information changes the meaning "to know something".
5. To recognize that proliferation of information requires selectivity
6. To identify the role of computers in assisting humans to select from a proliferation of information
7. To identify the use/role of computers in generating,storing,and selecting information

B. Historical Perspective

1. To trace the change from an agricultural society to an industrial society to an information based society (history should be presented from a social science rather than a name-date or technological perspective)

C. Roles that Information Plays in Society

1. To illustrate the organization, synthesis and repacking aspects of information
2. To distinguish physical vs. logical aspects.

II. How Information is Processed

A. Processing by Humans

1. To identify human capabilities for acquiring information
2. To categorize this processes by which humans process information (e.g. how we sense, code,store,organize,retrieve,respond)
3. To illustrate types and sources of information that humans need to live and work each day
4. To contrast how humans process information differently (e.g. cognitive, auditory,sight)

B. Processing by Computers

1. To identify ways in which computers receive or acquire data/information
2. To describe how computers process data/information (e.g. batch, networks, parallel processing, data communication)
3. To identify ways in which computers output information
4. To understand the effects of speed, capacity,size and reliability on on computer processing

C. Human-Computer Interaction

1. To list ways in which humans and computers are similar and different
2. To explain how humans and computers work together to accomplish things
3. To recommend what can be done to improve the working relationship (interface) between humans and computers

III. How Information is Used

1. To know how to access information when given a clearly defined subject
2. To find information about topics related to a given topic
3. To know how to organize a body of data into information
4. To know how to test validity of information
5. To know basic techniques in decision making, problem solving and model building
6. To know sources and uses of information involved in societal or group decision making
7. To identify a variety of kinds and types of information resources and to demonstrate skill in accessing information systems
8. To explain how newer technology can be used as tools in these processes

IV. How Information Affects Us

A. Careers and Education

1. To identify and describe career paths in the computing profession

2. To illustrate how computers have changed occupations
3. To identify sources for career path preparation

B. Issues

1. To identify major social,ethical and economic impacts and implications arising from information technology (in education,business,government)
2. To relate differential rates of technological changes and social change
3. To illustrate the problems of maintaining a democracy in a technological society

C. Trends

1. To project future developments based on past rates of change and effects of technology

It is recognized that a great deal of teacher training is necessary. Thoroughly tested curriculum material and preparing a number of trained teachers are the next steps for further evaluations and testing.

As a member of the AFIPS committee which is developing the program just described, I would welcome any suggestions you may have which would strengthen our efforts.

Children in an Information Age

BLAGOVEST SENDOV
Bulgarian Academy of Sciences, Sofia, Bulgaria

My task is to summarize and comment on the fundamental ideas and views expressed in the plenary papers of the International Conference "Children in an Information Age: Tomorrow's Problems Today". The wealth of these ideas and the variety of the experiences exchanged make this a difficult and important task.

I shall not dwell on the papers separately, as it is impossible and hardly necessary, since they will be published. I shall try to formulate certain conclusions, drawn from these papers, which were presented by well-known speakers with considerable experience in the subjects covered by the conference.

The theme of the Conference "Children in an Information Age: Tomorrow's Problems Today" allows the inclusion of a host of problems. Nevertheless, the problem of

Educating children in an information age

came up as the principal issue.

We refer to this most frequently by the term computer training, though the terms electronic and informatics training were also used. The latter was justified because a computer is only one of the devices within a system for the transfer, storage and processing of information.

Concentration on the problems of training, when talking of children in an information age, is understandable, bearing in mind the presence of invited speakers who are involved primarily with education and teaching. Nevertheless there is another possible explanation. We adults believe that education is the most important childhood and youth activity. On the other hand it is increasingly clear that in an information age education will continue throughout the lifetime of all active people.

The question of computer or information training is already a matter of state policy in many countries. The papers which outlined the strategies of different nations, such as the USSR, France, Bulgaria, Japan etc. were received with special interest. While organizational and financial problems play a major part in the implementation of these strategies, nevertheless, the content of the educational process cannot and should not be overlooked. Whatever the attitudes to these problems or their solution, a consensus exists to the effect that

No educational system can overlook the problem of computerization.

Special interest and activity has been shown by a number of international organizations, federations and unions concerning the problems of training children and young people in a period of rapid growth and improvement of electronic data processing equipment. Although the practical solution of these problems in each individual country depends on the system adopted, and on the position and resources of the country concerned, international cooperation can be extremely useful. UNESCO can play a particularly important role in this respect. The log, wide-ranging experience of the International Federation of Information Processing (IFIP) in the field of computer training can also make a considerable contribution in assisting cooperation.

And thus, we are confronted by attitude to the computer, or more generally speaking, towards information technology and education. This question cannot be avoided or overlooked. It can, however, be seen differently and approached by different means.

It should be noted that the computerization of education has:

Many enthusiastic supporters and an equal number of sceptical critics.

And this is quite natural, since it is a new, promising, and multi-faceted phenomenon. It is concerned with radical changes in production, management technology and many other changes in everyday life. On the other hand, the changes are so rapid and radical, that they affect basic human activities and centuries-old traditions. Hence the conditions conducive to both uncontrolled optimism and extreme pessimism. What do the papers presented to the conference show? We frequently hear categorical declarations for or against, with no serious background study, nor experimental tests; these conclusions are simply the outcome of speculative thinking. So one of the most important conclusions we can draw is:

We need well-designed, carefully conducted and precisely evaluated experiments.

Here the rapid development of computer technology runs counter to the natural training process and the comparatively long period needed for the assessment of results. On the other hand, information technology affects the education system in many ways. Information technology can be used as an instrument, while at the same time affecting substantially the content of education. After the initial euphoria, which is to be expected and is only natural, emphasis should be placed on systematic scientific and experimental work on the computerization of education, and on the establishment of specific principles concerning education in the information age.

It is generally accepted that if we really are entering a new information age, we are certainly at the beginning. The metaphor of second literacy and the analogy with printing is frequently used and it can give us some idea of the level of our information technology and how it stands in relation to the printed word. As I see it, these are the times of Guttenberg. From now on we should expect the analogous improvements which we witnessed in printing technology from the days of Guttenberg to its present state. This frequently used analogy rises the question of the role of books. In this connection the views of certain authors concerning books as a basic educative medium are not clear-cut. Books play a dominant role as a symbol of our contemporary civilization, and many people dread the very thought of this role being reduced in the future. Some also consider it a logical development to predit the end of books as the principal source of information and knowledge, passed down from one generation to another. The belief has been expressed that the dominating role of books as a teaching aid will be replaced in the not so distant future by a new electronic device for the storage transmission and processing of data. One of the papers also raised the question: Will people write in the information age?

It is difficult to offer clear-cut answers to this kind of question at this stage, though the question is quite justified. The existence of cheap and convenient word-processors will no doubt affect the writing habits of many people.

The theacher-computer relationship was the · one of the central issues debated at the conference. There was a general consensus that:

No computer can replace a teacher.

Many factors point to this conclusion. I very much welcomed one statement synthesizing the problem:

If a teacher can be replaced by a computer, this should be done immediately.

A disproportionate interest was initially shown in the automation of the education system, which was to be implemented by programme training without a teacher; this is considered by many specialists to be unsuitable, particularly for younger children.

It was pointed out that according to Pnage and Vygotsky the teaching of small children largely depends on an auto-regulated use of practical experience. As far as sensory-motor experience is concerned, computer programs are fully comparable with text books. No one recommends today that the beginnings of knowledge and experience of the environment should be presented to small children mainly through books. Thus, arguments against the use of computers in primary education are nothing new. They amount to the same arguments against text books at an early age.

It is interesting to note that the problem of computerization of education is bound up with the most up-to-date and important trends in the development of present-day computer technology in general. The efforts to expand the potential of computers are concentrated on the problem of creating so-called artificial intelligence. On the one hand, the creation of an artificial intelligence had to rely on the mechanisms can best be traced and studied within the education process and by observation of the effect of various strategies on children of different ages. On the other hand, the existence of an artificial intelligence will also stimulate learning by offering new opportunities.

The very concept of artificial intelligence still provokes arguments, arising mainly from unjustified expectation of claims to have created a thinking machine. I do not see why this term should provoke arguments of this kind, for we are not talking about creating intelligence, only an artificial intelligence. We are already accustomed to synthetics, synthetic wool, cotton, even woodwork, which are in many cases extremely useful. The same attitude should be applied to the concept of knowledge. There has recently been much talk about data banks and machines processing knowledge. Nevertheless knowledge always presupposes action, which is carried out following the decision of the individual who has this information. I believe therefore that it is right to speak of artificial knowledge in the context of machines. This could also be extended to the concept of thought.

It is essential that the problems of education are closely related to the basic principles of the development of computers, regardless of the fact that the simplest and cheapest personal computers are beginning to be used in education.

All the specialists who took part in the conference expressed a clear desire to determine the place of the computer in school and in education in general. This emerged frequently in the statement:

<u>A computer is only a tool</u>

It was noted that the computer did not develop to meet the need of education. This is why we need to justify attitudes to computers from the point of view of educational practice. On the other hand, computerization of production and processes make this instrument a new and powerful object to study and to learn how to use. It is here, to my opinion, that the most important problems arose:

<u>A reform of the system and the content of programmes in the information age.</u>

The rapid utilization of information technology in industrial production and in all aspects of human activity, i.e. the entry of society into the information age produces some immediate problems which cannot be avoided and also some of a long-term nature. Those demanding immediate solution involve the provision of computer literacy courses for students in the final grades at school. It should be noted that there is no agreement on the meaning of the concept "computer literacy". There would be some justification in asking whether we have to teach everyone to play about with a piano with one finger when the musically educated community is something quite different. An analogy could be drawn with the problem of mass training in programming in algorithm language which, owing to its mass scale, will hardly progress beyond the one-finger stage of piano-playing. No one is opposed to computer literacy, but serious reservations exist as to whether the content of this literacy programme should be based solely on a knowledge of programming.

The need for a fundamental change in the entire system and content of education throughout the various stages of the education system is a long-term plan. Owing to the rapid increase in the potential of information technology, the mass user of the computer will not be involved in programming in the current sense of the word. He will be using the same medium and means, but will have to be able to apply these to his specific needs. The existence of vast information sources, making data for artificial intelligence (artificial knowledge) available to everyone demands changes in training objectives and strategy. Natural intelligence, which can make use of artificial intelligence and artificial knowledge should be built up in a suitable manner. Human knowledge should be integrated and aligned with the basic principles as details and precise quantitative characteristics emerge from the machines. It was emphasized on many occasions that the main aim of organized education is to teach children to teach themselves:

Students should be taught how to learn and we should encourage and develop the desire and the need for continuing study.

The major goal of education is no longer the learning and memorizing of certain facts. This process is of course inevitable, but it is not the primary aim. The most important factor is the acquisition of skill in using information and artificial intelligence and together with this the development of motivation and the need for continuing accumulation of new knowledge.

The solution of the problem through reform of the system and the change in programme content is a difficult and important task in an information age. It is clear that the volume of separate facts should be considerably reduced to enable identification of the general principles, pinpointing connections between the facts.

Present-day informatics draw a distinction between data bases (information) and a base of knowledge. The view has been expressed that a base of knowledge is essentially a data base, given a certain structure, which permits conclusions to be drawn. This we previously defined as artificial knowledge. Real knowledge amounts to more than structuralized data. Real knowledge is the basis for creativity, which is arrived at through individual action.

This is why the basis of the educational system in an information age should be the encouragement and promotion of human creativity. The availability of a large number of computers should on the other hand not turn man into a computer slave.

The final goal of computerization should be to make people more human.

The use of contemporary information technology in education should not serve to increase the distinction between science and mathematics and the humanities. On the contrary, these technologies allow further humanization of human knowledge. Everything should be assessed from a humanist point of view.

The mass utilization of automated sources of information, based on knowledge etc. raises new problems in terms of the education of those who make use of them. The question of the reliability of the data obtained, and the need to check the degree of reliability requires special knowledge and skills. These means can be used successfully by a person with a particular view of the world familiar with the principles of philosophy, nature and society.

Many of the speakers attempted to project further into the future of the children in the information age. This is only natural in view of the problems considered, where change is so rapid. If you drive at night at great speed your lights show the way ahead for a considerable distance. Many voiced the opinion that the likelihood of foretelling the future with a reasonable degree of accuracy is small. Nevertheless every plan is based on a certain hypothetical prognosis for the future.

A participant in the conference expressed his satisfaction that the conference limited the discussion to global questions and the way ahead. "I did not hear anyone discuss the relative merits of Pascal or Basic", he said. "Perhaps", he added jokingly, "because everyone knows that Logo is best."

Although wide-ranging and long-term experiences were discussed at the conference, we all agree with the statement:

We are still at the beginning, the very beginning!

This is why we need systematic and prolonged investigations, and an intensive exchange of experience and opinion through international cooperation.

Let us hope that in two years time, when this Conference is held again, we shall have more and more interesting material to share.

Recommendations of the International Conference "Children in an Information Age: Tomorrow's Problems Today" Varna, Bulgaria, 6–9 May 1985

We, the participants from 45 countries in the International Conference and Exhibition on "Children in an Information Age: Tomorrow's Problems Today", organized by the Bulgarian Government with the co-sponsorship of UNESCO, IIASA, the Lyudmila Zhivkova International Foundation and the World Health Organization,

Take into account the great importance and the need to study the impact of computers on society in general and on children in particular,

Consider this conference an important new stage in the international study of:

° the social, cultural and economic consequences and effects of computers in education;

° the physiological, psychological and educational issues and methodological consequences of introducing the computer into the world of the child;

° educational software and hardware;

° national educational policies in applying computers in education.

We express our gratitude to the organizers of this conference for preparing this very stimulating and excellently organized scientific forum.

We find the idea of inviting scientists, educationists and decision-makers from different countries and from different fields connected with children and education very fruitful and promising.

We welcome the proposal of the Government of the People's Republic of Bulgaria and the Lyudmila Zhivkova International Foundation to organize an international research programme on the problems discussed by the conference with the support of UNESCO, IIASA, and WHO.

CIA-N

We are of the opinion that this international research programme could involve several workshops, symposia, etc. We note with gratitude the intention of the Bulgarian Government and the Lyudmila Zhivkova International Foundation to organize another international conference in 1987. Proposals were also made and discussed to organize:

° an international research and information centre where scientists from different countries will have the opportunity to experiment with the results of their studies and to compare their findings, and where there will be possibilities to exchange information on children and computers;

° an international comparative study of the psychological consequences of introducing computers into the world of the child under conditions of different cultures and traditions;

° a meeting of the editors of journals and magazines specializing in informatics and education in order to study the possibilities of exchanging information on children and computers;

° a study of the possibility of standardizing computer equipment and software products for educational purposes in order to facilitate international co-operation and exchange.

We also welcome the proposal of the conference organizers that this international research programme be recommended for discussion at the forthcoming XXIII Session of the UNESCO General Conference with a view to its possible inclusion among the activities of the future Intergovernmental Programme on Informatics which UNESCO envisages launching.

Last, but not least, we would like to express our common feeling of concern that nowadays many computer games for children have a competitive and aggressive character. We feel very strongly that the computer should not be turned into a device for children to participate in fantasy wars or to think in violent terms however innocent some of these games might seem. Products of new technology and computers in particular should be used for the purposes of educating children in peace and understanding and preparing them for the problems of tomorrow's world.

Varna
9 May, 1985

Appendix 1. Reports of Stream Rapporteurs

REPORT ON STREAM 1. SOCIAL, CULTURAL AND ECONOMIC CONSEQUENCES AND EFFECTS OF COMPUTERS IN EDUCATION

Rapporteur : B.Segerstahl (IIASA)

In this report on the presentations given in the sessions on SOCIAL,CULTURAL AND ECONOMIC CONSEQUENCES AND EFFECTS OF COMPUTERS IN EDUCATION I have to use the material available selectively as the papers presented touched on a very broad spectrum of specific topics.

Dr. Vacca set up a quantitative framework for the estimated growth in numbers of microcomputers. He pointed out that by using a version of the so-called evolutionary metaphor based on Volterra-Lotka equations, curves can be constructed to predict saturation for microcomputer populations. Dr.Vacca stressed the important fact that even in the most advanced countries most people read and write rarely and even more rarely computer, organize knowledge, draw or carry out exercises in logic.

In his presentation Dr. Clark examined claims about the learning benefits of technology, putting microcomputers into the broader perspective of all available technologies. His central argument was that when communication technologies are used for education they may increase instructional efficiency but do not influence learning. based on a broad review of past research and future directions for the use of communication technology in the USA, Clark presented five conclusions. These are :

1. No one medium enhances learning more than any other medium, regardless of the learning task, curriculum content, student characteristics or setting.

2. Any new delivering technology is likely to result in enhanced learning and motivation when it is the focus of a local or national cirriculum reform effort.

3. Education officials may wish to evaluate newer media for their effective-

CIA-O

ness in delivering instruction on the basis of cost, local availability and/or student appeal.

4. There is evidence in past research that we should continue to explore the effects of student and teacher attitudes and beliefs about new delivery technologies

5. Future investigations must focus on instructional technology and must be prepared to reach the conclusion that newer media should not be adopted in some instances.

Issues related to planning and managing the introduction of technology into programs for the education of children was the theme of the presentation given by Dr. Costello. He took his paradigms from conventional and modern treatises on management and illustrated these by reference to organizations concerned mainly with computer technology. In his paper Dr. Costello stated that concern with the education of children is universal and by its nature futuristic, experimental and controversial. Inadequate, insufficient or faulty planning can cause untoward havoc and it is consequently unacceptable to avoid planning discussions.

Mr. Yrjonsuuri stated three facts as starting points in his evaluation of the interaction between education and society:

- educational goals need reevaluation as society changes
- teaching aids change together with these general changes
- the interaction between education and society is changing.

These three facts can lead to substantial changes in the education system. Without consistent planning at the level of the individual, the nation and internationally, a coherent future framework might be difficult to create. This process of change is conditioned by changing goal definitions, the availability of resources and environmental conditions.

Dr. Azinian reported on her own and her colleague's work on trying to find out what computing activities were good for and how they influence the social system. Based on the facts and concepts analyzed, and depending on resources and socio-cultural needs, they suggest that the priorities of permanent education must be established, with emphasis on teacher education:

- a training of teachers' trainers (at university departments of education)
- avoiding the "oil spot" method with trained teachers
- practical teacher training courses. Theoretical aspects may be developed by reading and discussion workshops.

Dr. Kovacs presented in his paper a review of mass education in computer technology as undertaken in Hungary. This education was organized according to specific Hungarian needs and made use of TV, books, microcomputer-clubs, magazines and all other available resources to attract as big audience as possible.

He indicated that the methods developed in Hungary might be useful in other countries too and expressed the Hungarians' willingness to support these activities.

Dr. Richardson gave a concise review of :

a) the origins of computers and computer programs and what they do,

b) what computers have replaced in the past and

c) the relationship between computers and human beings and its pitfalls. Finally an assessment was made of the most rational future uses of the computer and artificial intelligence.

Dr. Martinov and his colleagues discussed microprocessor knowledge as an indicator of the nature of education today. He prescribed four components needed in the synthesis of knowledge and attitudes toward this new equipment.

1. It is necessary to form some opinion of the different methods of obtaining data from an object.

2. Algorithms and their utilization for describing solutions to problems and for the realization of processes.

3. The technical means inherent in the microprocessor equipment and the principle of programme control used in the processing of input data.

4. Programming as a means of solving problems depending on the objectives and the language selected for operating the microprocessor devices.

Dr. Yule focused his attention on the work going on in the field of computerization of measurement, diagnostcs and treatment of special groups of children. He pointed out that a lot of standardization and validation of existing methods and methods under development is needed before a solid base for a broader and more consistent introduction of new methods can be created.

CONCLUSIONS

Finally I want to make some personal remarks influenced by what I have heard and seen. The constraining framework for almost every speaker has been the assumption of a fixed and frozen physical layout in an educational environment. A lot of work goes into constraining and evaluating software for educational environments while almost nothing has been said about the need to evaluate different alternative hardware structures. Is the keyboard for instance really natural for a child?What influence will speech synthesis and recognition have in the future? Will the microcomputer system be built into completely different types of education al tools? There are a lot of questions still to be answered.

Throughout history new tools and methods have emerged and have been introduced into education.Is there something really new in the so-called micro-computer revolution or can we see this in a historical perspective as natural new step in a smooth evolutionary process.

The economic impact on society as a whole of alternative strategies for introducing computers in education is a question which is unsystematically and randomly raised but very little is known about the quantitative structure of this complex problem. It is however one of the fundamental basis for any efforts to create a long term policy for computers in education.

Is the mcirocomputer a drug? A logical counter alternative to a reality which is too chaotic and complex to be managed by the individual? If so, how should we manage and control the drug addiction aspects of microcomputerization ?

And finally. Are we perhaps so fascinated by this new tool and production system that we forget the supply and demand aspects of the society around it? Knowledge, information and creativity are broader intellectual concepts which could form the conceptual environment for our efforts to optimize our new tool.If you allow me a very simple- perhaps even oversimplified- metaphor : it is very important to know how to sharpen a knife ; it is important to know how to use a knife. But sometimes the most important thing is to forget about the knife and use a drill instead. The microcomputer is one tool in our toolbox. It is complicated, new and fascinating but it is a tool- not a goal.

REPORT ON STREAM 2. PHYSIOLOGICAL, PSYCHOLOGICAL AND EDUCATIONAL ISSUES AND METHODOLOGICAL CONSEQUENCES

Rapporteur : D.Harris (UK)

The focus of the papers was mainly on the psychological and educational issues. There were 26 papers presented from 14 countries. The papers covered a spectrum of dimensions:

nursery education	teacher training
idiosyncratic	national
subject based	across the curriculum
industrialisation	collaboration
participant	observer
natural language	computer language.

The latter pairing raised two interesting issues. There was a suggestion that the move to naturalistic languages may not enhance all learning, particularly where logical thinking was perceived as being important. The counter view was that computers in that case were being percieved as the modern version of learning Latin. There was also a serious reservation over the fact that a programming languages were in English which produced alienation in some countries; the alternative proposed was Latin.

The dimensions were covered in a range of activities: computer camps to which children went to enjoy programming and sports; automated didactic play; adventure games; learner-based approaches; algorithmic approach to mathematics; a topic-based curriculum based on maths, history, technology and language over an 8-year period using the computer as an adjunct; selection of learners most suited to informatics; free access workshops for the very young; a complex multi-peripheral learner station; and even the perceptions of earth by visitors from outer space

One feature that occurred in several contexts was the idea of collaboration. Collaboration between groups of learners is problem solving- problem solving was perceived by many to have much potential for enhancement through the use of computers and information systems. Collaboration in the design of software was by a group of experts including psychologists, educationists, psychiatrists,software engineers and sometimes teachers. The potential alienation of teachers was countered by strategies which made teachers an equal partner, where interactive communication was seen as an essential feature.

The most interesting idea of collaboration was initiated because of limited resources. Some teachers, administrators, pupils and parents were formed into an informatics community; that community was given courses and became the nucleus for the diffusion of ideas and learning to the rest of the community.

Two papers raised reservations about the potential of computers in learning. The existing research evidence was presented as providing a picture with limited cognitive gains and even more limited affective gains. Future workers are recommended to read the available reports, including the discouraging ones, before the inventing a square wheel.

The perceptions of learners and teachers were also identified as in need of investigation. Learners can be seen as having a participant or an observer work view which will have a considerable impact on their interaction with technology and with other learners. The teachers were recommended to think to the future in their decision-making rather than to the present, which in turn would require a change in the structure of learning and the learning environment if collapse of the whole educational edifice was to be prevented.

In many papers there was an underlying assumption of technological determination focused upon the computer. Other papers focused on information and the technology of information. Focus on the technology of information may enable a stranger bridge to be built between teachers and parents with a historical view of education and the future needs of learners living, learning and working in an information age.

REPORT ON STREAM 3. EDUCATIONAL SOFTWARE AND HARDWARE

Rapporteur : D.Tagg (UK)

In an invited paper Mike Newton gave a description of the work done in the British Open University especially with regard to computer courses. Twenty-five hundred out of 65,000 Open Univerisity undergraduate students take the computer courses. The TV and radio programmes are just two components of the whole courses. Also included are teaching notes, tutorials, assignments, examination and work on a microcomputer (each student has a specially designed one called HEKTOR) and on a terminal to a mainframe. Packs have also been produced for industrial applications and for education at school level, especially for teachers. The last include awareness courses, practice in using computers, case studies from schools, including use of CAL software, and courses to give guidelines for the assessment of hardware and software for classroom or individual use.

Four of the papers in the session were concerned with adaptive systems which could be used in a wide variety of fields.

Before this Donovan Tagg (UK) outlined some of the psychological, physical and social dangers in advancing too fat towards a state where everyone had a home computer through which he can communicate, learn, shop and do business.

Then the four reports, dedicated to different types of authoring systems were presented.Pavlov, Eskenazi and Mitkov (Buglaria) reported on a testing system, based on microcomputers, successfully applied to the examination of both children and adults and now being expanded by some adaptive features. The Asistp program product reported by Iosep, Macarie and Barbu (Roumania) is a complete system providing courseware generation, as well as teacher-pupil communication and student learning with considerable freedom given to the courseware authors. The Austrian experience in developing educational software was reported by Hager. Emphasis was put on learning programs, based on IBM PC, and developed using either traditional programming languages or the specially designed SEF author's language. Closely following these three was the report of Blahova and Blaho (Czechoslovakia), concerning their two-year experience in teaching a particular subject (principles of processing as an essential part of modern operating systems) through programming computer games.

I. Brown from London (UK) was concerned to make communication beween the learner and the screen and input device as simple, quick and effective as posssible. If a touch-sensitive screen is used there is two-way communication with the learner but this involves the child being very near the screen which could be hazardous. The use of overlays giving concept keyboards of a wide variety make input easier. If the areas for pressing are also identified by drawings then there is a good, easy two-way communication between learner and keyboard. The applications are numerous, from helping in special education, teaching children how to construct letters and numerals, to spell to create their own statements and stories with a limited vocabulary, to identifying and naming parts of an elaborate machine shown on the keyboard.

Hvorecky (CSSR) had analyzed the construction of programmes in a language such as PASCAL and decided that twice as many keys had to be pressed to conform with PASCAL syntax as to identify the particular program. This was discouraging to beginners and stopped many students from taking up computer science. He had devised a system which enabled the student to write programmes on the screen by putting up various preforms which the student fills in to suit his purpose.

Fanghaenal's paper was read by H.Sydow. It described the effects of the new information technology on the educational system in the GDR. The main changes were in general education at secondary school level. Aims included a broad-based, flexible an applicable fundamental knowledge with particular relevance to its uses in society. Students were also being trained to use mathematical models and algorithmic thinking, to produce algorithms which work and to interpret their results. New books, curricula and technical aids had been produced. The empahsis was on thinking about the new technologies and their applications. The use of computers could wait until more hardware and software was available.

Borkowski (Poland) showed how effectively small computers such as the Spectrum could be used in physics lessons. The background could be varied to create interest, calculationscould be demonstrated of such activities as dampled or forced oscillators, charging a capacitor or motion in a resisting medium. The computer could be used with real experiments to take the chores out of the calculation and analysis of experimental data- not to replace the real experiments. The computer enabled physics to be applied to real situations of interest to the students such as sports.

A variety of problems were raised during the third session. In the first part of his talk. Gerhold (USA) discussed some practical problems arising from the educational use of computer-hardware (no computers had been designed for education), software, teachers preparation, dependence of self-paced CBI on the educational structures.The second part was dedicated to his experience in developing instructional materials using IBM Pilot. How inaccessible techniques and concepts could be made accessible by the aid of computers- was the main idea in Neuwirt's (Austria) talk. Cerri (Italy), in his talk, considered the sequence 'CAL Rule-based systems- concept-based systems' as an essential trend thus emphasizing the importance of involving AI in the educational use of computers.

Harmathy (Hungary) shared his concrete experience of micro - computer applications to technical and scientific experiments, pointing out hardware and software requirements and illustrating it with a videofilm. Hansen's (Denmark) talk dealt with the matter of what questions teachers have to answer when faced with educational software and how to evlauate it, identifying the essential elements The last talk by Maniu, Rancea, Clamba and Rentsch (Romania) was concerned with teaching informatics in high schools and with emphasizing the importance of management and motivation - examples of problems were given (8 -queens, etc.) requiring a great number of operations but solvable by computers.

The papers in stream 3 considered a wide variety of aspects of hardware and software in computer education. The authors are to be congratulated on the high standard maintained, the interest generated and the excellent English of those for whom this is not the native language. Most authors found themselves short of time and there was no opportunity for discussion- at the most one or two questions.

REPORT ON STREAM 4. NATIONAL POLICIES

Rapporteur : K.Satoru (UNESCO)

In stream 4 (National Educational Policies) 8 sessions were held, which consisted of two invited paper sessions and six applied paper sessions.

In the first invited paper session on Tuesday morning, Mr. Gorny from FRG presented " ATEE'S (Association for Teacher Education in Europe) proposal for a teacher education syllabus "Literacy in Information Technology", in which he proposed practical aims, content and presentation in several course, areas, including "Information Technology and Society ".

The second invited paper given on Wednesday morning by Mrs. Martinengo from Italy, dealt with her experience in using the microcomputer as a teaching tool for handicapped children with learning disabilitied in Italian.

In the other six sessions a total of 25 papers were presented. Most of the papers presented the authors' experience in their own countries- developing, industrialized and in general geographically widespread countries- with a view to developing a national strategy in primary and secondary education by,for, and/or in, information technology. These problems were discusses by authors from the following countries: Australia, Austria, Bulgaria, Canada, Denmark, Egypt, Finland, FRG, GDR, Greece, Hungary, Iran, Italy, Morocco, Norway, Poland,Romania, Switzerland, UKMUSA, USSR.

Each session was followed by lively and useful discussion. Findings from those discussions include:

- the importance of this kind of exchange of experience
- the value of this face-to-face direct communication between participants either in formal discussions in sessions or informal ones in exhibition areas and in the halls.
- the necessity to adapt to every child's particular need and/or condition
- the need to consider socio-cultural differences
- the language problems are difficult, but not insoluble
- the adaptation of technology to the geographical differences
- the technical problems arising from inadequate computer facilities.

Appendix 2. Conference Committees

HONORARY COMMITTEE

Chairman: Corr. Member Prof. N. Todoriev, Chairman of the State Committee for Technical Progress, Bulgaria

Members:

Academician J. M. Gvishiani, Deputy Chairman of the State Committee for Science and Technology, USSR

Corr. Member Prof. S.V. Emelianov, Director of the International Research Institute of Management Problems, USSR

Prof. T. H. Lee, Director of the International Institute of Applied Systems Analysis, Austria

Dr. A. R. Kadura, Deputy General Director of UNESCO

Mr. V. Zhivkov, President of the International Foundation "Lyudmila Zhivkova", Bulgaria

Mr. John Vincent Atanasoff, USA

Mr. Robert Maxwell, UK

PROGRAM COMMITTEE

Chairman: Academician B. Sendov, Bulgaria

Members:

P. Bollerslev, Denmark

V. Boltianski, USSR

D. Costello

A. Ershov, USSR

P. Gorny, FRG

R. Gwyn, UK

E. C. Jacobson, UNESCO
G. Kovacs, Hungary
L. Varga, Hungary
J. Mentalecheta, UNESCO
O. Panov, Bulgaria
A. Pissarev, Bulgaria
N. J. Rushby, UK
G. Sacerdoti, Italy
S. Sharp, USA
G. Tchigovadze, UNESCO
T. Vasco, IIASA
S. Cerry, Italy

Appendix 3. Scientific Program and Speakers

<u>Monday, May 6th</u>

PLENARY SESSIONS

Plenary Speakers:

E. Velichov, USSR
S. Shiba, Japan
J. Hebenstreit, France
M. A. White, USA
T. Vasco, IIASA
M. Edmundson, UK
H. Hogbe-Nlend, Cameroon

OFFICIAL CEREMONY

Welcoming Address by Organizers and Sponsors of the Conference

Invited Plenary Keyspeaker: J. V. Atanasoff, USA

<u>Tuesday, May 7th</u>

PLENARY SESSION

Plenary Speaker: S. Larsen, Denmark

STREAM 1

Invited Speaker: A. DiSessa, USA

Speakers:

D. Costello
G. Kovacs, Hungary
H. Azinian, Argentina
P. Balkanski, Bulgaria
J. Filden, UK
Y. Yrjonsuuri, Finland
R. Vacca, Italy
V. Korcinov, Bulgaria
R. Clark, USA
S. Procopanko, Canada

I. L'Hermenier, France

W. Jule, WHO

I. Zwetanov, Bulgaria

P. Medow, Canada

T. Rumak, Poland

STREAM 2

Invited Speaker: N. Rushby, UK

Speakers:

G. Futscher, Austria

D. Harris, UK

E. Petrova, Bulgaria

R. Scanlon, USA

J. Whiting, Northern Ireland

T. Perl, USA

A. Walat, Poland

M. Ramlot, Argentina

S. Gascoigne, UK

G. Pipyov, Bulgaria

J. Lochheed, USA

T. Moisa, Rumania

V. Peeva, Bulgaria

S. Jacoub, France

STREAM 4

Invited Speaker: P. Gorny, FRG

Speakers:

A. Bork, USA

N. Nimmervoll, Australia

G. Gvaramia, USSR

S. Raasio, Finland

O. Pavlov, Bulgaria

R. El Hadity, Egypt

Z. Suray, Poland

A. Melmed, USA

S. Kwiatkowski, Poland

R. Nikolov, Bulgaria

A. Owais, Egypt

M. Zyoute, Morocco

A. Thompson, Scotland

I. Diamandi, Rumania

Z. Sabbagnian, Iran

ROUND TABLE. THE EDUCATION IN THE COMPUTERIZED WORLD

Chairman: B. Sendov, Bulgaria

Participants:

S. Shiba, Japan

M. Edmundson, UK

H. Hogbe-Nlend, Cameroon

S. Larsen, Denmark

A. DiSessa, USA

V. Boltianski, USSR

G. Kovacs, Hungary

<u>Wednesday, May 8th</u>

PLENARY SESSION

Plenary Speaker: M. Aston, UK

STREAM 2

Invited Speaker: V. Boltianski, USSR

Speakers:

R. Kentsch, Rumania
G. Broadman, USA
B. Papazova, Bulgaria
R. Lauterbach, FRG
H. Gratiot-Alphandary, France
R. Cohen, France
E. De Corte, Belgium
P. Fiddy, UK
R. Zankova, Bulgaria
M. Arora, Bahrain
N. Patrubani, Rumania
G. Paris, Hungary
A. Marchev, Bulgaria
K. Brelinska, Poland
E. Lemut, Italy

STREAM 3

Invited Speaker: M. Newton, UK

Speakers:

D. Tagg, UK
R. Pavlov, Bulgaria
M. Iosep, Rumania
V. Blahova, CSSR
B. Hager, Austria
I. Brown, UK
J. Hvorecky, CSSR
G. Fanghagel, GDR
M. Zyoute, Morocco
J. Borkowski, Poland
G. Gerhold, USA
E. Neuwirt, Austria
Z. Harmathy, Hungary
K. Hansen, Denmark
I. Maniu, Rumania

STREAM 4

Invited Speaker: G. Martinengo, Italy

Speakers:

L. Sandals, Canada
S. Mushkova, Bulgaria
E. Ramseiter, Switzerland
L. Caltinescu, Rumania
N. Alexandris, Greece
P. Jensen, Denmark
J. Wibe, Norway
R. Angelinov, Bulgaria
K. Wala, Poland
G. Gavrilescu, Rumania
G. Slavov, Bulgaria
A. Antonov, Bulgaria

TUTORIAL: ARTIFICIAL INTELLIGENCE IN EDUCATION

Invited Speaker: S. Cerri, Italy

PANEL DISCUSSION: COMPUTERS IN EDUCATION - WHAT WE MIGHT WIN OR LOSE

Chairman: S. Sharp, USA

Participants:

A. Bork, USA
P. Gorny, FRG
D. Harris, UK
S. Larsen, Denmark
O. Panov, Bulgaria

Thursday, May 9th

PLENARY SESSIONS

Plenary Speakers:

A. Pissarev, Bulgaria
S. Sharp, USA
B. Sendov, Bulgaria

Streamrapporteurs:

B. Segerstahl, IIASA
D. Harris, UK
D. Tagg, UK
K. Satoru, UNESCO